The AYRS~~~~~
BOOK OF
BURNS–LORE

ACKNOWLEDGEMENTS

In the first edition of the 'Burns-Lore', I acknowledged my indebtedness to many people who had assisted me with my research into the poet's life in Ayrshire. Alas, since then, several of them have 'shuffled off this mortal coil' and I realize how privileged I am to have shared their knowledge and had it recorded 'in guid black print' before it was forgotten. Prior to publication of this edition, I have thanked all of the others again in person.

There are two more people to whom I am pleased to express my thanks and appreciation. The first is Doctor John Strawhorn, Mauchline, Ayrshire's leading historian, whose several books on the country and on Burns are invaluable sources of information. The other is Mrs. Heather Ronald, Australia, whose husband is descended from 'The Ronalds of the Bennals'; by diligent research, Mrs. Ronald corrected misinformation repeated by many generations of Burns authors when they attributed bankruptcy to the wrong William Ronald, a small but important inaccuracy to Burns scholars.

Finally, I acknowledge the patience and thoroughness of my wife, Lilias, while sharing the checking of the manuscript and proof copies of this book.

INTRODUCTION

Since the first edition of The Ayrshire Book of Burns-Lore was published in 1985, it has been acknowledged by Burns enthusiasts as the most comprehensive source of information on the people and places of Ayrshire associated with Robert Burns. Amongst the plethora of books on the poet, it is truly distinct and has been recommended by other authors as an essential reference work on the poet's life in the County.

This new edition is even more comprehensive than the first; there are several new entries and photographs, and a series of eleven Special Features, the subjects of which could not be found easily elsewhere.

The 'Burns-Lore' is more than a catalogue of factual information; it is also a fund of traditions and anecdotes, myths and legends, claims and counter-claims, which have grown up around the story of the poet's life and have been handed down through the generations.

As stated in the Introduction of the first edition, too often even Ayrshire people are not aware that places with which they are familiar have an association with Burns and guided tours of the area unwittingly neglect locations of more importance and interest in the Burns story than the museums and restored properties they visit. If you would be knowledgeable about the poet's life in Ayrshire and able to find the places referred to in his works, let the 'Burns-Lore' be your guide.

Some readers may wonder at the varied spellings of the Burns family name. The father, William Burnes, adhered to the East of Scotland spelling of his forebears, and the family followed suit with Burnes or Burness during most of his lifetime. As early as July, 1780, the poet adopted the Ayrshire spelling, Burns, and after their father's death in 1784, Robert and his brother Gilbert, dropped the 'e' and 'ss' for good.

The map references given relate to the Ordinance Survey Landranger 70 (1:50,000) series.

Dedicated to
The Immortal Memory of
ROBERT BURNS
on the bi-centenary of his death

Other books by the author:

Ayrshire Heritage
Pictorial History of Arran

The AYRSHIRE BOOK OF BURNS–LORE

A. M. BOYLE

Alloway Publishing

© ANDREW M. BOYLE
First Published in 1985
by
Alloway Publishing Ltd.,
Darvel

Second Edition printed 1996

Printed in Scotland
by
Walker & Connell Ltd.,
Hastings Square, Darvel,
Ayrshire.

CONTENTS

Cover Picture - Kirk Alloway

CHRONOLOGICAL HIGHLIGHTS

Year	Occurrence	Reference
1732	Agnes Broun, the poet's mother, born on 15 March (Died 14 January, 1820).	Whitestone Cottage, Craigenton Farm
1744	Agnes Broun moved into Maybole to live with her maternal grandmother.	Maybole
1750	William Burnes, the poet's father, moved from the east of Scotland to Dundonald, Ayrshire.	Fairlie House
1752	William Burnes moved to Alloway.	Doonside, Doonholm Doonside Mill
1756	William Burnes and Agnes Broun met at Maybole Fair.	Maybole
1757	William Burnes constructed the cottage at Alloway. William and Agnes married at Maybole on 15 December	Burns Cottage, New Gardens
1759	Robert Burn(e)s born in the cottage on 25 January. (Died 21 July, 1796).	Burns Cottage, New Gardens
1760	Gilbert Burn(e)s born in the cottage on 28 September. (Died 8 April, 1827).	Lochlea Farm, Mossgiel Farm, Kilmarnock
1762	Agnes Burn(e)s born in the cottage on 30 September. (Died 17 October, 1834).	
1764	Annabella Burn(e)s born at the cottage on 14 November. (Died 2 March, 1832).	Tarbolton
1765	Robert and Gilbert attended school at Alloway Mill under Mr. Campbell. Campbell left and William Burnes joined other parents in employing John Murdoch to conduct a school at Alloway.	Alloway Mill, Simpson's Inn, Murdoch's House
1766	William Burnes rented Mount Oliphant Farm and the family moved in at Whitsun.	Mount Oliphant Farm
1767	William Burnes, Jnr., born at Mount Oliphant on 30 July. (Died 24 July, 1790).	Murdoch's House
1769	John Burnes born at Mount Oliphant on 12 July. (Died 4 December, 1783).	
1771	Isabella Burn(e)s born at Mount Oliphant on 27 June. (Died 4 December, 1858).	Bridge House, Kirk-Alloway
1772	Robert and Gilbert attended Dalrymple School.	Dalrymple
1773	Robert attended Ayr Grammar School under John Murdoch. Robert composed his first published song, Handsome Nell.	Ayr Grammar School, Murdoch's House, Purclewan Mill
1775	Robert attended Hugh Rodger's School at Kirkoswald and met Peggy Thomson.	Kirkoswald, Rodger's School, Ballochneil Farm, Peggy Thomson's House
1777	William Burnes rented Lochlea Farm and the family moved in at Whitsun.	Lochlea Farm
1779	Robert joined Tarbolton dancing class against his father's wishes.	Lochlea Farm, Tarbolton
1780	Robert and Gilbert, together with five other young men founded the Bachelors' Club, Tarbolton.	Bachelors' Club, Tarbolton

1781	Robert courted and proposed marriage to Alison (Ellison) Begbie who rejected him. He was initiated into Lodge St. David Tarbolton on 4 July and moved to Irvine to learn flax dressing in mid-summer. Dispute started between William Burnes and his landlord.	Carnell House, Bachelors' Club, Freemasonry, Irvine, Glasgow Vennel, Lochlea Farm, Old Place Farm
1782	Irvine flax dressing workshop destroyed by fire. Robert worked in other premises and then returned to Lochlea in March. In July he left Lodge St. David for Lodge St. James Tarbolton.	Irvine, Glasgow Vennel, Freemasonry
1783	Robert won £3 prize for flax dressing at Lochlea. Robert and Gilbert arranged with Gavin Hamilton to rent Mossgiel Farm. Robert started his first Commonplace Book. Dispute between William Burnes and his landlord found mainly in favour of Burnes.	Lochlea Farm Mossgiel Farm Shawwood
1784	William Burnes died at Lochlea on 13 February and was buried at Alloway. The Burnes family moved into Mossgiel in March. Robert became Depute Master of Lodge St. James, Tarbolton.	Lochlea Farm Mossgiel Farm Alloway Kirkyard Freemasonry
1785	Elizabeth Paton gave birth to an illegitimate child (Elizabeth Burns) on 22 May. Robert met Jean Armour in Mauchline. First Commonplace Book finished.	Largieside Mauchline, Mauchline Bleaching Green
1786	Jean Armour pregnant by Robert; her parents opposed to her common-law marriage to Robert and sent her to Paisley. Robert courted Highland Mary and made plans to emigrate to Jamaica. Kilmarnock Edition of Robert's work published on 31 July. Jean Armour gave birth to twins on 3 September. Mary Campbell died at Greenock in October. Robert abandoned plans to emigrate and on 27 November left Mauchline for his first visit to Edinburgh.	Kilmarnock Failford Stairaird Old Rome Garallan
1787	Robert returned to Mauchline in June amid national acclaim, Jean and Robert's infant daughter, Jean, died during October. Robert and Jean met again and Jean became pregnant. Robert returned to Edinburgh and went on tours of the Highlands and Stirlingshire.	Mauchline Kirkyard, Willie's Mill
1788	Robert returned to Mauchline during February. He found Jean lodging at Willie's Mill, took her to a house in Mauchline and they began married life together. Jean gave birth to twins on 3 March and both died within days. Robert received Excise instruction at Mauchline and Tarbolton. He took over Ellisland Farm, Dumfries on 11 June, leaving Jean at Mauchline while he built a house. In December Jean joined Robert at Isle, Dumfries.	Willie's Mill, Back Causeway, Mauchline Kirkyard, Beechgrove Cottage, Gavin Hamilton's House, Morton's Ballroom, Ronald's Inn
1789	Robert attended Gilbert's wedding to Jean Breckenridge of Kilmarnock on 21 June and paid a visit to Mrs. Dunlop at Dunlop House before returning home.	Dunlop House, Kilmarnock
1798	Gilbert Burns gave up Mossgiel and moved to Dinning, Nithsdale. His mother moved with him and the family of William and Agnes Burnes ended their connection with Ayrshire for several years. About 1843 the poet's youngest sister, Isabella Burns Begg returned to live at Bridge House, Alloway until her death in 1858.	Bridge House Kirk Alloway

ACHMACHALLA

It is referred to in the poem *HALLOWE'EN* - 'He sin gat *Eppie Sim wi' wean, That lived in Achmachalla.'* According to the Rev. James Muir, Minister of Kirkoswald, in his book, Burns To His Seventeenth Year, Achmachalla was a fictitious name for a dwelling called Fardincalla on the lands of Kirklands Farm, Kirkoswald, a half mile south of the village. The exact location cannot be traced.

ADAMHILL FARM   Map Ref. 430 304

Situated on the south side on the A719 Ayr/Galston Road, one mile east of the B730 Dundonald/Tarbolton Road. It is a neighbouring farm to Lochlea and was the home of the poet's friend, John Rankine and his daughter Anne. John Rankine was addressed in the poems *EPISTLE TO JOHN RANKINE* and *EPITAPH ON JOHN RANKINE*. In Burns lore he is known as '*rough, rude, ready-witted Rankine,*' as quoted from the Epistle. Late in life, Rankine moved from Adamhill to Galston where he lived in Old Manse Close. He died on 2 February, 1810, and is buried in Galston Kirkyard.

Anne Rankine, the daughter, was the same age as Burns and claimed to be *'Annie'*, the heroine of the song *THE RIGS OF BARLEY*. She said that she had expressed surprise to the poet at having been mentioned in his poems and that he had replied, - 'Oh ay! I was just wanting to give you a cast amang the lave (rest).' She married John Merry, Innkeeper, Cumnock, and lived most of her life there. In 1843, she died aged 84 years, and is buried in Cumnock Kirkyard. The poet did not identify the heroine of the song.

In his Reminiscences Of A Long Life (1906), A.B. Todd, Ayrshire poet and antiquarian who was a close friend of Anne Rankine's son, Hugh Merry, gives the following account of an incident at Adamhill as handed down to Merry - 'Tarbolton Kirk Session were informed that the local Assistant Minister, The Rev. John McMath, had got drunk at Adamhill in the company of John Rankine and Robert Burns. The Session arranged to visit the farm to enquire into the incident and Rankine plotted to save McMath. He gave the visitors refreshments which he repeatedly topped up with 'hot water' from a kettle by the fire. Unknown to the visitors he had filled the kettle, not with water, but with whisky. Eventually, when all of the Session were drunk, he had them loaded on to an open cart and dropped off at their homes in Tarbolton, in full view of the public.' There may have been some truth in the allegation against the Rev. McMath as he had to demit his post a few years later for excessive drinking. He was addressed by the poet in the poem *TO THE REV. JOHN McMATH*.

John Rankine's sister, Margaret, was the first wife of John Lapraik, the Muirkirk poet and friend of Burns.

Also see: Cumnock; Dalfram; Galston; Tarbolton.

AFTON LODGE   Map Ref. 416 257

Situated on the north side on the A758 Ayr/Mauchline Road, one mile east of Mossblown. The house is still inhabited. It was built in 1790 for Mrs. Catherine Stewart, formerly of Stair House. She was a daughter of James Gordon of Afton, New Cumnock and the name Afton Lodge arose from this connection.

Mrs. Stewart was the first of the upper classes to befriend Burns and encourage him in his writing. In 1791 the poet sent her a collection of 13 manuscripts of his later and then unpublished compositions, including *TAM O'SHANTER* and *SWEET AFTON*. The collection is now known as the Afton Manuscript. In his introduction to the collection, Burns wrote - 'To Mrs. General Stewart of Afton - the first person of her sex and rank that patronised his humble lays, this manuscript collection of poems is presented, with the sincerest emotions of grateful respect, by 'The Author.'

AFTON LODGE

Early biographers of Burns claimed that the song SWEET AFTON was composed as a compliment to Mrs. Stewart and that the 'Afton' referred to was a burn in the vicinity of Afton Lodge. As it was one of the collection in the Afton Manuscript, it may have been intended as a compliment but the circumstances gave rise to the erroneous claim regarding the river. The poet recorded that the song related to the River Afton, New Cumnock.

Also see: Afton River; Stair House.

AFTON RIVER   Map Ref. 630 050

The river flows north through Glen Afton, New Cumnock, and joins the River Nith at the map reference shown. It is referred to in the song *SWEET AFTON*.

The poet was familiar with the area and had several friends in Glen Afton. A cairn and picnic area on the west bank of the river commemorate his association with the district.

In a letter to Mrs. Dunlop of Dunlop dated 5 February, 1789, Burns wrote - 'There is a small river, Afton, near New Cumnock . . . . I intended a compliment . . . . to Afton as follows' (followed by the song *SWEET AFTON*). When the song was composed, Burns referred to the river as 'Clear Afton'. He later changed 'Clear' to 'Sweet'.

Local legend maintains that the song was written in an inn by the River Afton at New Cumnock. The poet had halted at the inn on his way from Ellisland to Mauchline and had gone to visit Mr. Logan of Laight, Glen Afton, for the evening. During his absence from

2

the inn, the landlady had spread news of the poet's presence, expecting to have a busy, lively night on his return. When Burns returned he appeared to be pre-occupied with his thoughts and went straight to his room. In the morning he sent a servant to Laight with a draft of the song Clear Afton which he had composed on his way back to the inn.

The inn cannot be traced. Local tradition maintains that the existing Castle Hotel was the inn concerned but this cannot be substantiated. About 1900, the inn in which Burns lodged was described as then being a farmhouse on the banks of the River Afton and that does not support the tradition concerning the Castle Hotel which has no history of having been a farmhouse.

Also see: Ashmark; Corsincon; Knockshinnoch; Laight; New Cumnock; Pencloe.

GLENAFTON
'Flow gently sweet Afton, amang thy green braes.'

AIKENBRAE FARM   Map Ref. 369 272 (approx)
The farm was demolished for the development of Prestwick Airport. It was situated to the south of the A739 Monkton/Tarbolton Road and north of the main runway of the airport. The steading was opposite the location of the present control tower.

The farm was the home of Matthew Paterson and his wife, Ann Ronald, both of whom are buried in Monkton Kirkyard.

Matthew Paterson was friendly with Burns in Tarbolton and was admitted into the Bachelors' Club early in 1782. It is not known where he lived in Tarbolton; members of the Paterson family farmed at Crofthead, Tunnoch and Skeoch in Tarbolton area, at Pant in Stair Parish and at Aikenbrae.

Isabella Burns Begg, the poet's youngest sister, recalled having danced with Matthew Paterson at a Bachelors' Club Ball in Tarbolton. She had been attending a sewing class in the village while her older brothers and sisters attended the ball. Although she was only 11 years old, and waiting to be accompanied home to Lochlea, her sister Annie (Annabella) took her into the ball to partner Matthew Paterson, whose intended partner had let him down.

Ann Ronald was a daughter of William Ronald, Laird of Bennals, Mossblown. She was referred to in the poem THE RONALDS OF THE BENNALS - 'Then Anna comes in, the pride of her kin.' The poet was keen to court Ann but was afraid of being rebuffed because of her family's superior social standing.

Also see: Bachelors' Club; Bennals; Monkton.

AILSA CRAIG   Map Ref. 020 997

A rocky island in the Firth of Clyde, 10 miles west of Girvan, Burns referred to it in the song DUNCAN GRAY - 'Meg was deaf as Ailsa Craig.'

In a letter dated 1788 from Mossgiel, the poet wrote to his maternal uncle, Samuel Broun, Kirkoswald - 'I am impatient to know if the Ailsa fowling be commenced for the season yet as I want 3 or 4 stones of feathers.'

Local tradition maintains that while he was lodging at Ballochneil Farm, Kirkoswald in 1775, and attending Rodger's School in the village, the poet and his friend John Niven went to Ailsa Craig with Douglas Graham of Shanter Farm, the man who was later to be the model for Tam O' Shanter in the poem of that name. It is also said that Graham's boat was called 'The Tam' and that it was from the name of the boat that the poet chose the name Tam for the subject of his poem.

Also see: Ballochneil Farm; Laigh Park Farm; Shanter Farm.

ALLOWAY

Situated on the B7024 Ayr/Maybole Road, 2 miles south of Ayr town centre.

Now within the Burgh of Ayr, Alloway was originally a separate village. It commands a place of honour in the Burns story as the poet's birthplace.

When Burns was a boy in Alloway, Kirk-Alloway was dilapidated but still at least partially roofed. The Old Doon Bridge was the only bridge over the river in the vicinity of the village until he was 13 years of age when his future father-in-law, James Armour, built the bridge at Doonfoot in 1772. The village was only a hamlet but most of the mansion houses on the south bank of the Doon had been built and their grounds laid out.

The main roads in the area were similar to what they are at present. Armstrong's 1775 map of Ayrshire shows that by then a road existed from Ayr through Alloway and on to Old Doon Bridge, generally on the line of the present B7024 Ayr/Alloway/Maybole Road. Another road is shown from Ayr to Doonfoot and beyond, generally on the line of the A719 Ayr/Dunure Road, over the bridge of 1772.

In 1755/56 the poet's father, William Burnes, had constructed the road now called Greenfield Avenue, which runs parallel to the River Doon and links the roads referred to in the preceding paragraph.

The modern bridge over the River Doon at Alloway was not built until 1815. At that time the road from Kirk-Alloway to the Old Doon Bridge and beyond was re-aligned to cross the new bridge.

Before the road systems described were constructed, the original track from Ayr to Old

Doon Bridge and into South Ayrshire, ran to the west of both Burns Cottage and Kirk-Alloway and it was probably existing as a track when the poet was a boy.

The many places of interest associated with the poet in the vicinity are dealt with separately.

Also see: Alloway Mill; Bridge House; Burns Cottage; Doonholm; Doon River; Doonside; Doonside Mill; Greenan Bridge; Greenfield Avenue; Kirk-Alloway; Monuments, etc.; Newark; New Gardens; Old Doon Bridge; Tam O'Shanter's Journey.

ALLOWAY MILL   Map Ref. 324 187

Situated on the north bank of the River Doon, about 300 yards from the mouth of the river. It is still extant but no longer a working mill.

Tradition maintains that about 1755/56, while the poet's father was working at Doonholm, Alloway and before he met his future wife, Agnes Broun, he was attracted by a girl he met regularly at Alloway Mill, He wrote a letter to the girl but placed it in his kist (trunk) rather than give it to her. When he met Agnes he destroyed the letter.

In 1765, when the poet was 6 years of age, he attended a school at Alloway Mill conducted by a William Campbell. The building in which the school was held is not known and has probably been demolished.

The school should not be confused with one conducted at Alloway by John Murdoch, later of Ayr Grammar School. Murdoch's school was held in a tenement situated near Burns Cottage and demolished in 1878.

Also see: Ayr Grammar School; John Murdoch's House.

ANNBANK

Situated on the B742 Mossblown/Coylton Road, one mile south of Mossblown.

William Cunningham of Annbank and Enterkine was referred to as 'Annbank' in the poem THE FETE CHAMPETRE - 'Annbank, wha guessed the ladies' taste, He gies a Fete Champetre.'

Also see: Enterkine.

ANN ORR'S ALE HOUSE   Map Ref. 499272

Situated on the east side of Cowgate, Mauchline, at its junction with Mansefield Road. No longer extant, it was the meeting place of Mauchline Young Men's Society formed by Robert and Gilbert Burns along the lines of Tarbolton Bachelors' Club. The rules of the new club were almost the same as those of the Bachelors' Club with one important difference - whereas in the latter, fines for non-attendance, etc., were spent on drink for the members, at Mauchline they were used to purchase books.

Also see: Bachelors' Club; McLelland's Inn; Mauchline.

ARDLOCHAN

An area at the north end of Maidenhead Bay, a half mile north of Maidens village.

John Niven, blacksmith, designated as from Ardlochan or Damhouse of Ardlochan, is accepted as having been the model of the 'smith' in the poem TAM O'SHANTER - 'That ev'ry naig was ca'd a shoe on, The smith and thee gat roarin fou on.'

The site of Niven's smiddy (smithy) is unknown. At any part of Ardlochan it would have been within a half mile of Shanter Farm, home of Douglas Graham, the model for 'Tam' in the poem TAM O'SHANTER.

Tradition maintains that John Niven was the first blacksmith in Ayrshire to introduce a cart with wheels that rotated on a fixed axle. This serves as a reminder that generally at the time of Burns, pack animals or sledges were in use and carts were only being introduced.

DAMHOUSE OF ARDLOCHAN
circa 1900

John Niven was father of Robert Niven, farmer and miller, Ballochneil, Kirkoswald. Burns lodged at Ballochneil in 1775 while attending school in Kirkoswald. The poet must have known John Niven.

Also see: Ballochneil Farm and Mill; Damhouse of Ardlochan; Maidens; Shanter Farm.

ARMOUR'S HOUSE   Map Ref. 498 273

The parental home of the poet's wife, Jean Armour, until shortly before her marriage, was situated on the west side of Cowgate, Mauchline, about 30 yards south of Loudoun Street. The Whitefoord Arms stood on the west side of the Cowgate/Loudoun Street junction and the Armour house was immediately behind it, separated from it by a narrow lane.

The house was owned by the poet's father-in-law, James Armour, a prosperous master mason and contractor. His standing in the community is illustrated by the Mauchline Church records which show that he rented one of the most expensive pews at a cost of 10/8 per year. He is reputed to have been involved in the building of Dumfries House, Cumnock: Skeldon House, Dalrymple, and numerous bridges throughout Ayrshire. His wife was Mary Smith, daughter of another Mauchline stone mason.

Also see: Cowgate; Greenan Bridge; Whitefoord Arms.

ASHMARK   Map Ref. 611 106

Situated in Glen Afton, New Cumnock, 2 miles south of the town. It was the home of

John Murdoch, whose daughter, Mary Murdoch lived with her aunt, Mrs. Logan, wife of the poet's friend, John Logan of Laight.

Mary Murdoch has been suggested as the heroine of the song *SWEET AFTON* - *'My Mary's asleep by thy murmuring stream.'* The poet did not identify the heroine. Nothing else is known of Mary Murdoch.

John Murdoch of Ashmark should not be confused with John Murdoch, schoolmaster, who taught Burns at Alloway and Ayr.

Also see: Afton River; Laight; New Cumnock.

Jean Armour Burns and Grand-daughter

ASSLOSS HOUSE   Map Ref. 440 398

Situated on Assloss Road, Kilmarnock, a half mile south of Glasgow Road, at a part two miles east of Kilmarnock Town Centre. The house is still occupied.

It was the home of Major William Parker, fellow mason and friend of Burns. He was Right Worshipful Master of Lodge St. John Kilmarnock No. 24 (now No. 22) when the poet was made an Honorary Member, and was referred to in the MASONIC SONG composed by Burns for the occasion - *'Ye sons of old Killie, assembled by Willie.'*

In a letter dated 8 September, 1786, to Robert Muir, Kilmarnock, the poet enclosed a copy of the poem THE CALF and suggested that it be read to Mr. W. Parker.

The poet sent his regards to Messrs. W. and H. Parker in a letter dated 26 August, 1787, to Robert Muir, Kilmarnock. 'H. Parker' was William's brother, Hugh, a Kilmarnock banker who was himself addressed by Burns in the poem EPISTLE TO HUGH PARKER.

Also see: Freemasonry; Kilmarnock.

AUCHENBAY FARM   Map Ref. 486 235

Situated on the Ochiltree/Barskimming Road, 2 miles north of Ochiltree. The farm was the home of John Tennant, second son of John Tennant of Glenconner. It is reasonable to presume that Burns visited the farm. John Tennant of Auchenbay was referred to in the poem *EPISTLE TO JAMES TENNANT* - *'An' Auchenbay, I wish him joy.'*

In a letter dated 22 December, 1788, the poet wrote to John Tennant and thanked him for a case of whisky received. The letter was addressed to Tennant as c/o Mr. Robb, Innkeeper, Ayr.

When the Burnes family lived at Mount Oliphant, Alloway, the Tennant family lived at the neighbouring farm of Laigh Corton. During 1773, John Tennant attended Ayr Grammar School with Burns and both lodged with John Murdoch, School Master, in his home in Sandgate, Ayr.

John Tennant of Auchenbay later took over the neighbouring farm of Steelpark and eventually farmed at Shield Farm, St. Quivox and at Girvan Mains. Late in life he purchased the lands of Creoch, Ochiltree, then described as 'a considerable estate.'

Also see: Glenconner Farm; Laigh Corton Farm; Murdoch's House.

AUCHENBLANE   Map Ref. 262 079

Situated on the east side on the A77 Maybole/Kirkoswald Road, one mile north of Kirkoswald.

Ann Gillespie, wife of John Davidson the prototype of Souter Johnie, is described as having been born at Wester Auchenblane Farm. No farm of that name exists at present but it was probably part of the present Auchenblane Farm which is at the map reference shown.

The poet's maternal grandmother died at Craigenton Farm, Turnberry when his mother, Agnes Broun, was only 10 years of age. Ann Gillespie worked at Craigenton for 2 years and helped Agnes, who was the eldest of the family, to look after her 5 brothers and sisters.

Also see: Craigenton Farm; Glenfoot; Souter Johnie's Cottage.

AUCHINCRUIVE   Map Ref. 382 236

The house and estate are on the south side of the A758 Ayr/Mauchline Road, one mile east of the A77 Ayr by-pass.

Now called Oswald Hall, the house is part of the Scottish Agricultural College. It was the home of Mrs. Mary Oswald, subject of the poem *ODE SACRED TO THE MEMORY OF MRS. OSWALD OF AUCHINCRUIVE*. In January, 1789, Burns and his horse were settling into an inn in Sanquhar on a wet, stormy night en route from Ellisland to Mauchline when the funeral cortege of Mrs. Oswald arrived on its way to Auchincruive. The poet had to leave and make his way 11 miles through the storm to the next inn at New Cumnock.

Auchincruive was also the home of Mrs. Lucy Oswald. Burns wrote the song *O' WAT YE WHA'S IN YON TOWN* to Jean Lorimer but changed the reference from 'Jeanie' to 'Lucy' and sent a copy of it to Mrs. Lucy Oswald. Before her marriage, Mrs. Oswald was Lucy Johnson, and under that name wrote the tune to which Burns set his song *TO MARY IN HEAVEN*.

Lucy Oswald's husband, Richard Oswald, was referred to in the poem *SECOND HERON ELECTION BALLAD* - 'An' there'll be wealthy young Richard.'

LUCY JOHNSON OSWALD

AUCHINLECK

Situated on the A76 Mauchline/Cumnock Road, 2 miles north of Cumnock. The Rev. John Dun, Minister of Auchinleck, wrote a reply to the poem *ADDRESS TO THE DIEL* in a volume of sermons published in 1790. The publisher was John Wilson, Kilmarnock, who also printed the Kilmarnock edition of the poet's work.

Local tradition maintains that John Murdoch, the school teacher who taught Burns at Alloway and Ayr Grammar School, belonged to Auchinleck where his father was Session Clerk of the Parish Church. This can neither be proved nor disproved.

Also see: Auchinleck House; John Murdoch's House; The Deil's Answer.

SPECIAL FEATURE - THE DEIL'S ANSWER TO HIS VERRA FRIEND, ROBERT BURNS

The Rev. John Dun, Parish Minister of Auchinleck, composed the following reply to the poem 'Address To The Deil'. Many of the Clergy had frowned on Burns' poem but Rev. Dun may have written his reply with tongue in cheek.

1 So zealous Robin, stout an' fell -
   True champion for the cause of Hell -
   Thou beats the righteous down pell-mell,
   Sae firm an' frothy,
   That o' a seat where devils dwell,
   There's nane mair worthy.

2 Gif thou gang on the gate thou's gaun,
   Ilk fearless fiend shall by thee stan',
   That bows aneath my high comman';
   Sae, be nae frichtet,
   For I shall send my helpin' han',
   To see thee richtet.

3   Thou does as weel's could be expected
     O' ane wha's wit lay lang neglected,
     Some Godly folk your rhyme I trowe
     Ca' worthless blether;
     But be na feart, ye's get your due,
     When we forgether.

4   Sae feart I'm for the gospel gun;
     To see my frien's I canna win;
     But tell such chiels as, my son,
     I'll see them soon,
     An' thee an' me's hae curious fun,
     E'er a' be done.

5   The Endor witch wha liv'd lang syne,
     Was ae richt honest frien' o' mine,
     An' Haman, wha in tale shall shine
     For zeal an' spite;
     But nane o' them did feats like thine
     In black an' white.

6   As Judas, too, richt bauld an' leal,
     Wha served wi' perfect heart the deil,
     An' play'd his pairt, I'm sure, as weel
     As ony breathing;
     'Till aince he hanged himsel', puir chiel -
     But that was naething.

7   In Hell, when I read o'er your sang,
     Where rhymes cam' thund'rin wi' a bang,
     Quoth I, trouth, I'll see Rab e'er lang,
     An' that's be seen,
     Gif Nick should on me ride the stang
     To Aberdeen.

8   Now Rab, my lad, cheer up thy saul,
     In Goshen thou shalt tent thy faul,
     An' gif thou's still as stout an' baul',
     As I'm a deil,
     Thou's no gi'e up 'till thou's richt aul',
     Sae fare thee weel.

Re. John Dun.

AUCHINLECK HOUSE

Map Ref. 507 230

Situated north of the B7036 Auchinleck/Ochiltree Road, one mile west of Auchinleck. The house, built c.1760, is extant and undergoing much-needed restoration.

It was referred to in a suppressed stanza of the poem *THE VISION* - '*Nearby arose a mansion fine, The seat of many a muse divine.*' In a footnote to the poem, Burns indicated that the reference was to Auchinleck House.

By his reference, the poet intended a compliment to the Boswell family, particularly to his contemporary, James Boswell, famed as the biographer of Doctor Johnson. Burns and Boswell never met although the poet tried to arrange a meeting.

AUCHINSKIETH

Map Ref. 456 337

The mansion house, now called Dallars, is situated 300 yards west of the A76 Kilmarnock/ Mauchline Road at Crossroads. It is within 2 miles of the poet's former home at Lochlea Farm. In a note to a suppressed stanza of the poem THE VISION Burns indicated that the following description related to Auchinskieth - '*Where Cessnock pours in gurgling sound.*'

The present house was built in 1779, before the poem was composed. In Armstrong's 1775 map of Ayrshire it is spelled Auchinskeigh. It is not known when the name was changed to Dollars and subsequently to Dallars.

The Rev. Dr. James Mackinlay, Minister of Laigh Kirk, Kilmarnock, who is referred to in the poem *THE ORDINATION,* was tutor to the family of Sir William Cunningham at Auchinskieth while he was a probationary minister.

In a letter from Ellisland, dated 16 October, 1789, to Captain Riddell, Dumfries, Burns asked for a letter to be forwarded on his behalf to Sir William Cunningham of Robertland and Auchinskieth.

Also see: Laigh Kirk; Robertland.

AYR FROM THE NORTH
circa 1900

AYR

Situated on the Ayrshire coast, at the mouth of the River Ayr. It is an important centre in the Burns Country, indeed, the name is almost synonymous with Burns.

The poet was very familiar with the town of his day and many of its inhabitants. In the Statistical Account of 1775, the population of Ayr Parish was only 2964, compared with Irvine's 4025; it grew during the succeeding 25 years but not to a marked degree; by 1791 the population of the burgh was 3871 and the Parish 4647. As Burns knew it, apart from the Fort and St. John's Church, Ayr consisted of Sandgate, South Harbour Street, High Street to Alloway Street and Mill Street. Alloway Street was the Cow Vennel or Gate and Carrick Street was Carrick Vennel. Until 1786 the Auld Brig was the only bridge over the river, and only a few streets had been developed north of the river.

High Street was the market street, badly fouled by the litter and offal of the various trades. The fish, meal and butter markets of today are accurate indications of the original sites. Horses and cattle were sold on open ground now occupied by Burns Statue Square.

The poet made numerous references to Ayr, the most famous being in the poem *TAM O'SHANTER* - *'Auld Ayr, whom ne'er a town surpasses, For honest men and bonie lassies.'*

The numerous places of interest for their association with Burns are dealt with separately.

Also see: Alloway; Ayr Auld Kirk; Ayr Grammar School; Ayr River; Bridge House; Brigs of Ayr; Burns Cottage; Doonholm House; Doon River; Doonside House; Doonside Mill; Ducat Stream; Greenan Bridge; Kirk-Alloway; Monuments etc; Murdoch's House; Museums, etc; New Gardens; Old Doon Bridge; Park House; Simpson's Inn; Tam O'Shanter's Journey; Wallace Tower; Water-Fit.

AYR AULD KIRK
Attended by the poet as a boy.

AYR AULD KIRK   Map Ref. 339 218

Situated off the east side of High Street, Ayr, and on the south bank of the River Ayr.

The church dates from the 17th century when Oliver Cromwell gave a grant of £600 to the people of Ayr to replace the Church of St. John which he had requisitioned.

Robert Burns was baptised in the cottage at Alloway by the Rev. Dr. William Dalrymple, Minister of the Auld Kirk. The poet and his parents were regular attenders at the Kirk until Alloway had a new place of worship to replace 'Kirk-Alloway'.

Rev. Dr. Dalrymple was referred to in the poem *THE TWA HERDS - 'Dalrymple has been lang our fae.'* He was also referred to in the poem *THE KIRK'S ALARM as 'Dalrymple mild.'* He was the uncle of the poet's patrons, James Dalrymple of Orangefield and Robert Aiken of Ayr.

A board at the main gate of the kirk shows that the following people associated with the poet are buried in the kirkyard:-

1. Robert Aiken - An Ayr lawyer who was a close friend of the poet. Burns referred to

him as his 'first kind patron' and as 'orator Bob.' The poem *THE COTTER'S SATURDAY NIGHT* was dedicated to Aiken.

2. Provost William Ferguson - A retired medical practitioner and Provost of Ayr. He employed the poet's father, William Burnes, as head gardener at Doonholm, Alloway. He also leased Mount Oliphant Farm to William Burnes and lent him £100 to buy stock.

3. Doctor Charles - Described at the gateway as 'A playmate of the poet's boyhood.' Doctor George Charles, was born in 1757 and died on 21 July, 1831, aged 74 years. He was provost of Ayr from 1798 to 1804. When recalling their friends in Ayr, Gilbert Burns wrote - 'Dr. Charles of Ayr, who was a little older than my brother, and with whom he had a longer and closer intimacy than with any of the others, which did not, however, continue in after-life.' On writing to William Niven, Maybole, from Mossgiel on 30 August, 1786, Burns addressed it c/o Thomas Piper, Surgeon, to be left at Dr. Charles's shop, Ayr.

4. John Ballantine - Provost of Ayr and friend and patron of Burns.

5. Rev. Dr. William McGill - Minister of Ayr. He was referred to in the poem *THE KIRK'S ALARM* as *'Doctor Mac'* and in the poem *THE TWA HERDS* - *'McGill has wrought us meikle wae.'* Rev. McGill was friendly with the poet's father and highly regarded by the poet. In a letter dated December, 1789, to Graham of Fintry, Burns described McGill as - 'one of the worthiest, as well as one of the ablest, of the whole priesthood.'

6. Rev. Dr. William Dalrymple - As described earlier.

7. David McWhinnie - An Ayr lawyer who raised 20 subscriptions for the poet's Kilmarnock Edition. Burns wrote to him from Mossgiel in a letter dated 17 April, 1786.

8. John Kennedy - Keeper of the 'drowsy dungeon-clock' of Ayr Tolbooth which was referred to in the poem *THE BRIGS OF AYR*.

Also see: Castlehill; Dungeon-Clock; Whitehill.

AYR GRAMMAR SCHOOL Map Ref. 335 222
It is known that in 1773 Burns attended the school for 3 weeks but there is conflicting evidence on the location of the school he attended.

A plaque on the east wall of the shop at No. 4 Sandgate, Ayr, purports to indicate the site of the grammar school attended by the poet. The same location is shown for the school in a street plan of Ayr for the period 1534 to 1624.

In Dr. John Strawhorn's History of Ayr Academy (1983), the site of the school attended by Burns is indicated as being in Fort Street, opposite the west end of Academy Street, on the site of the present Academy. This site is supported by Armstrong's 1775 map of Ayrshire and is accepted as correct.

John Murdoch, who had taught Robert and Gilbert Burnes at Alloway from 1765 to 1768, and then moved to Dumfries, returned to Ayr in 1773 and was appointed English Master at Ayr Grammar School. In the autumn of 1773, Robert attended the school for 3 weeks to improve his English and French and was also encouraged to try Latin.

The poet was accompanied by John Tennant, Jnr., of Laigh Corton Farm, Alloway and later of Auchenbay Farm, Ochiltree. While attending the school, the boys shared lodgings in John Murdoch's home in Sandgate. In manhood, John Tennant recalled having been kept awake by the poet reciting verses he had composed.

John Tennant's uncle, David Tennant, youngest brother of John Tennant, Snr., of Laigh Corton and Glenconner Farms, was English Teacher and later Head English Teacher at Ayr Grammar School.

It was David Tennant who recommended John Murdoch, an 18 year old former pupil of Ayr Grammar School, to the poet's father, William Burnes, in 1765, as a teacher for the children of Alloway.

Soon after William Burnes moved to Alloway, he became friendly with Alexander Paterson who had been Latin Master of the Grammar School from 1751 and became Rector in 1761. The friendship probably arose from their both being from the east coast of Scotland. Paterson lent Burnes books to help with his efforts to educate his sons, Robert and Gilbert. After Paterson's death in 1768, his widow continued to lend books to the Burnes family and did much to increase the scope of the poet's literary experience.

Also see: Auchenbay Farm; Ayr; Laigh Corton Farm; Murdoch's House.

AYR RIVER   Map Ref. 323 227
The river rises in the hills north-east of Glenbuck, on the Ayrshire/Lanarkshire border, and flows westwards for about 33 miles to enter the Firth of Clyde in Ayr, at the map reference shown.

Burns was familiar with most of the course of the river and it features prominently in Burns lore. Many locations, such as Ballochmyle, Barskimming, Failford, Stair, Leglen Woods and the town of Ayr are well known names in Scottish literature due to their association with the poet.

There are many direct references to the river in the poet's works and in the poem *THE BRIGS OF AYR,* he described its course from its source to the sea.

Also see: Ayr; Ballochmyle; Barskimming; Bridge Holm; Brigs of Ayr; Ducat Stream; Failford; Glenbuck; Leglen Woods; Ratton-Key; Stair; Stairaird.

BACHELORS' CLUB   Map Ref. 432 272
The premises known as the Bachelors' Club are situated in Sandgate, Tarbolton, a few yards from The Cross. The building was purchased by The National Trust for Scotland in 1938 and is now open to the public as a museum.

When Burns was in Tarbolton Parish, the building was used as an ale house by one John Richard. The stair at the rear of the building, giving access to the upper storey, has been reversed from its original position.

Burns, his brother Gilbert, and 5 other young men met in the premises on 11 November, 1780 and founded a debating society called the Bachelors' Club. The poet was elected President for the first meeting.

The 5 young men who joined Robert and Gilbert were Hugh Reid, Alexander Brown, Thomas Wright, William McGavin and Walter Mitchell. Members admitted later included the poet's friend David Sillar and Matthew Paterson who eventually married Ann Ronald, referred to by Burns in the poem *THE RONALDS OF THE BENNALS.*

On 4 July, 1781, Burns was initiated into Lodge St. David Tarbolton at a meeting in the Bachelors' Club building.

Also see: Freemasonry; History etc. of Bachelors' Club; Manson's Inn; Tarbolton.

**Sandgate, Tarbolton, with the Bachelors' Club
on the left and Cross Keys Inn on the right**

SPECIAL FEATURE - THE HISTORY OF THE RISE, PROCEEDINGS AND REGULATIONS OF THE BACHELORS' CLUB

(Although the Bachelors' Club was formed in 1780, it was not until 1782 that, wishing to keep a proper account of their constitution and proceedings, they bought a book in which to record them. Doubt has been expressed as to who worded the document. Dr. Currie, the poet's first biographer, thought it to be 'evidently the work of our poet', while others have suggested that it was written by David Sillar. The language is very akin to that used by Burns in his First Common-Place Book, written during the same period. It may be that Burns worded the Rules, Regulations and preamble originally, in loose-leaf form, and that Sillar copied them into the new book, adding the introductory verse which is generally attributed to him.)

Of birth or blood we do not boast,

Nor gentry does our club afford;

But ploughmen and mechanics we,

In Nature's simple dress accord.

'As the great end of human society is to become wiser and better, this ought therefore to be the principle view of every man in every station of life. But as experience has taught us, that such studies as inform the head and mend the heart, when long continued, are apt to exhaust the faculties of the mind, it has been found proper to relieve and unbend the mind of some employment or another, that may be agreeable enough to keep its powers in exercise, but at the same time not so serious as to exhaust them. But superadded to this, by far the greater part of mankind are under the necessity of 'earning the substance of human life by the labour of their bodies', whereby not only the faculties of the mind, but the nerves and sinews of the body, are so fatigued, that it is absolutely necessary to have recourse to some amusement or diversion, to relieve the wearied man worn down with the necessary labours of life.'

'As the best of things, however, have been perverted to the worst of purposes, so, under the pretence of amusement and diversion, men have plunged into all the madness of riot and dissipation; and instead of attending to the grand design of human life, they have begun with extravagance and folly, and ended with guilt and wretchedness. Impressed with these considerations, we, the following lads in the parish of Tarbolton, viz. Hugh Reid, Robert Burns, Gilbert Burns, Alexander Brown, Walter Mitchel, Thomas Wright and William McGavin, resolved, for our mutual entertainment, to unite ourselves in a club, or society, under such rules and regulations, that while we shall forget our cares and labours in mirth and diversion, we might not transgress the bounds of innocence and decorum: and after agreeing on these, and some other regulations, we held our first meeting at Tarbolton, in the house of John Richard, upon the evening of the 11th November, 1780, commonly called Hallowe'en, and after choosing Robert Burns president for the night, we proceeded to debate on this question - 'Suppose a young man, bred a farmer, but without any fortune, has it in his power to marry either of two women, the one a girl of large fortune, but neither handsome in person, nor agreeable in conversation, but who can manage the household affairs well enough; the other of them a girl every way agreeable in person, conversation, and behaviour, but without any fortune; which of them shall he choose?' Finding ourselves very happy in our society, we resolved to continue to meet once a month in the same house, in the way and manner proposed, and shortly thereafter we chose Robert Ritchie for another member. In May, 1781, we brought in David Sillar, and in June, Adam Jamieson as members. About the beginning of the year 1782, we admitted Matthew Patterson and John Orr, and in June following we chose James Patterson as a proper brother for such a society. The club being thus increased, we resolved to meet at Tarbolton on the race night, the July following, and have a dance in honour of our society. Accordingly we did meet, each one with a partner, and spent the evening in such innocence and merriment, such cheerful and good humour, that every brother will long remember it with pleasure and delight.'

This lengthy preamble is followed by the rules and regulations of the club. There being ten in all, the following are of most interest:-

1st. The club shall meet at Tarbolton every fourth Monday night, when a question on any subject shall be proposed, disputed points of religion only excepted, in the manner hereafter directed.

6th. There shall be no private conversation carried out during the time of debate......All swearing and profane language, and particularly all obscene and indecent conversation is strictly prohibited.

10th. Every man proper for a member of this society, must have a frank, honest, open heart; above anything dirty or mean, and must be professed lover of one or more of the female sex. No haughty, self-conceited person, who looks upon himself as superior to the rest of the club, and especially no mean-spirited, worldly mortal, whose only will is to heap up money, shall upon any pretence whatever be admitted. In short, the proper person for this society, is a cheerful honest-hearted lad, who, if he has a friend that is true, and a mistress that is kind, and as much wealth as generally to make both ends meet - is just as happy as this world can make him.'

Other subjects known to have been debated by the Bachelors' Club are:-

1. 'Whether is the savage or the peasant in a civilized country in the most happy condition?'

2. 'Whether do we derive more happiness from friendship or love?'

3. 'Whether between friends who have no reason to doubt each other's friendship, there should be any reserve?'

4. 'Whether is a young man of the lower ranks of life likeliest to be happy who has got a good education and his mind well informed, or he who has just the education and information of those around him?'

When Robert and Gilbert Burns moved from Lochlea Farm, Tarbolton, to Mossgiel Farm, Mauchline, and entered the social life in Mauchline, they ended their involvement in the Bachelors' Club. The club survived for a few years but without the poet's talent and charisma it went into steady decline. Eventually, after dissent amongst its members, it was disbanded and its records burned. Fortunately, the preamble and regulations survived.

BackCauseway, Mauchline, circa 1920 with Burns's House on the left and Nance Tannock's Inn on the right.

BACK CAUSEWAY
Map Ref. 498 273

The street in Mauchline now called Castle Street, which runs west from The Cross at the map reference shown, was originally called Back Causeway. At the time of Burns, it was the main thoroughfare into Mauchline from the north.

It was in Back Causeway that Burns and Jean Armour set up home in 1788. The house was then owned by Archibald Meikle, known locally as Baldy Muckle, described as 'A tailor in Machlin.' In 1915, the house was bought by the Glasgow & District Burns Clubs' Association. In 1969, The Burns house Museum was opened in its present form.

The neighbouring house was bought in 1788 by the poet's friend and physician, Doctor John Mackenzie, who may have occupied it as either a house or surgery. It was purchased by the Burns Federation in 1917 and forms part of the museum with the Burns House. Doctor Mackenzie married Helen Miller, daughter of John Miller of the Sun Inn, Mauchline. Helen was Miss Miller of the poem *THE BELLES OF MAUCHLINE*.

Nance Tannock's Inn was also in Back Causeway.

Robin Gibb, Beadle and Bellringer of Mauchline Parish Kirk, lived in a house called 'Brownlea' in Back Causeway. It was situated on the east side of the street, at its junction with the Knowe. Gibb was referred to by Burns as 'Clinkumbell' in the poem *THE HOLY FAIR - 'Now Clinkumbell, wi rattlin tow, Begins to jow and croon.'* Mary Morrison may also have lived in 'Brownlea'.

Also see: Mary Morrison's House; Mauchline; Nance Tannock's Inn; Museums, etc.; Sma' Inn; Sun Inn.

BAILIE GREENSHIELD'S HOUSE   Map Ref. 424 378

This house is no longer extant. It was situated on the north side of Grange Street, Kilmarnock, on the site now occupied by the Department of Employment offices at No. 17.

Bailie Thomas Greenshield of Townend had a brewery on the Grange Street site and his house was part of the complex. Burns is reputed to have visited the house and dined with his friend, the Bailie, while visiting Kilmarnock on market days.

Also see: Kilmarnock.

BALLOCHMYLE HOUSE circa 1850

BALLOCHMYLE   Map Ref. 522 264

The mansion house and estate are situated on the west side on the B705 Mauchline/ Catrine Road, one mile south of Mauchline. The house is semi-derelict and the estate is occupied by Ballochmyle Hospital.

When Burns moved into Mossgiel Farm, Mauchline, in 1784, Ballochmyle was owned by Sir John Whitefoord. The men had met as fellow-masons and continued to do so. Sir John suffered financially by the collapse of the Ayr Bank in 1772 and was eventually forced to sell Ballochmyle. When the family moved out, Burns composed the song *FAREWELL TO BALLOCHMYLE*, also called *THE BRAES OF BALLOCHMYLE*. In a copy of Johnson's Musical Museum presented to captain Riddell of Glenriddell, Burns added the following footnote to the song - 'I composed the verses on the amiable and excellent family of Whitefoord leaving Ballochmyle.' The 'Maria' referred to in the song was Sir John's daughter, Mary Anne Whitefoord.

The Braes of Ballochmyle is the wooded north bank of the River Ayr between Catrine and the Howford Bridge on the A76 Mauchline/Auchinleck Road.

In 1785, Ballochmyle was bought by Claud Alexander. His sister, Wilhelmina Alexander, was the heroine of the song *THE LASS OF BALLOCHMYLE*. Shortly after the Alexanders moved in, Burns was walking by the River Ayr where it flows through the estate when he saw Miss Alexander walking alone. He composed the song soon afterwards and sent a copy of it to her but she failed to even acknowledge receipt. In later life, when Burns was recognised as a poetic genius and Wilhelmina Alexander was an elderly spinster, she was pleased to acknowledge that she had been 'The Bonie Lass'.

BALLOCHMYLE FOG HOUSE
Where Burns met 'The Bonie Lass'

Claud Alexander erected a wooden summer-house, called the Fog House, to commemorate the site where Burns had met Wilhelmina. Unfortunately, it was destroyed by fire by vandals in 1944.

Also see: Catrine; Cloncaird, Mossgiel Farm.

BALLOCHNEIL FARM AND MILL   Map Ref. 223 065
Situated on the east side of the A77 Ayr/Girvan Road, 2 miles south of Kirkoswald. The ruin of the original Ballochneil can be seen behind the existing cottage of that name.

At the time of Burns, the tenant of Ballochneil was Robert Niven, son of John Niven, blacksmith, Ardlochan or Damhouse of Ardlochan, Maidens.

Robert Niven of Ballochneil is thought to have been the prototype of the 'miller' in the poem *TAM O'SHANTER*. Douglas Graham, Shanter Farm, Maidens, prototype for Tam in the poem *TAM O'SHANTER*, also farmed Laigh Park, a neighbouring farm to Ballochneil.

Hugh Brown, miller, Damhouse of Ardlochan, Maidens, a neighbour of Douglas Graham's Shanter Farm, is also said to have been the prototype for the 'miller' of the poem.

Samuel Broun, the poet's maternal uncle, was son-in-law of Robert Niven and lived at Ballochneil. According to Dr. Robert Chambers, the Brouns lived in a room attached to the mill.

In 1775, Burns attended Hugh Rodger's school in Kirkoswald and while doing so he lodged at Ballochneil. It is disputed whether he lodged with his uncle or with the Niven family. Tradition maintains that he shared a bed with Robert Niven's son, John Niven, who was a fellow pupil at Rodger's school and thereafter a life-long friend of the poet.

Also see: Ardlochan; Damhouse of Ardlochan; Kirkoswald; Laigh Park Farm; Maybole; Park Farm; Rodger's House and School.

OLD BALLOCHNEIL FARM circa 1900

BARQUHARRIE FARM   Map Ref. 503 191
Situated 1½ miles south of the A70 Ayr/Cumnock Road, a half mile east of Ochiltree. It was the home of George Reid, husband of Agnes Tennant, eldest daughter of John Tennant of Glenconner. John Tennant and his family were all close friends of the poet.

Burns borrowed a horse from George Reid to carry him from Mauchline to Edinburgh and in a letter dated 29 November, 1786, from Edinburgh he apologised to Reid for the delay in returning 'the pownie'.

Also see: Auchenbay Farm; Glenconner Farm; Orangefield.

BARR MILL
Map Reg. 510 368

The mill is no longer extant. It was situated on the south bank of the River Irvine, between the river and what is now Henrietta Street, Galston. The area is still known as Barr Mill.

In a copy of Johnson's Musical Museum presented by Burns to Captain Robert Riddell of Glenriddell, Dumfries, the poet wrote foot-notes to most of the songs. After the old Scottish song I Had A Horse And I Had Nae Mair, he wrote - 'This story is founded on fact. A John Hunter, ancestor to a very respectable farming family, who live in a place in the parish (I think) of Galston, called Barr Mill, was the luckless hero who 'had a horse and had nae mair.' For some little youthful follies he found it necessary to make a retreat to the West Highlands, where he 'feed himself to a Highland laird', for that is the expression of all the oral editions of the song I have heard. The present Mr. Hunter, who told me the anecdote, is the great grandchild of our hero.'

It is thought that Burns met Mr. Hunter at a meeting of Loudoun Newmilns Masonic Lodge. It appears from his "Parish (I think) of Galston" that he was not familiar with Barr Mill which is surprising as he was well acquainted with the Galston/Newmilns area.

BARR VILLAGE

Situated on the B734, 6½ miles south-east of Girvan. It is referred to in the poem *THE KIRK'S ALARM* - *'Barr Steenie! Barr Steenie! What mean ye? What mean ye?'* This is a reference to the Rev. Stephen Young, Minister of Barr from 1780 to 1819. The kirk was on the site of the present kirkyard but can not be traced. The fabric of the original kirk was probably used in the building of the present kirk. Rev. Young is thought to have been buried in the kirkyard.

An aunt of Burns, described as from Kirkoswald and probably the wife of his maternal uncle, Samuel Broun, is recorded as having said that the poet wrote the song *MY NANIE, O'* to a girl called Agnes McIlwraith of Pinvalley, whom he had met at Kirkdamdie Fair. At least three other girls are said to have been the heroine of the song.

Kirkdamdie Fair, also called Kirkdominie Fair, was the largest feeing fair in south Ayrshire. It was ancient in origin and was held annually on the last day of May on the grounds of a ruined church on the north bank of the River Stinchar, 1½ miles south-west of Barr.

Also see: Coldcothill Farm; Doura Farm; Kirkoswald; Peggy Thomson's House; Pinvalley; Ship Inn; Stinchar River.

BARSKIMMING
Map Ref. 483 254

The house and estate are situated north of the Mauchline/Stair Road, 1½ miles south-west of Mauchline. The present mansion was built in 1883. When Burns was in Mauchline, Barskimming was the home of Sir Thomas Miller of Glenlee who became Lord Barskimming and later Lord Glenlee. The poet was very familiar with the estate and often walked by the River Ayr which flows through it. Lord Barskimming and the estate are referred to in the 20th stanza of the poem *THE VISION* - *'Thro' many a wild, romantic grove . . . An aged judge I saw him rove.'*

Patrick Miller of Dalswinton, Dumfries, patron of Burns and landlord of Ellisland Farm, was Lord Barskimming's brother.

Lord Barskimming's son, Sir William Miller, succeeded to the Barskimming title; he was referred to as 'Barskimming's guid Knight' in the poem *SECOND ELECTION BALLAD*. He also succeeded to the title Lord Glenlee.

Also see: Barskimming Mill; Bridge Holm.

BARSKIMMING MILL   Map Ref. 492 254
Situated on the River Ayr, south of the Mauchline/Stair Road, 2 miles south-west of Mauchline. The mill building still exists but it stopped milling flour in the 1950's. When Burns was in Mauchline, the miller was the poet's friend, James Andrew. Andrew is buried in Stair kirkyard.

On the north side on the Mauchline/Stair Road, opposite the road leading to the mill, there is a grass area in a bend of the River Ayr, called Bridge Holm or Miller's Holm. The poet and James Andrew were walking together on the Holm when Burns composed the poem *MAN WAS MADE TO MOURN*.

Also see: Bridge Holm; Kate Kemp's House.

BEECHGROVE COTTAGE AND HOUSE   Map Ref. 499 272
The cottage was situated on the west side of Cowgate, at its junction with Catrine Road, Mauchline. The site is now occupied by a property called Grove cottage. It was the home of Peter Morrison, carpenter, cabinet maker, and friend of Burns. He made the furniture for Ellisland Farm, Dumfries and in a letter dated 22 January, 1789, Burns wrote and asked him to speed up his work.

Local tradition maintains that while Burns was at Mossgiel he was in the habit of joining the Morrison family for lunch after Sunday morning church services and that on one such visit he composed the poem *ADDRESS TO THE HAGGIS*. It is thought that only the last stanza was composed initially as a grace before a meal and that the poem was completed later. Other traditions maintain that the poem was written in Edinburgh or at a social evening at Craigie.

Beechgrove House, still occupied and with the same name, is on the south side of the cottage. When Burns was in Mauchline it was owned by his friend, Gavin Hamilton, and was later occupied by Hamilton's son, Doctor Dugald Hamilton.

BEGBIE'S INN
The inn was in Kilmarnock town centre. The area has been completely re-developed and the site is now under a supermarket in Kilmarnock shopping centre. Begbie's was referred to in the poem *THE ORDINATION - 'Then aff to Begbie's in a raw, An' drink divine libations.'* In the Rob Rhymer manuscript of the poem, Burns changed the name to 'Crookes', another town centre inn of the period.

Begbie's Inn later became The Angel Hotel and was extant as such for many years.

Also see: Crookes's

BENNALS FARM   Map Ref. 405 263
Situated one mile north of the A758 Ayr/Mauchline Road at the east end of Mossblown. It was the home of William Ronald and his wife and two daughters, the subjects of the poem *THE RONALDS OF THE BENNALS*. The elder daughter, Jean Ronald, was courted by the poet's brother Gilbert Burns but she married John Reid, Langlands Farm, Tarbolton. The poet was keen to court the younger daughter, Ann Ronald, but was afraid of being rebuffed because of the family's wealth and standing. Ann married Matthew Paterson, a

Tarbolton acquaintance of the poet and a member of The Bachelors' Club.

In a letter dated November, 1789, to his brother, William Burns, the poet informed him - "Mr. Ronald is bankrupt." Mistakenly, writers have related this to Mr. Ronald of Bennals, whereas, the Mr. Ronald who went bankrupt was a tobacconist in Mauchline.

Also see: Aikenbrae Farm; Blackbyre; Braehead; Ford; Langlands Farm; Monkton.

BLACKBYRE

Burns referred to Blackbyre in the poem *THE RONALDS OF THE BENNALS* - *'The laird o' Blackbyre wad gang through the fire'* - but gave no indication of the location of the property. There is no Blackbyre in the immediate vicinity of Bennals at present nor was there in Armstrong's 1775 map of Ayrshire.

Also see: Bennals Farm.

BLACKSIDEND   Map Ref. 585 298

Blacksidend Hill is located 3 miles north-east of Sorn. It is referred to in the poem *A MAUCHLINE WEDDING* - *'The rising sun o' er Blacksideen, Was just appearing fairly.'* The 1342 feet high hill lies almost due east from Mossgiel and from the farm Burns would see the sun rising from behind it.

Also see: Mossgiel Farm; Sun Inn.

BOGHEAD FARM   Map Ref. 435 298

Situated on the south side of the A719 Ayr/Galston Road. 1½ miles east of the B730 Dundonald/Tarbolton Road. It is a neighbouring farm to Lochlea and was occupied by James Grieve who was referred to in the poem *EPITAPH ON JAMES GRIEVE* - *'Here lies Boghead amang the dead, In hopes to get salvation.'* In the dispute between the poet's father, William Burnes, and his landlord, David McLure, over Lochlea, James Grieve acted as arbitrator on behalf of McLure.

Also see: Lochlea Farm.

BOWLING GREEN HOUSE   Map Ref. 428 382

An inn, the site of which was on the east side of Portland Street, Kilmarnock, opposite the north side of West George Street. It was demolished when the former East George Street was developed. The inn took its name from the nearby Kilmarnock Bowling Green which, between 1780 and 1790, was located in the area now occupied by the shop premises at the north-east corner of Portland Street and West George Street.

Many of the poet's friends, including Tam Samson, frequented the inn and bowling green. Tam Samson was referred to in the poems *TAM SAMSON'S ELEGY* and *TAM SAMSON'S EPITAPH*. Legend maintains that the poems were composed and recited for the first time in the inn. Tam Samson had been out shooting and was late in returning. Burns was in the inn and was told by Tam's nephew, Charles Samson, that Tam had said that he would be happy to die out shooting on the moors. Burns retired for a short time and by the time Tam returned, the poet was able to read the poem *TAM SAMSON'S ELEGY*. After protests from Tam, the poet composed and recited *TAM SAMSON'S EPITAPH* and its 'Per Contra' to let the world know that Tam was hale and hearty.

The innkeeper was Sandy Patrick, Tam Samson's son-in-law.

Also see: Kilmarnock; Laigh Kirk; Ochiltree; Tam Samson's House.

BRAEHEAD

The location is referred to in the poem *THE RONALDS OF THE BENNALS* - '*The laird o' Braehead has been on his speed, For mair than a tow-mond or twa, man.*' The poet gave no indication of the property to which he was referring and the subject has caused much speculation. There is no property called Braehead in the immediate vicinity of Bennals but there are several in neighbouring parishes.

MARGARET CHALMERS

BRAEHEAD FARM Map Ref. 496 248

Situated on Haugh Road, Mauchline, 2 miles south of the town. Margaret 'Peggy' Chalmers, friend of Burns, lived at the farm, probably while the poet was at Mossgiel but it is not known whether or not they met at that time. The dates between which the family lived at Braehead are not known. She was born at Fingland, Kirkcudbrightshire, and moved to Mauchline when financial difficulties forced her father to sell his estate.

Burns visited Peggy Chalmers at Harvieston, near Dollar, in October, 1787, during his Highland tour. She claimed later that he had eventually proposed marriage to her and the tone of his letters to her suggests that he probably did so. Peggy was referred to in the love songs, *MY PEGGY'S FACE* and *WHERE BRAVING ANGRY WINTER'S STORM*.

BRAEHEAD HOUSE

BRAEHEAD HOUSE, KILMARNOCK Map Ref. 434 381

The house was situated to the north of London Road, Kilmarnock on the eminence overlooking Kilmarnock Water. It was demolished several years ago. The present Braehad Court and Kilmarnock Technical College occupy the site. Braehead was the home of William Paterson, Town Clerk of Kilmarnock and friend of Burns. The neighbouring property on the south side of London Road was Rosebank, home of Thomas Samson, subject of the poems *TAM SAMSON'S ELEGY* and *TAM SAMSON'S EPITAPH*. Tam Samson's nephew, Charles Samson, was clerk to William Paterson.

Braehad House, Kilmarnock is unlikely to have been the 'Braehead' referred to in the poem *THE RONALDS OF THE BENNALS* as the poem was composed before the poet frequented Kilmarnock.

At the time of Burns, the house sat on a hill on the outskirts of the town, overlooking the town centre, Kilmarnock Water and the Laigh and High Kirks.

Also see: Kilmarnock; Tam Samson's House.

BARSKIMMING BRIDGE and KATE KEMP'S HOUSE

BRIDGE HOLM Map Ref. 491 254

Situated on the south bank of the River Ayr, immediately west of Barskimming Bridge on the Mauchline/Stair Road, 2 miles south-west of Mauchline. It is also known as Miller's Holm. Burns composed the dirge *MAN WAS MADE TO MOURN* while walking on the Holm.

Also see: Barskimming; Barskimming Mill; Haugh; Kate Kemp's House.

BRIDGE HOUSE Map Ref. 330 195

The house is no longer extant. It was situated on the east side of the A719 Ayr/Doonfoot Road, near the main entrance to Belleisle Park. About 1843, the poet's youngest sister, Isabella Burns Begg, who had been married and living in East Lothian, moved into Bridge House. She lived there until her death in 1858, aged 87 years, and was buried in Alloway Kirkyard beside her father, William Burnes. She was survived by her unmarried daughters, Agnes and Isabella Begg who lived on in Bridge House. Agnes died in 1883 and Isabella in 1886. The death of Isabella Begg marked the end of the last direct family link with the poet in Alloway.

During Isabella Burns Begg's years in Bridge House, her home was a place of pilgrimage for Burns enthusiasts. She gave a vast amount of information about her famous brother, Robert Burns, but as she was 12 years younger than the poet her accounts of his life, especially until he reached manhood, cannot be relied upon for accuracy. Isabella always spoke highly of her brother, especially of his interest in and attention to the younger members of the family.

SPECIAL FEATURE - A CHILDREN'S STORY - by ROBERT BURNS

ISABELLA BURNS BEGG

(When Isabella Burns Begg was interviewed by Dr. Robert Chambers, author of a Life of Burns (1851/52), she recounted a story composed by Burns as a teenager for his wee brothers and sisters at Lochlea. Chambers published the story in his book, Nursery Rhymes of Scotland.)

THE MARRIAGE OF ROBIN REDBREAST AND JENNY WREN

"There was an auld grey poussie baudrons (cat), and she gaed awa' doon by a water side, and there she saw a wee Robin Redbreast happin' (hopping) on a brier (briar); and poussie baudrons says, "Whare's tu gaen, wee Robin?" And wee Robin says, "I'm gaun awa' to the King to sing him a sang this guid Yule mornin'." And poussie baudrons says, "Come here, wee Robin and I'll let ye see a bonnie white ring roun' my neck." But wee Robin says, "Na, Na! grey poussie baudrons; Na, Na! Ye worry't (savaged) the wee mousie, but ye'se no worry me." So wee Robin flew awa' till he cam' to a fail fauld-dike (turf fold wall), and there he saw a grey greedy gled (hawk) sittin'. And the grey greedy gled says, "Whare's tu gaen, wee Robin?" And wee Robin says, "I'm gaen awa' to the King to sing him a sang this guid Yule mornin'." And the grey greedy gled says, "Come here, wee Robin, and I'll let ye see a bonnie feather in my wing." But wee Robin says, "Na, Na! grey greedy gled; Na, Na! ye pookit (plucked) a' the wee lintie (linnet), but ye'se no pook me." So wee Robin flew awa' till he cam' to the cleuch (cleft) of a craig (crag), and there he saw slee (sly) Tod Lowrie (fox) sittin'. And slee Tod Lowrie says, "Whare's tu gaen, wee Robin?" And wee Robin says, "I'm gaen awa' to the King to sing him a sang this guid Yule mornin'." And slee Tod Lowrie says, "Come here, wee Robin, and I'll let ye see a bonnie spot on the tap o' my tail." But wee Robin says, "Na, na! slee Tod Lowrie; Na, Na! Ye worry't (savaged) the wee lammie (lamb), but ye'se no worry me." So wee Robin flew awa' till he cam' to a bonnie burnside, and there he saw a wee callant (boy) sittin.' And the wee callant says, "Whare's tu gaen, wee Robin?" And wee Robin says, "I'm gaun awa' to the King to sing him a sang this guid Yule mornin'." And the wee callant says, "Come here wee Robin, and I'll gie ye a wheen grand moolins (crumbs) oot o' my pooch (pocket)." But wee Robin says, "Na, na! wee callant, Na, Na! Ye speldert (tore apart) the gowdspink (goldfinch), but ye'se no spelder me." So wee Robin flew awa' till he cam' to the King, and there he sat on a winnock-sole (window sill) and sang the King a bonnie sang. And the King says to the Queen, "What'll we gi'e wee Robin for singin' us this bonnie sang?" And the Queen says to the King, "I think we'll gi'e him the wee Wren to be his wife." So wee Robin and the wee Wren were married, and the King and the Queen and a' the coort danced at their waddin'; syne (soon) he flew awa' hame to his ain waterside and happit (hopped) on a brier (briar).

'I'll be a brig when ye're a shapeless cairn'
(The 'New' bridge being dismantled after its collapse in 1877)

BRIGS OF AYR
Map Ref. 336 223 and 338 222

The two bridges span the River Ayr in Ayr town centre. They are referred to in the poem *THE BRIGS OF AYR*. The Auld Brig, probably built about 1232, is still in use as a busy footbridge. Until 1786 it was the only bridge over the river in or near the town. It was extensively restored in 1910. The history of the bridge and the story of its restoration can be read in the book Brig Of Ayr by James A. Morris (1910).

The New Brig of the poem was on the site of the bridge furthest downstream at present. The new bridge referred to in the poem, having been built in 1786, collapsed in a flood in 1877, as prophesied by the Auld Brig in the poem - 'I'll be a brig when ye're a shapeless cairn.'

Also see: Ducat Stream.

BURNS COTTAGE

BURNS COTTAGE
Map Ref. 335 186

Situated on the west side on the B7024 Ayr/Maybole Road, in Alloway Village, 2 miles south of Ayr town centre. In 1756, the poet's father, William Burnes, feuded 7½ acres of land from Doctor Alexander Campbell, Ayr. He built a cottage on the land and called the property New Gardens, intending to work the ground as a market garden.

Robert Burns was born in the cottage on 25 January, 1759. When he was 9 or 10 days old, the south gable of the house was blown down in a storm and - *'Twas then a blast o' Janwar win', Blew hansel in on Robin'* - as the poet recorded in his song *THERE WAS A LAD*.

When the poet was one day old he was baptised in the cottage by the Rev. William Dalrymple of Ayr Auld Kirk. The witnesses were John Tennant and James Young. Nothing is known of James Young. It is generally accepted that John Tennant was the farmer at Laigh Corton and later Glenconner, a friend of both the poet and his father. It is much more likely that the witness was John Tennant, blacksmith, Alloway, whose smiddy (smithy) was close to Burns cottage. The site of the smiddy, still called Smithy Cottage, is at No. 6 Main Street, Alloway. The blacksmith's wife is thought to have been a midwife at the poet's birth and also the *'gossip'* who *'keekit in his loof'*, according to the song *THERE WAS A LAD*.

A woman called Betty Davidson, an elderly relation of the poet's mother, lodged with the family in the cottage. Burns later recalled that she had a fund of stories about the supernatural and the young Burns probably had his imagination fired by her tales.

In 1766, when Burns was 7 years of age, the family moved from the cottage to Mount Oliphant Farm, about 2 miles away. William Burnes retained the cottage and rented it out until 1781. The Ayrshire Register of Sasines shows that on 4 August, 1781, the property was transferred from William Burnes, Farmer, Lochlea (to which they had moved from Mount Oliphant) to the Incorporation of Shoemakers, Ayr.

From 1781 to 1881, the shoemakers rented it out as an ale house and it fell into a state of some disrepair. It was not totally neglected as in 1847 the building which now houses the museum was built as a meeting hall. In 1881 the property was purchased by the Burns Monument Trustees. The Trustees restored the cottage and it was opened to the public in March, 1901 in the form in which we now know it.

It is interesting to note that the first recorded dinner to pay tribute to the memory of Robert Burns - the first Burns Supper - was held in the cottage. During the summer of 1801 a group of the poet's friends and admirers sat down to dinner, including sheep's head and haggis. The poem *ADDRESS TO A HAGGIS* was read and several toasts were drunk. A portrait of the poet painted on wood and intended as a sign for the cottage was presented to the company and an Ode On The Anniversary of Burns was read by its author, The Rev. Hamilton Paul, a noted Burns scholar. Nine gentlemen were present:-

William Crawford, Doonside, Ayr.

John Ballantine, lawyer, Castlehill, Ayr, to whom the poem *THE BRIGS OF AYR* was dedicated.

Robert Aiken, lawyer, Whitehill, Ayr, to whom the poem *THE COTTER'S SATURDAY NIGHT* was dedicated.

Dr. Patrick Douglas, Garallan, Cumnock, the poet's patron who arranged a post for him in Jamaica.

Primrose Kennedy, Drummelland, Maybole.

Hugh Ferguson, barrackmaster, Ayr.

David Scott, banker, Ayr.

Thomas Jackson, rector of Ayr Academy.

The Rev. Hamilton Paul, Burns scholar, elected Chaplain and Laureate.

The gathering resolved to meet again in the cottage on 29 January, 1802. It was thought then that the poet's birthday was 29 January. They duly met as arranged, joined by Provost William Bowie of Ayr and other 8 leading citizens.

The cottage was extensively refurbished in 1993. It is open to the public, as is a Burns museum in its grounds.

Also see: Alloway; Castlehill House; Doonside House; Garallan House; Museums, etc; New Gardens; Whitehill.

CAPRINGTON   Map Ref. 405 363

The castle and estate are situated 2 miles south-west of Kilmarnock, between the A759 Kilmarnock/Troon Road and the B7038 Kilmarnock/Ayr Road.

In a note to a suppressed stanza of the poem *THE VISION*, the poet indicated that the following lines refer to Caprington - '*And Irwine, marking out the bound, Enamour'd of the scenes around, Slow runs his race, A name I doubly honor'd found, With knightly grace.*'

The poet must have been familiar with the estate. In 1786, when Jean Armour's father took out a warrant against him, Burns went into hiding with his uncle and aunt at Fairlie Estate within a short distance of Caprington. As an admirer of the Scottish patriot, William Wallace, he would have known of the legends connecting Wallace with Caprington.

The Whistle, subject of the poem of that name, is held at Caprington.

Also see: Fairlie House; Old Rome; The Whistle.

SPECIAL FEATURE - THE STORY OF 'THE WHISTLE'

Burns's poem, 'The Whistle', is an account of a drinking contest held on 16th October, 1789, at Friar's Carse, near Dumfries. The gentlemen who took part were Robert Riddell of Glenriddell, Alexander Fergusson of Craigdarroch, and Sir Robert Lawrie of Maxwelton, all Dumfriesshire gentlemen noted for their heavy drinking habits.

The prize for the contest was a small, silver-mounted ebony whistle with a long history of bacchanalian revelry. It had been brought to Scotland by a Danish courtier who came with Prince George of Denmark when the latter married Princess (later Queen) Anne in 1683. The courtier revelled in his prowess as a toper and, when challenged, would place the whistle at the centre of a table round which the contestants sat, consuming drink for drink. As participants retired or lapsed into a drunken stupor, the winner was he last able to blow the whistle.

The Dane lost the whistle, eventually, in a contest against a Lawrie of Maxwelton, who, in turn, lost it to a Riddell of Glenriddell. The Lawrie and Riddell contestants in 1789 were descendants of the earlier Scottish winners.

Burns attended the Friar's Carse contest but did not take part. His friend, John McMurdo, was appointed judge of the bout, two gentlemen were witnesses, and Burns was the ballad-maker. The poet's wife and a Friar's Carse servant testified later that the poet had walked home sober.

The winner of the contest was Fergusson of Craigdarroch who drunk 'upwards of five bottles of claret' before his victory blast on the whistle.

By marriage, the whistle passed into the possession of the Cuninghame family of Caprington Castle, Kilmarnock. It is still kept at Caprington.

CARNELL HOUSE   Map Ref. 467 323

Situated east of the A719 Ayr/Galston Road, one mile south-west of its junction with the A76 Kilmarnock/Mauchline Road, and on the west bank of the River Cessnock. The house is still occupied. It is about 2 miles from Lochlea Farm and was called Cairnhill when Burns lived in the area.

In 1781, when the poet was 22 years of age, he courted a girl called Alison (Ellison) Begbie who worked at Carnell. She lived at Old Place Farm on the east bank of the Cessnock, about one mile downstream from Carnell. The poet wrote five romantic letters to Alison and she is thought to have been the heroine of the songs *THE LASS OF CESSNOCK BANK* and *BONNIE PEGGY ALISON* (And I'll Kiss Thee Yet). He proposed marriage to her but was rejected.

In a dispute between the poet's father, William Burnes, and his landlord, David McLure, over the terms of the lease of Lochlea Farm, Burnes claimed an allowance for the purchase of 12 tons of limestone annually from Cairnhill Lime Quarry, to fertilise the fields of the farm.

Cairnhill Lime Kilns, which the poet must have visited regularly, were situated about 300 yards north of the A719 Ayr/Galston Road and 400 yards east of the Fiveways/ Riccarton Road.

Also see: Mary Morison's House; Old Place.

CARNGILLAN Map Ref. 432 257

Situated on the B743 Ayr/Mauchline Road, at its junction with the B730 Tarbolton/Stair Road. A clump of trees in the field, about 100 yards north-west of the junction was the site of a dwelling in which was born James Humphrey, subject of the poem 'ON A NOISY POLEMIC'. In the poem, Burns referred to him as 'a bletherin' bitch' because of his liking for gossip and noisy controversy. As a stonemason, he worked at Lochlea and Mossgiel. As an aged, indigent man, he took advantage of his 'fame' by begging from visitors to Mauchline. He died in 1844, aged 84, and is buried in Mauchline kirkyard.

CARRICK

An ancient division of Ayrshire, being that part of the county south of the River Doon. The other divisions are Cunninghame and Kyle. The poet made several references to Carrick, the best known being in the song *MY FATHER WAS A FARMER* - *'My father was a farmer upon the Carrick border.'*

An entry by the poet in his First Commonplace Book, dated August 1784, referred to Kyle, Carrick and Cunninghame - 'My dear native country, the ancient Baileries of Carrick, Kyle and Cunninghame... We have never had one Scotch poet of any eminence, to make the fertile banks of Irvine, the romantic woodlands and sequestered scenes of Ayr, and the healthy, mountainous source and winding sweep of Doon, emulate Tay, Forth, Ettrick and Tweed.'

Also see: Cunninghame; Kyle.

CASSILIS DOWNANS Map Ref. 341 128

Green hillocky land west of the B742 Dalrymple/Maybole Road, about 2 miles south of Dalrymple. Cassilis is pronounced 'Castles'. It was referred to in the opening stanza of the poem *HALLOWE'EN* - *'Upon that night, when fairies light, On Cassilis Downans dance.'* The area takes its name from Cassilis House which is located at the map reference shown.

CASTLEHILL HOUSE Map Ref. 354 202

The house was situated east of the A713 Ayr/Dalmellington Road, 1½ miles south of Ayr town centre. The house is no longer extant but gave its name to the Castlehill district of Ayr. It was the home of John Ballantine, lawyer and banker who became Provost of Ayr in 1787. Ballantine was a friend and patron of Burns and corresponded with him over several years. The poem *THE BRIGS OF AYR* was inscribed to Ballantine.

Also see: Ayr Auld Kirk; Burns Cottage.

CATRINE

Situated on the B705 Mauchline/Auchinleck Road, 2½ miles south of Mauchline, and on the banks of the River Ayr. It was referred to in the poem *FAREWELL TO BALLOCHMYLE* or *THE BRAES OF BALLOCHMYLE* - *'The Catrine woods were yellow seen, The flowers decayed on Catrine lea.'* It was also referred to in the poem *THE BRIGS OF AYR* - *'Learning and Worth in equal measure strode, From simple Catrine, their long-loved abode.'* 'Learning and Worth' is a reference to Professor Dugald Stewart of Catrine House. In 1786, Professor Stewart introduced Burns to Lord Daer in Catrine House. The meeting is commemorated in the poem *ON MEETING LORD DAER.*

In 1788, Claud Alexander of Ballochmyle, in partnership with the industrial reformer, David Dale, established a cotton mill in the valley of the River Ayr at Catrine and the village was developed to house mill workers. Due to its beautiful location and design, Catrine was a model village for the first 150 years of its existence. Burns must have witnessed the development of the village.

Also see: Ballochmyle; Catrine House.

JOHN BALLANTYNE

CATRINE HOUSE   Map Ref. 532 257
Situated on the west side of Townhead, Catrine at its junction with Newton Street. The house was built in 1682 and is still occupied. It was the country home of Dugald Stewart, Professor of Moral Philosophy in Edinburgh University and patron and friend of Burns. On 23 October, 1786, together with Doctor Mackenzie of Mauchline, Burns was invited to lunch at Catrine House where Professor Stewart introduced him to Lord Daer, second son of the Earl of Selkirk. The meeting was commemorated by the poet in the poem *ON MEETING LORD DAER - 'A ne'er to be forgotten day, Sae far I sprackl'd up the brae, I dinner'd wi' a Lord!'*

As the house stands on the floor of a steep-sided valley, the poet's expression 'sprackl'd up the brae' has caused confusion in interpretation. He could have been referring to going up the Howford Brae south of the River Ayr on his likely route to Catrine House (Catrine Village did not exist and it is unlikely that a road existed on the line of the B705 Mauchline/Catrine Road) or referring to his homeward journey. It has been suggested that the poet was referring to his 'ascent of the social ladder' but the use of the word 'sprackl'd' (clambering with difficulty) in this context is hardly in keeping with the character of the poet.

Burns and Professor Stewart were both freemasons. At a meeting of Lodge St. James Tarbolton held in Mauchline on 25 July, 1787, over which the poet presided in his role of Depute Master, Professor Stewart was made an Honorary Member of the Lodge. When the poet was in Edinburgh, the Professor was kind to him and helped to introduce him to prominent members of society.

Also see: Catrine.

CATRINE HOUSE

CESSNOCK RIVER
Map Ref. 472 375

The Cessnock joins the River Irvine from the south, between Hurlford and Galston, at the map reference shown. It was referred to in the song *THE LASS OF CESSNOCK BANK*, which was probably inspired by the poet's early love, Alison (Ellison) Begbie. She lived at Old Place Farm, Crossroads, on the east bank of the Cessnock and worked at Carnell House on the west bank of the river, one mile upstream from her home. The river was also referred to in a suppressed stanza of the poem *THE VISION - 'Where Cessnock flows with gurgling sound.'* On a summer evening, walk by the winding, gurgling Cessnock near Carnell and it is easy to imagine the poet and his lass strolling together, unaware that two centuries later they would still be remembered.

The poet's friend, John Goldie of Kilmarnock - *'O Gowdie, terror o' the Whigs'* - subject of the poem *EPISTLE TO JOHN GOLDIE*, was born at Craig Mill on the Cessnock.

Also see: Auchinskeith; Carnell House; Craig Mill; Old Place.

CLONCAIRD
Map Ref. 357 076

Situated on the Water of Girvan, west of the B7045 Kirkmichael/Straiton Road, one mile south of Kirkmichael. It was the home of James Whitefoord, relative of the poet's patron and friend, Sir John Whiteford of Ballochmyle. Cloncaird was referred to as 'Glencaird' in the poem *THE FETE CHAMPETRE* - *'Their vote shall be Glencaird's man.'*

It is not known whether the reference was to Sir John or James Whiteford but was probably the latter. Sir John had moved to Edinburgh when he sold Ballochmyle in 1785 and the poem was not written until 1788.

COILSFIELD HOUSE   Map Ref. 447 265

The house is no longer extant. It was situated north of the A758 Ayr/Mauchline Road, one mile east of the B730 Tarbolton/Stair Road. It was the home of Colonel Hugh Montgomerie, later 12th Earl of Eglinton, who was referred to as 'Sodger Hugh' in the poem *THE AUTHOR'S EARNEST CRY AND PRAYER.*

Highland Mary Campbell is thought to have worked at Coilsfield as a dairy maid. In the poem *HIGHLAND MARY*, the poet referred to the house as *'The castle o' Montgomery,'* a reference to the family, and indicated that it was on the 'banks and braes and streams around' that he parted from Mary.

A large thorn tree which stood on the west bank of the Fail Water, about 200 yards north of the mansion house, was known as Mary's Thorn and was reputed to be a trysting place for Burns and Mary Campbell. When the tree collapsed it was cut up and distributed throughout the world.

Coilsfield was demolished and replaced by a new mansion which was called Montgomerie House. The house is no longer extant, having been destroyed by fire. 'Montgomerie's Peggy', heroine of the song of that name and one of the most mysterious figures in the works of Burns, worked at Coilsfield while the poet was at Lochlea. Gilbert Burns said that the poet was in the habit of meeting Peggy at Tarboth Mill (Tarbolton or Willie's Mill). Burns wrote - "though I began the affair merely in a 'gaiete de coeur', or, to tell the truth . . . a vanity of showing my parts in courtship, particularly my abilities at a 'billet-doux' . . . When I had battered myself into a very warm affection for her, she told me one day in a flag of truce, that her fortress had been for some time before the rightful property of another." Peggy was engaged to be married to another and Burns ended this courtship.

In a dispute between the poet's father, William Burnes, and his Lochlea landlord, the arbiter on behalf of Burnes was one, Charles Norval of Coilsfield. All that is known about Norval is that he was a gardener at Coilsfield. Tradition maintains that the man referred to as 'whipper-in' in the poem *THE TWA DOGS* - *'Our whipper-in, wee blastit wonner'* - was Hugh Andrew, Huntsman at Coilsfield.

Also see: Fail; Failford; Mauchline Burn; Montgomerie House; Stairaird; Tarbolton Mill.

COLDCOTHILL FARM   Map Ref. 454 308

Situated a half mile south of the A719 Ayr/Galston Road, 2½ miles east of the B730 Dundonald/Tarbolton Road. It is a neighbouring farm to Lochlea and was said by the poet's brother, Gilbert Burns, to have been the home of Agnes Fleming whom Gilbert said was the heroine of the song *MY NANIE O'*.

Doura Farm, which also neighbours Lochlea, has also been referred to as the home of Agnes Fleming.

The Ayrshire Register of Sasines shows that when the Burnes family lived in Lochlea, a family called Steven lived in Coldcothill. The Register also shows that one John Fleming was tenant of Doura. It is thought that Agnes Fleming's home was at Doura and that she worked at Coldcothill.

A massive plane tree, said to have been a trysting place for Burns and Agnes Fleming, stood on the hill above Coldcothill until 1949.

The poet's youngest sister, Isabella Burns Begg, said that the heroine of the song *MY NANIE, O'* was Peggy Thomson of Kirkoswald; the poet's aunt, Mrs. Brown of Kirkoswald, said that it was Agnes McIlwraith of Pinvalley, Barr; local tradition in Girvan maintains that it was Nannie Brown, daughter of the proprietor of the Ship Inn, Girvan; and Rev. Hamilton Paul, a 19th century Burns scholar, said that it was an Agnes Sheriff of Kilmarnock. The poet did not identify the heroine.

Also see: Doura Farm; Girvan River; Kirkoswald; Lugar River; Minnybae Farm; Pinvalley; Peggy Thomson's House; Ship Inn; Stinchar River.

COMMONSIDE   Map Ref. 415 244

Situated on the B744 Annbank/Tarbolton Road, one mile east of Annbank. The poet's friend and fellow-rhymer, David Sillar, set up an adventure school at Commonside after he had failed to obtain a post as permanent teacher at Tarbolton school. The post as teacher was given to John Wilson, immortalised by Burns as *'Doctor Hornbook'* in the poem *DEATH AND DOCTOR HORNBOOK*. The Commonside school failed after a short time and David Sillar moved to Irvine. Later in life he inherited wealth and became a respected businessman and member of Irvine Town Council.

Also see: Irvine; Spittalside.

CORSINCON   Map Ref. 671 147

A conical shaped hill, 1547 feet high, situated east of the A76 New Cumnock/Sanquhar Road, 3 miles south of New Cumnock. It is referred to in one of the poet's most beautiful songs which gets less appreciation than it deserves, *O' WERE I ON PARNASSUS HILL -* *'On Corsincon I'll glow'r and spell, And write how much I love thee.'* When the song was composed, Burns and Jean Armour were recently married but separated. He was living alone at Isle, Dumfries, preparing Ellisland Farm for her arrival from Mauchline. From the words we can picture Burns in the solitude looking lovingly and longingly northwards to Corsincon and beyond towards Mauchline and thinking of his young wife. The hill is also referred to in the poem *DOES HAUGHTY GAUL INVASION THREAT -* *'The Nith shall run to Corsincon.'*

COWGATE   Map Ref. 498 273

Cowgate is a street in Mauchline town centre. It extends south from Loudoun Street, 50 yards west of the Cross. When Burns was in Mauchline area, it was the main route into the village from the south.

It was referred to in the poem *THE HOLY FAIR* - *'While "common-sense" has taen the road, An' aff an' up the Cowgate.'* Tradition maintains that "common-sense" was a reference to the poet's physician and friend, Doctor John Mackenzie. Shortly before the poem was composed, the doctor had written an article, either on the subject of common-sense or signed 'common-sense' as a nom-de-plume, and possibly in reply to something said or written by Burns. On the day of Mauchline Holy Fair he had arranged to dine with the Earl of Dumfries at Dumfries House, Cumnock, and the poet saw him heading out of the village by the Cowgate, just as the Rev. Dr. William Peebles of Newton-on-Ayr was mounting the rostrum to give his oration.

Jean Armour's parental home was in Cowgate, as was Beechgrove Cottage where the poem *ADDRESS TO A HAGGIS* is said to have been composed. The poet's favourite tavern, The Whitefoord Arms, was on the west side on the junction of Cowgate and Loudoun Street and Poosie Nancie's Inn, the setting of the cantata Love and Liberty (The Jolly Beggars) is on the east side on the junction. Ann Orr's Ale House, where Burns attended meetings of Mauchline Young Men's Society, was on the east side of Cowgate, at its junction with Mansefield Road.

Also see: Ann Orr's Ale House; Armour's House; Beechgrove Cottage; Mauchline; Poosie Nancie's Inn; Whitefoord Arms.

COWGATE circa 1875

COYLE WATER   Map Ref. 396 215

Joins the River Ayr from the south at the map reference shown, a half mile upstream from the bridge carrying the B744 Annbank/Belston Road. It is referred to in the poems *THE BRIGS OF AYR* - '*When from the woods where springs the brawling Coil*'. It is also referred to in the song *THE SOLDIER'S RETURN* - '*I thought upon the banks o' Coil*'. Tradition maintains that Millmannoch on the river is the location described in the song as the meeting place of the soldier and his sweetheart.

The name is derived from Coilus, King of the Picts (said to be the original of Old King Cole of the nursery rhyme). The name Kyle for an ancient division of Ayrshire is also derived from Coilus/Coil. In the poem *THE VISION*, Burns referred to his poetic Muse as Coila.

Also see: Coylton; Kyle.

COYLTON

The modern village is situated on the A70 Ayr/Cumnock Road, 5 miles east of Ayr. the hamlet now called Low Coylton, one mile to the south on the Coylton/Drongan Road, was the original village. The ruined remains of the original parish church are at Low Coylton.

The Rev. David Shaw, referred to by Burns in the poem *THE TWA HERDS* as one of *'baith the Shaws'*, was Minister at Coylton from 1749 to 1810. He was Moderator of the General Assembly of the Church of Scotland in 1776. Although he lived until he was 91 years of age he was reputed never to have required spectacles for reading or writing. He is buried in the kirkyard at Low Coylton.

The ruined Kirk at Low Coylton -
including the graves of Rev. Shaw and Nellie Kilpatrick's parents.

Alan Kilpatrick and his wife, Margaret Good, parents of Nellie Kilpatrick, the girl to whom Burns addressed his first song, *HANDSOME NELL*, are also buried in Low Coylton kirkyard. Alan Kilpatrick was miller at Purclewan Mill near Mount Oliphant when the Burnes family lived at the farm; he was born at Millmannoch, between Low Coylton and Drongan.

Tradition maintains that Millmannoch is the location described in the song *THE SOLDIER'S RETURN*. The song relates how the returning soldier - 'thought upon the banks o' Coil' - then - 'reach'd the bonie glen' - and - 'pass'd the mill and trysting thorn'. Millmannoch is recognisable from the description and to describe it as he did, the poet must have been familiar with the area.

On the east side of the Low Coylton/Drongan Road, a half mile south of Low Coylton and 200 yards north of Millmannoch (map ref. 431 185), a thorn bush surrounded by a metal fence is said to be the 'trysting thorn' of the song *THE SOLDIER'S RETURN*.

Also see: Purclewan.

CRAIGENGILLAN HOUSE
Map Ref. 474 028

The house is still occupied. It is situated one mile north of Loch Doon, Dalmellington. It was the home of John McAdam, who was addressed in the poem *TO MR McADAM OF CRAIGEN-GILLAN* - *'I'll cock my nose aboon them a', I'm roos'd by Craigen-Gillan.'*

McAdam had written to Burns who responded with the poem, written extempore in Nance Tannock's Inn, Mauchline. In the poem, John McAdam's son, Quinton McAdam, was referred to as 'young Dunaskin's laird.' Quinton was also referred to in the poem *SECOND HERON ELECTION BALLAD* as '*o' lads no the warst.*'

In a letter from Edinburgh to Doctor Mackenzie, Mauchline, dated 11 January, 1787, Burns made reference to one of John McAdam's daughters as 'the beauty-famed and wealth-celebrated Miss McAdam, our Country-woman.'

CRAIGENTON FARM

CRAIGENTON FARM   Map Ref. 231 055

Situated 2 miles east of Turnberry and to the east of the 'C' class road from Kirkoswald to Girvan. The poet's maternal grandparents and great grandparents farmed at Craigenton. His mother, Agnes Broun, daughter of Gilbert Broun and Agnes Rennie was probably born at Whitestone Cottage, Culzean, and moved to Craigenton as an infant when her father joined her grandfather in the farm. She was the eldest of 6 children and her mother died when she was 10 years old. After looking after her brothers and sisters for two years, with the help of Ann Gillespie who later married John Davidson, prototype of Souter Johnie, Agnes went to live with her maternal grandmother, Mrs. Rennie, in Maybole.

Gilbert Broun married 3 times and it is thought that Agnes became estranged from her father and step-mothers, resulting in the poet having little or no contact with his grandfather.

The poet's maternal grandparents and great grandparents are buried in Kirkoswald kirkyard.

Also see: Kirkoswald; Maybole; Whitestone Cottage.

CRAIGIE VILLAGE   Map Ref. 428 324

Situated between the A77 Ayr/Kilmarnock Road and A719 Ayr/Galston Road. 1½ miles east of the B730 Dundonald/Tarbolton Road.

The poet's friend, the Rev. George Bannatyne, was minister of Craigie Parish Church from 1744 to 1764. After leaving Craigie, he was minister of St. George's Church, Glasgow.

As Bannatyne left Craigie 13 years before Burns moved to the nearby farm of Lochlea, it is not known when or how they became acquainted.

The Rev. Andrew Shaw, referred to in the poem *THE TWA HERDS* as one of *'baith the Shaws'*, was minister at Craigie from 1765 to 1810. He is buried in Craigie kirkyard. John Wilson, *'Doctor Hornbook'* of the poem *DEATH AND DOCTOR HORNBOOK*, was school master at Craigie before he moved to Tarbolton in 1781.

The village should not be confused with Craigie House, Ayr, parental home of the poet's friend and patron, Mrs. Dunlop of Dunlop. Craigie House took its name from the Wallace family's ancient seat, Craigie Castle near Craigie Village.

Sir John Wallace, Laird of Craigie and ancestor of Mrs. Dunlop is referred to in the poem *THE VISION* as - *'The chief on Sark, who glorious fell in high command.'* In 1448, Sir John was wounded in a battle on the banks of the River Sark on the Scottish/English border and died 3 months later at Craigie Castle.

CRAIG MILL   Map Ref. 482 329

Situated on the north bank of the River Cessnock, a few hundred yards east of the A76 Kilmarnock/Mauchline Road. The mill is no longer extant and only the track leading to it and the remnants of the man-made wall of the lade can be traced. It was the parental home of John Goldie or Gowdie, friend of Burns and referred to in the poem *EPISTLE TO JOHN GOLDIE* - *'O' Gowdie terror o' the Whigs.'* Goldie was born at Craig Mill in 1717. He moved to Kilmarnock and started in business as a cabinet maker and later became a prosperous wine merchant with a shop at Kilmarnock Cross. He earned some fame as a writer of religious essays and as a theorist on religious beliefs.

Tradition maintains that Goldie visited Burns at Mossgiel during harvest time in 1785. Burns was working in a field and when Goldie arrived the poet sat down with him behind a stook and recited a few of his compositions. Goldie suggested that Burns should visit him at his home in Kilmarnock; he did so and was introduced to the leading citizens of Kilmarnock, many of whom remained his friends. John Goldie stood surety to John Wilson, printer, for the printing of the Kilmarnock Edition of the poet's work.

CROOKES'S

In the 'Rob Rhymer' manuscript of the poem *THE ORDINATION*, Burns changed the name 'Begbie's' to 'Crookes's' in the lines originally composed as *'then aff to Begbie's in a raw, An' drink divine libations.'* The line is normally published as 'Begbie's'. The place referred to as 'Crookes's' is unknown. It is generally said to have been an inn in Kilmarnock town centre. Another feasible theory is that it referred to the home of a family called Crookes who were prominent in the leather trade in the town in the 18th century. In support of this theory, the third line of the poem is quoted - *'An' ye wha leather rax an' draw'* - but it must be regarded as of little evidential value.

Also see: Begbie's Inn.

CROSS KEYS INN   Map Ref. 431 272

The building is no longer extant. It was situated on the south side of Cunningham Street, Tarbolton, on the site now occupied by a public garden. At a meeting in the inn on 8 July, 1782, Lodge St. James Tarbolton was reconstituted. For several years thereafter, the Lodge met in the inn and Burns was an enthusiastic and regular attender. As Depute Master of the Lodge from 1784 to 1788, he occasionally presided over the meetings.

On 9 August, 1844, the poet's three surviving sons were made Honorary Members of Lodge St. James at a meeting in Cross Keys Inn.

Also see: Freemasonry; Manson's Inn; Museums, etc., Tarbolton.

Cunningham Street, Tarbolton, circa 1900 with the Cross Keys Inn on the left and Doctor Hornbook's House third from the right

ROBERT BURNS Jnr.

COL. W. NICHOL BURNS
The poet's third son.

LIEUT. COL. JAMES GLENCAIRN BURNS
The poet's fourth son

CROSSRAGUEL
Map Ref. 275 084

Jean Kennedy, the model for *'Kirkton Jean'* of the poem *TAM O'SHANTER*, was the daughter of Alexander Kennedy, Farmer, Crossraguel. No Crossraguel Farm exists at present and it is concluded that Alexander Kennedy had a small farm or was a farm worker in the vicinity of Crossraguel Abbey.

The 13th century abbey is situated on the east side of the A77 Maybole/Girvan Road, one mile south of Maybole. It was a ruin when Burns was a boy in the area. He made no reference to it in his works.

Jean Kennedy, and her sister Anne, kept an inn in Kirkoswald known locally at The Ladies' or Leddies' House. In the poem *TAM O'SHANTER*, Burns referred to it as *'The Lord's House.'*

Also see: Kirkoswald; The Ladies' House.

CULZEAN CASTLE
Map Ref. 232 013

Situated on the Ayrshire coast, 13 miles south of Ayr. The property is now owned by the National Trust for Scotland and is open to the public. The existing castle was built from 1777 onwards by Robert Adam for the 10th Earl of Cassilis. It was built on the site of an ancient stronghold of the Kennedy family. Culzean is referred to as 'Colean' in the poem *HALLOWE'EN - 'Or for Colean the rout is ta' en.'*

CUMNOCK

Situated at the junction of the A76 Mauchline/Dumfries Road and the A70 Ayr/Muirkirk Road. The poet was very familiar with Cumnock and district, passing rhough regularly on his journeys between Mossgiel and Ellisland. The town was referred to in the poem *DEATH AND DOCTOR HORNBOOK - 'The rising moon began to glowre, The distant*

Cumnock Hills out-owre.' In a note to a suppressed stanza of the poem *THE VISION*, the poet indicated that the following line refers to Cumnock - *'Where Lugar leaves his moorland plaid.'*

Anne Rankine, later Mrs. Merry, and probably the 'Annie' of the song *THE RIGS OF BARLEY*, lived in the town after her marriage and is buried in the old cemetery.

William Simson, friend and fellow poet of Burns was appointed school master at Cumnock in 1788, having previously been School Master at Ochiltree. He is buried in Cumnock old cemetery, near Anne Rankine.

Also see: Adamhill Farm; Dumfries House; Garallan; Logan House; South Auchenbrain Farm.

CUNNINGHAME

An ancient division of Ayrshire, being that part of the county north of the River Irvine. Kyle and Carrick are the other ancient divisions of the county. Cunninghame was referred to in the cantata *LOVE AND LIBERTY*, better known as *THE JOLLY BEGGARS* - *'Till I met my old boy in a Cunningham Fair.'* It was also referred to in a letter dated 17 July, 1787, from Burns to Mrs. Dunlop of Dunlop - 'The farther corners of Cunningham, a place I little know.'

An entry by the poet in his first Common-Place Book, dated August, 1784, referred to Cunninghame, Kyle and Carrick - 'My dear native country, the ancient baileries of Kyle, Carrick and Cunninghame. We have never had one Scotch poet of any eminence, to make the fertile banks of Irvine, the romantic woodlands and sequestered scenes on Ayr, and the healthy, mountainous source and winding sweep of Doon, emulate Tay, Forth, Ettrick and Tweed.'

Also see: Carrick; Kyle.

DALFRAM   Map Ref. 655 267

The house is no longer extant. It was situated on the south side of the B743 Muirkirk/ Sorn Road, 2½ miles west of Muirkirk. It was the birthplace in 1727 and home of John Lapraik, Ayrshire rhymer and an acquaintance of Burns; he was addressed in the three *EPISTLES TO J. LAPRAIK*. Although generally described as being from Dalfram, he was the farmer at Laigh Dalfram Farm, the site of which is marked by a cairn on the north bank of the River Ayr, about 100 yards south-east of Townhead Farm on the Muirkirk/ Sorn Road. The cairn was erected in 1914 by the Lapraik Burns Club of Muirkirk.

As a result of having lost money in the collapse of the Ayr Bank in 1772, Lapraik moved from Laigh Dalfram to Muirsmill, then to Netherwood, back to Muirsmill, and to Nether Wellwood, all in the same area of Muirkirk Parish, and latterly into Muirkirk village. He is buried in Muirkirk kirkyard.

Lapraik's wife was Margaret Rankine, sister of John Rankine of Adamhill Farm, Tarbolton - 'rough, rude, ready-witted Rankine' - and an aunt of Anne Rankine, who was probably 'Annie' of the song *THE RIGS OF BARLEY*. It may have been through this connection that Burns and Lapraik first knew of each other.

According to his first epistle to Lapraik, Burns was at a 'rockin' (social evening) in Mauchline when he heard a song being sung which appealed to him. On enquiring about the song he was told that it was by a man, Lapraik, from Muirkirk.

In a copy of Johnson's Musical Museum presented by Burns to Captain Riddell of Glenriddell, Dumfries, the poet made the following footnote to the song *WHEN I UPON THY BOSOM LEAN* - 'this song was the work of a very worthy, facetious old fellow, John Lapraik, of Dalfram, near Muirkirk. He has often told me that he composed this song one day when his wife had been fretting over their misfortunes.'

Also see: Adamhill Farm; Muirkirk; Muirsmill.

DALJARROCK HOUSE   Map Ref. 188 881

Situated one mile west of the A714 Girvan/Newton Stewart Road, 2 miles north of Pinwherry. The house is still occupied. It was the home of Robert Kennedy, father-in-law of Gavin Hamilton, the poet's friend and patron in Mauchline. Kennedy's daughter, Peggy Kennedy, was the heroine of the poem *YOUNG PEGGY* - *'Young Peggy blooms our boniest lass.'*

DALRYMPLE

Situated on the B742 Maybole/Coylton Road, 5 miles north of Maybole, and on the banks of the River Doon. It is the village nearest to the farm of Mount Oliphant where the poet lived from 7 to 18 years of age. In 1772, when Burns was 13 years old, he attended Dalrymple Parish School. Robert and his brother Gilbert could not both be spared from the work of Mount Oliphant, so for one term they attended on alternate weeks to improve their writing.

The site of the school is now occupied by the White Horse Hotel.

DALSANGAN MILL   Map Ref. 480 307

Now Dalsangan Farm, it is situated on the Crosshands/Fiveways Road, about 400 yards north of the B744 Crosshands/Largie Toll Road. The ancient mill was referred to as a working mill as early as 1205. It was a meal mill until the mid-19th century and tradition maintains that it was the mill used by Burns while he was at Mossgiel Farm. The miller was called Morton.

The water for Dalsangan Mill came from Loch Brown which lay in the depression west of the A76 Kilmarnock/Mauchline Road and south of the B744 Crosshands/Largie Toll Road. The loch was drained for the construction of the Kilmarnock/Dumfries railway line about 1847.

Tradition maintains that Burns played curling on the loch and that Tam Samson of Kilmarnock occasionally went shooting on its shores.

Also see: Mossgiel Farm; Tam Samson's House.

DALWHATSWOOD   Map Ref. 542 381

Situated in Cemetery Road, Newmilns, almost a mile north of Main Street, It was formerly spelled Dalquhatswood. It was the home of John Arnot who subscribed to the first Edinburgh Edition of the poet's works and to whom the poet wrote one letter, post-dated as 'about the latter end of 1785.' In the Glenriddell Manuscript, the poet described Arnot as 'one of the most accomplished sons of men I ever met with - Alas! Had he been equally prudent.' There is no other reference to Arnot in the works of Burns. It is not known where or when the men became acquainted.

DAMHOUSE OF ARDLOCHAN   Map Ref. 221 088

Situated on the north end of Maidenhead Bay, a half mile north of Maidens village. Hugh

Brown, miller, designated as of Ardlochan Mill or Damhouse of Ardlochan, is thought to have been the model for the 'miller' of the poem *TAM O'SHANTER* - *'That ilka medler wi' the miller, Thou sat as lang as thou had siller.'*

Damhouse of Ardlochan is still occupied. The mill, which was between the house and the shore, is no longer extant but the course of the lade and other features can be identified. It was the mill nearest to Shanter Farm and is certain to have been used by Douglas Graham, model for 'Tam' in the poem *TAM O'SHANTER.*

Hugh Brown was related to the poet's mother and the poet probably visited him while in the area.

Douglas Graham of Shanter also farmed Laigh Park Farm, neighbouring Ballochneil Farm and Mill, Kirkoswald, and another tradition maintains that Robert Niven the Ballochneil miller was the model for the miller of the poem *TAM O'SHANTER.* Burns lodged at Ballochneil in 1775 while attending Hugh Rodger's school, Kirkoswald.

Also see: Ardlochan; Ballochneil Farm and Mill; Laigh Park Farm; Maidens; Shanter Farm.

Cunningham Street, Tarbolton, circa 1910 with Doctor Hornbook's House third from the right.

DOCTOR HORNBOOK'S HOUSE AND SCHOOL   Map Ref. 431 273

John Wilson, immortalised by Burns as 'Doctor Hornbook' in the poem *DEATH AND DOCTOR HORNBOOK*, was school master at Tarbolton from 1781 to 1790. He was also session clerk of the church and secretary of Lodge St. James Tarbolton. Before he moved to Tarbolton, Wilson had been schoolmaster at Craigie, near the poet's home at Lochlea and Burns probably knew him or at least knew of him at that time. John Wilson's house is still inhabited. He lived in either No. 20 or No. 22 Cunningham Street, Tarbolton; the houses are semi-detached and it is not known for certain which one he occupied. They are now single storied houses with slated roofs but were originally of two storeys with thatched roofs. He sold 'remedies' from his home, advertising his services in a ground

45

floor window.

The school in which Wilson taught is no longer extant. It stood on the south side of Cunningham Street, a few yards west of Wilson's house, and on the west side of what is now the vehicle entrance to Tarbolton Church and cemetery.

It has been said that the poem *DEATH AND DOCTOR HORNBOOK* brought such ridicule on John Wilson that he had to give up his job as school master, shut up 'shop' and leave Tarbolton. In fact, as fellow members of Lodge St. James and Wilson having been Lodge secretary when Burns was Depute Master, the two men were on good terms. In 1790, when Wilson decided to change his employment and leave Tarbolton, he wrote to Burns at Ellisland Farm, Dumfries. By then Burns was famous and Wilson sought his advice and assistance in obtaining a clerical post in Edinburgh. In a letter dated 11 September, 1790, the poet sent a very kindly worded reply, advising against the post but enclosing a reference to a lawyer in Edinburgh. Wilson accepted the advice and moved to Glasgow where he worked as a schoolteacher. He became session clerk of Gorbals Parish Church and is buried in Gorbals kirkyard.

Also see: Freemasonry; Johnie Ged's Hole; Tarbolton.

DOONHOLM HOUSE   Map Ref. 338 175

Situated south of Doonholm Road, Alloway, and west of the A77 Ayr/Maybole Road. The house is still occupied. It was the home of Doctor William Ferguson, Provost of Ayr. The poet's father, William Burnes, worked as head gardener at Doonholm. He had previously worked at the neighbouring Doonside House.

Doctor Ferguson owned Mount Oliphant Farm and in November, 1765, leased it to William Burnes as from Whitsun, 1766. He also lent the poet's father £100 to help him to stock the farm.

Doonholm was later the home of John Hunter, an Ayr lawyer who was probably the gentleman referred to in the poem *EPITAPH FOR J.H.*

Also see: Ayr Auld Kirk; Mount Oliphant Farm; Doonside House.

DOON RIVER   Map Ref. 324 195

The river flows generally west through Ayrshire and enters the Firth of Clyde 2 miles south of Ayr town centre, at the map reference shown. The river is close to Burns Cottage and Mount Oliphant. Until he moved to Lochlea in 1777, aged 18 years, the poet must have been very familiar with the banks and braes, holms and woods of its lower reaches.

There are numerous references to the river in the poet's works, the most famous being in the versions of the song *THE BANKS O'DOON - 'Ye banks and braes o' bonie Doon, How can ye bloom sae fresh and fair?'* It is also famed for its place in the poem *TAM O'SHANTER - 'Before him Doon pours all his floods.'*

DOONSIDE HOUSE   Map Ref. 335 176

The house is no longer extant. It was situated on the south bank of the River Doon, east of the B7024 Ayr/Maybole Road. It was the home of John Crawford, who employed the poet's father, William Burnes, as a gardener. About 1752, 2 years after he came to Ayrshire from the east of Scotland, during which time he had worked at Fairlie House, Dundonald, William Burnes entered employment at Doonside.

Also see: Doonside Mill; Fairlie House; Doonholm House.

DOONSIDE MILL Map Ref. 334 177

Situated on the north bank of the River Doon, a few hundred yards east of Old Doon Bridge. Although originally called Doonside Mill, it is known as the Dutch Mill. Even in 1754, when the lands of Alloway were feued off by public roup, it was referred to as the Dutch Mill.

About 1752, the poet's father, William Burnes, moved to Alloway from Fairlie House, Dundonald, and took up employment as a landscape gardener at Doonside House and later Doonholm House. Local legend maintains that from 1752 until he was married and set up home in New Gardens (Burns Cottage) in December, 1757, he lodged at Doonside Mill, although this can not be verified.

Legend also maintains that the only 'public' clock in the area was on a building on Mill Brae, above the Mill, and that William Burnes was in the habit of walking up the brae to see the time on the clock.

Also see: Doonholm House; Doonside House.

DOUGLASTON

Douglas Graham of Shanter Farm, model for *'Tam'* in the poem *TAM O' SHANTER*, was born at Douglaston Farm. No farm of that name exists at present but part of the village of Maidens retains the name Douglaston. In Armstrong's 1775 map of Ayrshire, the name Douglaston is shown in the area now occupied by Maidens. The name Maidens would be unknown to Burns; it is derived from twin rocks on the shore and did not appear on a map until 1828.

William Sloan, referred to as *'Haverel Will'* in the poem *HALLOWE'EN*, was born at Douglaston in December, 1758. On the recommendation of the poet's uncle, Samuel Broun, he was employed as a gaudsman at Mossgiel. He returned to Kirkoswald Parish and was apprenticed as a shoemaker with John Davidson, the model for *Souter Johnie* in the poem *TAM O' SHANTER*. Sloan eventually settled in Dalmellington.

Also see: Ardlochan; Damhouse of Ardlochan; Glenfoot; Kirkoswald; Maidens; Shanter Farm; The Cellars.

DOURA FARM Map Ref. 447 305

Situated a half mile south of the A719 Ayr/Galston Road, at a part 2½ miles east of the B730 Dundonald/Tarbolton Road. It is a neighbouring farm to Lochlea and was said by the Rev. Charles Rodgers in his Books of Burns to have been the home of Agnes Fleming.

The poet's brother, Gilbert Burns, said that Agnes Fleming lived at Coldcothill Farm, a neighbouring farm to Doura and that she was the heroine of the song *MY NANIE, O'*.

The Ayrshire Register of Sasines shows that when the Burnes family lived in Lochlea, a family called Steven lived in Coldcothill. It also shows that one John Fleming was tenant of Doura. It is thought that Agnes Fleming's home was at Doura and that she worked at Coldcothill.

Other girls are also said to have been the heroine of the song. The poet gave no indication of the girl he had in mind.

Also see: Coldcothill Farm; Girvan River; Kirkoswald; Lugar River; Minnybae Farm; Peggy Thomson's House; Pinvalley; Ship Inn; Stinchar River.

DRUKKEN STEPS   Map Ref. 329 404
The Drukken Steps were situated in Eglinton Estate, between Irvine and Kilwinning, at the map reference shown. The site is now covered by the Irvine by-pass dual carriageway. The ancient name of the site was St. Bryde's Well. In 1927 a plaque was placed near the Drukken Steps to commemorate the area as a favourite walk of Burns and his friend Richard Brown during the period when the poet was living in Irvine. In a letter to Brown dated 30 December, 1787, the poet wrote - 'Do you recollect a Sunday we spent in Eglinton Woods?'

In 1976, on the construction of Irvine by-pass, Irvine Burns Club had the plaque re-located on a cairn in Mackinnon Terrace, Irvine, 700 yards south-east of its original position at the Drukken Steps.

Also see: Eglinton; Irvine.

DUCAT STREAM   Map Ref. 341 218
An ancient ford on the River Ayr, in the vicinity of the modern Turner's Bridge, Ayr. It can still be detected at low tide, especially when the river is also low. It is referred to in the poem *THE BRIGS OF AYR* - *'There's men o' taste would tak the Ducat Stream.'* In a note to the poem, Burns indicated that it was 'a noted ford, just above the Auld Brig.'

The name of the ford is probably derived from the 'Doo-Cot' or 'Dove-Cot' of the ancient priory which stood on the site of the Auld Kirk of Ayr.

DUMFRIES HOUSE   Map Ref. 542 204
Situated north of the A70 Ayr/Cumnock Road, one mile west of Cumnock. The house was built between 1754 and 1759 and is still extant. John Kennedy, friend and correspondent of Burns, was factor to the Earl of Dumfries at Dumfries House. He was related to Gavin Hamilton, the poet's Mauchline friend and patron. Burns sent Kennedy copies of his poems and Kennedy was probably the first person to be shown the poem *TO A MOUNTAIN DAISY*. John Kennedy was the subject of the poems *LINES TO JOHN KENNEDY* and *TO JOHN KENNEDY, DUMFRIES HOUSE*. In the second postscript (last stanza) of the poem *THE KIRKS ALARM*, he was referred to as *'Factor John'* - *'Factor John! Factor John! Whom the Lord made alone, And ne'er made another thy peer.'*

The poet's father-in-law, James Armour, is reputed to have been engaged in the building of Dumfries House.

DUNASKIN
Situated on the A713 Ayr/Dalmellington Road, about 2½ miles west of Dalmellington. In the poem *TO MR. McADAM OF CRAIGENGILLAN* Burns referred to Mr. McAdam's son, Quinton McAdam, as - 'young Dunaskin's laird.' Together with Barbeth, Straiton and Dalmellington, Dunaskin formed the estate of Mr. McAdam.

Also see: Craigengillan House.

DUNDONALD
Situated on the B730 Irvine/Tarbolton Road, at its junction with the A759 Troon/Kilmarnock Road. Burns must have been familiar with the village as he had to pass through it on his journeys between Lochlea and Irvine. In 1786, when Jean Armour's father took out a warrant against him, Burns hid out near Old Rome in Dundonald Parish.

The Rev. Dr. Robert Duncan, *'Duncan Deep'* of the poem *THE TWA HERDS* was minister of Dundonald from 1783 until his death in 1815. He is buried in Dundonald kirkyard. The present church was built on the site of the previous church in 1803.

The Rev. Dr. Thomas Burns, the poet's nephew, while minister of Monkton Parish, assisted in the running of Dundonald Parish

When the poet's father, William Burnes, moved to Ayrshire from the east of Scotland, he lived and worked at Fairlie House in Dundonald Parish. On 26 November, 1752, Dundonald Parish Church Session gave him a character reference.

Also see: Fairlie House; Monkton; Old Rome.

Sandgate, Ayr with the Tolbooth Steeple, circa 1820

DUNGEON-CLOCK   Map Ref. 337 220

The clock was on the steeple of Ayr Tolbooth or town jail which stood in the middle of Sandgate between Academy Street and Cathcart Street. A plaque on the wall of the Registry Office, Sandgate, indicates the site of the Tolbooth. The building and its clock were removed in 1826. The dungeon-clock was referred to in the poem *THE BRIGS OF AYR - 'The drowsy dungeon-clock had numbered two.'*

John Kennedy, described as keeper of the dungeon-clock, is amongst those listed as associates of Burns who are buried in Ayr Auld Kirkyard. Nothing further is known about him.

DUNLOP HOUSE   Map Ref. 427 494

Situated on the 'C' class road from Dunlop to Neilston, one mile east of Dunlop. The original house is no longer extant, the present one having been built in 1834. It was the home of Mrs. Frances Dunlop of Dunlop, patron and friend of Burns. They corresponded regularly over many years and the poet visited the house on at least 5 occasions, staying overnight on 3 visits.

In 1786, Mrs. Dunlop was given a copy of the poem *THE COTTER'S SATURDAY NIGHT* and was so taken with it that she wished to read more of its author's work. She sent a messenger to Mossgiel with a letter for Burns, asking him to send her a half-dozen copies of his poems (Kilmarnock Edition) and inviting him to visit her home. Thus started a friendship and regular correspondence which was to last for the rest of the poet's life, except for a period of estrangement when Mrs. Dunlop took offence at the content of a letter and broke off the exchange of letters. In a letter to Mrs. Dunlop dated 26 October, 1788, Burns wrote of his intention to visit Dunlop Cow Fair at Hallowe'en.

When Burns and Jean Armour were married and moving into Ellisland Farm, Dumfries, Mrs. Dunlop's son, Major Andrew Dunlop, gave them a present of a cow.

Also see: Craigie Village.

MRS. FRANCES DUNLOP

EGLINTON Map Ref. 324 422

Eglinton castle has been almost completely demolished and the estate largely split up. The remnants of the castle are at the map reference shown, east of the A737 Irvine/Kilwinning Road, 2 miles north of Irvine town centre. It was the seat of the Montgomeries, Earls of Eglinton and Winton.

Colonel Hugh Montgomerie was referred to in the poem *THE AUTHOR'S EARNEST CRY AND PRAYER* as *'Sodger Hugh'*. Archibald Montgomerie, 11th Earl, subscribed for 42 copies of the poet's first Edinburgh Edition and Burns replied to the Earl's subscription enquiry in a letter dated 11 January, 1787.

When Burns was in Irvine, Eglinton estate was heavily wooded. In a letter dated 30 December, 1787, to his sailor friend, Richard Brown, the poet recalled their time together in Irvine and wrote - *'Do you recollect a Sunday we spent together in Eglinton Woods...?'* The woods in which they walked were probably on the site of the modern Castlepark housing estate. A cairn and plaque in Mackinnon Terrace, Irvine, commemorate the favourite walk of Burns and Brown.

Also see: Drukken Steps; Irvine.

ELBOW TAVERN Map Ref. 497 274

The tavern was situated at the west end of The Knowe, Mauchline, on its south side. A lane, on the same line as an existing lane, ran from Kilmarnock Road to The Knowe and on to Loudoun Street. The bend in the lane at The Knowe was known as The Elbow and as that was where the tavern sat, so arose the name. Legend maintains that the tavern was conducted by an old sailor known locally as 'The Old Tar'.

Joseph Train, who was born at Gilmilnscroft, Sorn, in 1779, and collected material on Burns from contemporaries of the poet, recorded the poet's close friend, John Richmond, as having said that Highland Mary Campbell was of low morals. Richmond claimed that while she was associating with Burns she was also the mistress of one of the Montgomerie family, a brother of the Earl of Eglinton. According to Richmond, the poet's friends warned him about Mary but he would not be convinced. One night the friends took Burns to the Elbow Tavern, knowing that Mary was in a back room with Montgomerie. Eventually, Mary emerged from the room and was jeered by the poet's friends. A few minutes later, Montgomerie came out of the back room and left the tavern. Burns was obviously upset at the time but, to the dismay of his friends, he continued his friendship with Mary a few days later. Richmond is quoted as having said that Burns returned to Mary, 'Like the dog to its vomit.'

It must also be recorded that a nephew of Richmond said after his death that his uncle had been an inveterate liar.

Also see: Failford; Mauchline Burn; Stairaird; Richmond's House.

ENTERKINE Map Ref. 423 237

Situated on the north bank of the River Ayr, one mile east of Annbank. The original house has been demolished and a new one built nearby. It was the home of William Cunningham of Annbank and Enterkine, son-in-law of the poet's patron, Mrs. Stewart of Stair and Afton Lodge. Cunningham was referred to in the song *THE FETE CHAMPETRE* - *'Annbank, wha guessed the ladies' taste, He gies a Fete Champetre.'*

According to John McVie in his book Burns and Stair (1927), the event referred to as The Fete Champetre was probably held on the holm on the north bank of the River Ayr, immediately below the original Enterkine House. The purpose of the event was for Cunningham to introduce himself to the nobility of Ayrshire, although Burns implies that Cunningham intended to stand for election as a Member of Parliament and wished to ingratiate himself for that purpose.

Also see: Afton Lodge; Stair House.

FAIL Map Ref. 421 287

A hamlet on the A719 Ayr/Galston Road, at its junction with the B730 Dundonald/ Tarbolton Road. It is referred to in the poem *THE TARBOLTON LASSIES* - *'Gae doon by Faile, and taste the ale. And tak a look o' Mysie.'* There is nothing to indicate the identity of 'Mysie'.

Also see: Lochlea Farm; Tarbolton.

FAILFORD

Situated on the A758 Ayr/Mauchline Road, 2½ miles west of Mauchline. It is generally accepted as the scene of one of the most romantic incidents in the life of Robert Burns. In

1786, the poet had become estranged from Jean Armour over the breaking of their marriage arrangement when her parents found her to be pregnant by Burns and had their 'contract' defaced. Highland Mary Campbell worked as a nursery maid for Gavin Hamilton, the poet's friend and patron, and after breaking with Jean he began to associate with Mary. About the same time he had been offered a job in Jamaica and was preparing for his departure. He asked Mary to go with him to the West Indies as his wife. In May, 1786, Burns and Mary met for what proved to be the last time; she was leaving for her home in Argyll to make arrangements for her departure with Burns. The poet described the meeting in a letter to George Thomson, song collector, in October, 1792 - 'We met by appointment on the second Sunday of May, in a sequestered spot, by the Banks of Ayr, where we spent the day in taking farewell before she should embark for the West Highlands, to arrange matters for our projected change of life.' Mary died at Greenock and they never met again.

At their parting, Burns and Mary exchanged bibles as a token of their love, and possibly, betrothal. By old Scottish custom, the bibles would be exchanged across running water. The bible Burns gave to Mary is now on display in the musuem at Burns Cottage, Alloway. The bible given to Burns has not been traced.

Monument to the parting of Burns and Highland Mary

A monument erected in 1921 on the west bank of the Fail Water near where it joins the River Ayr, at Failford, commemorates the parting. The location is generally accepted as being in the vicinity of the poet's 'sequestered spot.' Other locations said to have been the scene of the parting are Stairaird, a few hundred yards up the River Ayr from Failford, where the Mauchline Burn joins the River Ayr, and a wood near Kingencleugh, Mauchline, on the north bank of the River Ayr.

Also see: Gavin Hamilton's House; Kingencleugh; Mauchline Burn; Monuments, etc.; Stairaird; Tarbolton.

FAIL WATER Map Ref. 459 262

It joins the River Ayr from the north at Failford, 3 miles west of Mauchline, at the map reference shown. It is referred to in the poem *THE BRIGS OF AYR* - *'From where the Feal wild-woody coverts hide.'* The parting of Burns and Highland Mary Campbell is generally accepted as having been in the vicinity of where the Fail Water joins the River Ayr at Failford.

Also see: Failford.

The River Fail where it joins the River Ayr at Failford

FAIRLIE HOUSE Map Ref. 385 358

Situated to the north of the A759 Troon/Kilmarnock Road, 1½ miles west of Gatehead. The original house is no longer extant. About 1750, the poet's father, William Burnes, moved from the east of Scotland to Ayrshire and took up employment as a gardener at Fairlie House, home of Alexander Fairlie of Fairlie. He worked at Fairlie for about 2 years before moving to Doonside, Alloway.

Fairlie was referred to in a suppressed stanza of the poem *POOR MAILIE'S ELEGY* - *'She was the flower o' Fairlie lambs.'* Alexander Fairlie was a well-known agricultural reformer and his 'Fairlie lambs' were renowned for their excellence.

The poet's uncle and aunt, James Allan and his wife, Jean Broun, lived in a cottage on Fairlie estate where James was employed as a carpenter. Jean Broun was a half-sister of the poet's mother, Agnes Broun. James died in 1789 and Jean moved into Old Rome cottages on the Kilmarnock/Troon Road near Gatehead. She re-married an Adam Blair of Dundonald and died in 1821, aged 71 years. James and Jean's son, Sandy Allan (1780-1854) founded the Allan Shipping Line.

In 1786, Jean Armour's father, James Armour, took out a warrant against Burns, hoping to get money to maintain Jean and the twins she was expecting by the poet. Burns went into hiding with his uncle and aunt at Fairlie.

Tradition in the area maintains that William Burnes met the poet's mother, Agnes Broun, while she was visiting her half-sister, Mrs. Allan, at Fairlie. In fact, whereas William Burnes was at Fairlie between 1750 and 1752, Mrs. Allan was not born until 1750. She was 18 years younger than the poet's mother and only 7 years of age when William and Agnes were married.

Also see: Craigenton Farm; Dundonald; Old Rome.

FENWICK

Situated on the A77 Kilmarnock/Glasgow Road, 4 miles north of Kilmarnock. The village is referred to in the poem *THE ORDINATION* - *'As lately Fenwick, sair forfairn, Has proven to its ruin.'* This is a reference to the ordination of the Rev. William Boyd as pastor at Fenwick on 25th June, 1782, and the public disquiet and controversy aroused by the appointment.

FORD

Referred to in the poem *THE RONALDS OF THE BENNALS* - *'The Laird o' the Ford will straught on a board,If he canna get her at a' man.'* The location referred to can not be identified. There is no property called Ford in the vicinity of Bennals Farm. It may be an abbreviation of Failford or Failford House, both on the A758 Ayr/Mauchline Road. The close proximity of the River Ayr and its numerous ancient fords makes identification difficult.

Also see: Bennals Farm.

FREEMASONRY

Robert Burns was associated with the following Masonic Lodges in Ayrshire:-

1. Lodge St. David Tarbolton No. 174

The poet was initiated into the Lodge on 4 July, 1781, aged 22 years. He was passed and raised on 1 October, 1781. This Lodge was disbanded in 1843 and re-constituted in Mauchline in 1877 as Lodge St. David (Tarbolton) Mauchline No. 133, which holds the original charter.

2. Lodge St. James Tarbolton Kilwinning No. 135

This Lodge had amalgamated with Lodge St. David on 25 June, 1781. On 8 July, 1782, they broke away again and re-constituted Lodge St. James. Although he had been the first man initiated into the amalgamated Lodge, the poet left St. David's for St. James'. On 27 July, 1784, he was elected Depute Master, a post he held until 1788. As Depute Master he presided at many meetings of the Lodge. The chair, gavel, and minute books used by the poet are displayed in the lodge.

3. Lodge Loudoun Kilwinning Newmilns No. 51

The poet was made an Honorary Member of the Lodge at a meeting in the Loudoun

Arms, Newmilns, on 27 March, 1786. His friend and patron, Gavin Hamilton, Mauchline, then Right Worshipful Master, introduced him to the Lodge. The minute of the meeting records - "John Morton, merchant in Newmilns, is answerable for Mr. Robert Burns's admission money."

4. Lodge St. John Kilmarnock Kilwinning No. 24 (now No. 22)

The poet was made an Honorary Member of the Lodge at a meeting on 26 Octber, 1786. The minute of the meeting records - "Robert Burns, poet in Mauchline, a member of St. James, Tarbolton, was made an Honorary Member of this Lodge, (signed) Will Parker." The Lodge met in the Old Commercial Inn, Croft Street. 'Will. Parker' was Major William Parker, Assloss House, Kilmarnock, friend of Burns and Right Worshipful Master of the Lodge. THE MASONIC SONG composed by Burns and sung by him at the meeting refers to the Kilmarnock Lodge and Major Parker - 'Ye sons of old Killie, assembled by Willie.'

5. It is almost certain that during his stay in Irvine, as a new and enthusiastic Freemason, Burns would attend meetings of Lodge St. Andrew Irvine which were held in The Wheat Sheaf Inn, High Street.

FULLARTON HOUSE   Map Ref. 345 303

A mansion house which was situated on the eastern outskirts of Troon, one mile west of the A78 Ayr/Irvine Road. It was demolished a few years after the Second World War, except for an ancient courtyard that has been modernised. Fullarton was the home of Colonel William Fullarton who is referred to in the poem *THE VISION* - *'Hence Fullarton, the brave and young' and as 'Brydon's brave ward.'*

After service in the army, Fullarton returned to his estate and became a noted agricultural reformer. In a treatise on agriculture he acknowledged his indebtedness to Burns for a method of dehorning cattle - 'Mr. Robert Burns, whose general talents are no less conspicuous than the poetic powers which have done so much honour to the country of his birth.'

Fullarton visited Burns at Ellisland during 1791 and the poet wrote to him from Ellisland in a letter dated 3 October, 1791.

Legend in Troon maintains that Burns visited Colonel Fullarton at Fullarton House but this can not be substantiated. As he was able to give an accurate description of the location of Orangefield House, Prestwick, in a suppressed stanza of the poem *THE VISION*, Burns may have visited his friend and patron James Dalrymple at Orangefield. If he did so, it is reasonable to suppose that he may have also visited the neighbouring estate of Fullarton at the same time. However, the matter is no more than conjecture.

Also see: Orangefield House.

GALSTON

Situated on the A71 Kilmarnock/Edinburgh Road, 5 miles east of Kilmarnock and on the banks of the River Irvine. The town is referred to in the poem *THE HOLY FAIR* - *'The rising sun, owre Galston muirs, Wi' glorious light was glintin.'* The muirs referred to lie south-east of Galston and Newmilns. Legend maintains that Burns composed the poem *THE FAREWELL* while trudging over the muir on his way home from Newmilns to Mossgiel.

The Rev. George Smith, Minister of Galston, was referred to in the poems *THE HOLY FAIR* - *'Smith opens out his cauld harangues'* and *THE TWA HERDS* - *'Forby turn-coats amang oursel, There's Smith for ane.'* Rev. Smith was also *'Cessnock-side'* of the poem *THE KIRK'S ALARM*. He was great grandfather of Robert Louis Stevenson. He is buried in the kirkyard.

John Rankine of Adamhill Farm, friend and confidant of Burns moved into Galston and lived in Old Manse Close. He died on 2 February, 1810, and is buried in Galston kirkyard.

Also see: Adamhill Farm; Barr Mill; Craig Mill; Milrig.

GARALLAN HOUSE   Map Ref. 549 183

Situated on the B7046 Cumnock/Skares Road, 2 miles west of Cumnock. The house has been greatly altered but is still occupied. It was the home of Doctor Patrick Douglas, Surgeon in Ayr. Doctor Douglas owned an estate in Port Antonio, Jamaica and offered Burns the post of book-keeper on the estate, resulting in the poet arranging to sail to the West Indies on the ship 'Nancy' in 1786. After the successs of the first edition of his poems, Burns was encouraged to go to Edinburgh and he abandoned his plans to emigrate. Burns visited Doctor Douglas on 13 August, 1786, probably at Garallan House. Doctor Douglas was one of nine men who met in Burns Cottage, Alloway, during the summer of 1801 to pay tribute to the memory of Burns.

Also see: Burns Cottage.

GARPAL WATER   Map Ref. 682 263

Joins the River Ayr from the south at the map reference shown, one mile west of Muirkirk. The burn is referred to in the poem *THE BRIGS OF AYR* - *'Or haunted Garpal draws his feeble source.'* In his notes to the poem, Burns wrote - 'the banks of Garpal Water is one of the few places in the west of Scotland where those fancy-scaring beings, known by the name of Ghaists, still continue pertinaciously to inhabit.'

A woman called Tibbie Pagan lived in a cottage on the banks of the burn, making a living by singing, song writing and running a sheebeen. It is often said that she wrote the song Ca' The Yowes To The Knowes and that Burns heard the song, liked it, improved it and gave us the song we know. In fact, Burns wrote to George Thomson, song collector, in 1794, that he had heard the song sung by a minister called Clunie.

The poet knew the area well by passing through on his journeys between Mauchline and Edinburgh and by his visits to John Lapraik at Muirsmill.

Also see: Dalfram; Muirsmill.

GAVIN HAMILTON'S HOUSE   Map Ref. 497 274

Situated in Mauchline town centre, north of Loudoun Street and adjoining Mauchline Castle on its west side. It is still occupied. The house was the home of the poet's friend and patron, Gavin Hamilton, a lawyer in Mauchline, and the man to whom Burns dedicated the Kilmarnock Edition of his poetry. Gavin Hamilton leased Mossgiel Farm from the Earl of Loudoun and used the farmhouse as a summer residence. When the poet's father, William Burnes, was engaged in litigation with the owner of Lochlea Farm, Robert and his brother Gilbert arranged secretly with Hamilton for the sub-lease of Mossgiel.

In the compositions and correspondence of Burns, Hamilton features prominently. He is addressed in the poems *TO GAVIN HAMILTON, ESQ.* and *EPITAPH FOR GAVIN*

HAMILTON. He is referred to in *HOLY WILLIE'S PRAYER* and his character is described in complimentary fashion in the poem *TO THE REV. JOHN McMATH*.

Burns was a frequent visitor to Hamilton's home and one particular visit deserves to be mentioned. He called in at the house on his way to church and learned that Gavin Hamilton was suffering from gout and could not attend the service. Hamilton challenged the poet, for a wager, to produce a poetic account of the sermon, in no fewer than 4 stanzas, by the time he returned after the service. The Rev. James Steven, a visiting minister, used as his text, Malachi Ch. IV, Verse 2 - 'And ye shall go forth, and grow up, as calves of the stall.' Burns responded to the challenge and won the wager with what are now verses 2 to 5 of the poem *THE CALF*. Doctor Mackenzie of Mauchline visited Hamilton while Burns was there and asked for a copy of the poem. The poet sent a copy to the doctor during the evening, by which time he had added the first and sixth verses to complete the poem.

Over several years, Gavin Hamilton was in dispute with the Rev. William Auld, minister of Mauchline Parish Church and his church session over minor religious misdemeanours alleged against him. Burns supported him and brought derision on the minister and session with several satirical poems.

Gavin Hamilton's House flanked by Mauchline Kirk and Castle

One traditional version of the marriage of Burns and Jean Armour maintains that the ceremony was performed by John Farquhar-Gray, Justice of the Peace, Gilmilnscroft, Sorn, in Gavin Hamilton's home or office. The exact location of Hamilton's office is unknown but it is thought to have been in Back Causeway (Castle Street) or in Loudoun Street.

Burns first met Highland Mary Campbell when she worked for Gavin Hamilton as a nursery maid. Mary was born in 1763, at Auchamore, which is now part of Dunoon. She moved to Ayrshire to find work and her movements are not clear; speculation has placed her in Irvine and Dundonald as well as Mauchline. In 1785 she took up employment in Gavin Hamilton's home but her stay must have been short as by May, 1786, she is thought to have been working at Coilsfield House, near Tarbolton.

In 1786 the poet had become estranged from Jean Armour over the breaking of their marriage contract when her parents knew she was pregnant by Burns. By frequenting Gavin Hamilton's home, he obviously knew Mary Campbell and he appears to have begun to court her after his break-up with Jean. Burns and Mary parted by the River Ayr in May, 1786; he had asked her to accompany him to the West indies and she had gone home to arrange for her departure. Mary died at Greenock before they met again.

Also see: Failford; Gilmilnscroft House; Kilwinning; Mauchline Castle; Morton's Ballroom; Ronald's Inn; Stairaird.

GIGRIEHILL

The exact location is now unknown. It was a small farmhouse situated between Millburn and Lochlea Farms in Tarbolton Parish. A tradition in Tarbolton maintains that one Barbara Tweedie, wife of a weaver, who lived at Gigriehill, claimed to have been the model for 'Willie Wastle's wife' of the poem called *WILLIE WASTLE* or *SIC A WIFE AS WILLIE HAD*. There is no evidence to support the tradition. The song was written about 1792, eight years after Burns left Lochlea.

It has also been claimed that the models for Willie Wastle and his wife lived near Ellisland, Dumfries, but if models for the couple and 'Linkumdoddie' of the song did exist - and they may have been imaginary - they are most likely to have been located near the River Tweed and Logan Water, as described in the song. Tradition in the latter area locates the site of 'Linkumdoddie' and identifies the persons concerned; this tradition is supported by the fact that when the song was written, the poet was familiar with the area.

Tarbolton Parish is sufficiently rich in associations with Burns to make pointless such imaginative conjecture. Such specious claims debase factual Burns lore.

GILMILNSCROFT HOUSE   Map Ref. 556 254

Situated one mile east of the B713 Sorn/Catrine Road, one mile south of Sorn. It was the home of John Farquhar-Gray, Justice of the Peace, who was the man most likely to have married Burns and Jean Armour in 1788, although it can not be verified. There is no record of where the ceremony was performed and various claims have been made. Joseph Train (1779 - 1852), Ayrshire Historian, whose father was employed by Farquhar-Gray and who lived at Sorn as a boy, said that the ceremony was conducted by Farquhar-Gray in Gavin Hamilton's lawyer's office in Mauchline. Mrs. Alexander, daughter of John Richmond and Jenny Surgeoner, both close friends of Burns and Jean Armour, claimed that the marriage took place in Ronald's Inn, Mauchline; and another traditional version maintains that it was in Morton's Ballroom, Mauchline. It is unlikely that evidence will ever by produced to prove any of the versions. The poet knew John Farquhar-Gray. At a meeting of Lodge St. James Tarbolton, held in Mauchline on 25 July, 1787, and over which Burns presided in his capacity as Depute Master, Farquhar-Gray was made an Honorary Member.

Also see: Gavin Hamilton's House; Morton's Ballroom; Ronald's Inn.

GIRVAN RIVER   Map Ref. 181 982

The River flows south-west through south Ayrshire and enters the Firth of Clyde in Girvan, at the map reference shown. In all editions of his works up to and including 1794, Burns showed the first line of his song *MY NANIE, O* as - *'Beyond yon hills where Stinchar flows.'*

In a letter to George Thomson, song collector, in 1792, Burns wrote - 'The name of the river is horribly prosaic - I will alter it.' He then gave the choice of Girvan and Lugar. Thomson chose Lugar and so it has remained.

In the town of Girvan, tradition maintains that the heroine of the song was Nannie Brown, daughter of the innkeeper of the Ship Inn which stood on the west side on Old Street, a short distance south of the cemetery wall.

Also see: Coldcothill Farm; Doura Farm; Kirkoswald; Lugar River; Minnybae Farm; Pinvalley; Ship Inn; Stinchar River.

GLASGOW VENNEL
in the mid 19th century with the poet's lodging on the right

GLASGOW VENNEL   Map Ref. 324 388

Situated on the east side of Townhead, Irvine, about 300 yards south of The Cross. The Vennel was previously called Smiddy Bar. About mid-summer 1781, when Burns was 22 years of age, he went from Lochlea Farm to Irvine to learn flax dressing. In the popular account of the poet's sojourn in Irvine, he went into partnership in a flax dressing workshop in Glasgow Vennel with a relation of his mother called William Peacock and lodged in a house in the Vennel, a few doors from the workshop. Peacock turned out to be a scoundrel. At New Year, 1782, the heckling shop was accidentally destroyed by fire and after working in another workshop for a few weeks, the poet returned home to Lochlea in March, 1782. In a joint venture by Irvine Development Corporation and Cunninghame District Council, Glasgow Vennel has been beautifully restored and is now an attractive stop on the Burns Heritage Trail.

The flax heckling workshop in which the poet worked with Peacock has been restored; there is no doubt about its authenticity but there has been doubt as to whether it was ever destroyed by fire as said by Burns. The workshop now has an exhibition of flax heckling tools and an audio-visual display on the story of Burns in Irvine. The house adjoining the heckling shop facing on to Glasgow Vennel is thought to be on the site of Peacock's home; the original house on the site had been demolished and reconstructed before 1826. The premises are now a shop cum exhibition room. The recently restored house at No. 4 Glasgow Vennel is indicated as the house in which Burns lodged. When the poet was in Irvine, the house at No. 4 was called Temple Dean; its history is uncertain but either it, or possibly another on the site was badly damaged by fire on 13 September, 1925. The initials and date 'R B 1782' have been carved on a lintel in the house but the authenticity of the carving as the work of Burns can not be substantiated. There has been some doubt as to the house in which Burns lodged. It has been said that he lived in part of the heckling shop or in Peacock's home until they separated, but the tradition generally accepted is that he lodged in a room of the house at No. 4 Glasgow Vennel.

A restored building at No. 3 Glasgow Vennel is called The Buchanite Meeting House. The Buchanites were a quasi-religious group led by a Mrs. Elspeth Buchan who settled in Irvine for about 2 years until assaulted by a riotous mob and officially expelled from the burgh by the magistrates in 1784. Burns gave an account of the Buchanites to his cousin, James Burness, Montrose, in a letter dated 3 August, 1784. A very attractive local girl called Jean Gardner with whom Burns had been friendly, left Irvine with the Buchanites. Jean and her parents lived in the Seagate, probably in the second house on the right from High Street.

The house on the north corner of the junction of Glasgow Vennel and Townhead, now the Porthead Tavern, was the home of Provost Hamilton whose family befriended the poet while he was in Irvine. The Provost's son, later Doctor Hamilton of Irvine, not only subscribed to the poet's Kilmarnock Edition but stood surety with others to John Wilson, the printer, for the cost of its production.

Also see: Drukken Steps; Eglinton, Freemasonry; Irvine; Monuments; etc.; Museums, etc.

GLENBUCK VILLAGE   Map Ref. 750 295
Situated one mile north of the A70 Muirkirk/Douglas Road, 3 miles east of Muirkirk. The village, now almost completely demolished, was referred to in the poem *THE BRIGS OF AYR* - '*And from Glenbuck, down to the Ratton-key, Auld Ayr is just one lengthened, tumbling sea.*' In his notes to the poem, Burns refers to Glenbuck as 'the source of the River Ayr.' In a letter to Mr. W. Chalmers, Ayr, shortly after he had ridden from Mauchline to Edinburgh, and enclosing 2 poems, Burns wrote - 'I enclose you two poems which I have carded and spun since I passed Glenbuck.'

GLENCONNER FARM   Map Ref. 495 194
Situated one mile south of the A70 Ayr/Cumnock Road, about one mile west of Ochiltree. It was the home of John Tennant and his family. When the Burnes family lived at the cottage in Alloway and at Mount Oliphant Farm, the Tennant family were their neighbours and friends at Laigh Corton Farm. John Tennant is generally said to have been a witness to the baptism of Robert Burns. In fact, the witness may have been his cousin, also John

Tennant, who was the blacksmith at Alloway and whose smiddy (smithy) adjoined the Burnes cottage. The blacksmith's wife is thought to have been the 'gossip' referred to in the song *THERE WAS A LAD*.

In Burns lore, John Tennant of Laigh Corton and Glenconner is often referred to as '*Auld Glen*', from the poem *EPISTLE TO JAMES TENNANT* in which the poet called him - '*Guid auld Glen, The ace and wale of honest men.*' Burns also expressed his high opinion of him in a letter to Mrs. McLehose (Clarinda) dated March, 1788 - 'a worthy intelligent farmer, my father's friend and my own.'

When the Tennant family moved from Laigh Corton, and John Tennant took over Glenconner, he also became Land Factor to the Duchess of Glencairn. The Duchess was the mother of James Cunningham, 14th Earl of Glencairn, the poet's patron and friend.

While preparing his work for publication in the Kilmarnock Edition, Burns took a manuscript copy to Glenconner and read it to the Tennant family for their opinions and approval. The family recalled the visit with great pleasure.

In 1787, when the poet was offered the tenancy of Ellisland Farm, Dumfries, he had John Tennant accompany him on an inspection of the property. Unfortunately Tennant advised him to accept.

All of the older members of the Tennant family were closely acquainted with Burns from childhood and he referred to each of them in the poem *EPISTLE TO JAMES TENNANT*:-

JAMES - the eldest son and the person to whom the poem was addressed. He was miller at Ochiltree Mill.

WILLIAM - he was ordaind as a minister and became an army chaplain. In the poem he was '*Preacher Willie*'.

JOHN JNR. - he farmed Auchenbay Farm, Ochiltree and was referred to as 'Auchenbay'. He became a wealthy farmer and landowner. In 1773 he attended Ayr Grammar School with Burns and shared a bed with him while they were lodging with their school teacher, John Murdoch.

DAVID - he went to sea, rose to command a naval ship and lost his right hand in battle. He was offered and refused a knighthood. In the poem he was referred to as - '*The manly tar, my Mason-Billie*'.

CHARLES - As a young man he was sent to Kilbarchan to learn weaving. The poet referred to him as '*Wabster Charlie*'. He patented a method of bleaching linen, set up the vast St. Rollox Chemical Works in Glasgow and became a very rich businessman. For almost 200 years his descendants have been amongst the most illustrious in the land; they have included the Lords Glenconner and Crathorne; Margo Tennant, second wife of Henry Asquith P.M.; and the late Baroness Elliot of Harwood.

ALEXANDER - referred to as 'Singing Sannock', he emigrated to Cape Town where one of his grandsons rose to be Speaker of The House of Assembly.

Agnes - '*auld acquaintance Nancy*' of the poem. She married George Reid of Barquharrie Farm neighbouring Glenconner.

KATHERINE - '*cousin Kate*' of the poem. She was John Tennant's niece.

The history of the Tennant family from the 17th century to the 1970s is recorded in the

Rev. Wm. TENNANT

JOHN TENNANT, JNR

CHARLES TENNANT

DAVID TENNANT

ALEXANDER TENNANT

very interesting book Tennant's Stalk by Nancy (Tennant), Lady Crathorne.

Also see: Auchenbay Farm; Auld Nick Horn; Ayr Grammar School; Barquharrie Farm; Burns Cottage; Laigh Corton Farm; Ochiltree.

GLENFOOT   Map Ref. 222 078

The house is no longer extant. It was situated on the east side of the A719 Ayr/Turnberry Road, opposite Kingshill Cottage.

It was the home of John Davidson, the model for 'Souter Johnie' of the poem *TAM O'SHANTER*. Douglas Graham, model for 'Tam' of the poem, lived at the neighbouring Shanter Farm.

In 1785, John Davidson moved from Glenfoot to a cottage in Kirkoswald. The cottage is now owned by The National Trust for Scotland and open to the public as a museum.

John Davidson's wife, Ann Gillespie, worked for the poet's maternal grandfather, Gilbert Broun, at Craigenton Farm and assisted the poet's mother, Agnes Broun, to look after the family when Gilbert Broun's first wife died. Agnes Broun was only 10 years of age when her mother died.

As indicated by the name 'Souter Johnie', Davidson was a shoemaker. He travelled into Ayr on market days, in connection with his trade, and possibly did so with his neighbour, Douglas Graham. As was the practice with farmers and traders on market days, a few 'drams' would be consumed before the journey home.

Davidson was well known for his quick answers and canny sayings. An anecdote traditionally told about him is that when he was asked what would happen if the day ever came when the craft of shoemaking might end he replied - 'my craft will continue as long as calves are born with heads and bairns are born barefooted'.

Also see: Auchenblane; Kirkoswald; Shanter Farm; Souter Johnie's Cottage.

GREENAN BRIDGE   Map Ref. 327 191

Now called Doonfoot Bridge, it is situated on the River Doon, a few hundred yards from its mouth and on the A719 Ayr/Dunure Road, 2 miles south of Ayr town centre. The present bridge was built in 1861.

Armstrong's 1775 map of Ayrshire shows a road from Ayr to south-west Ayrshire on the line of the present A719 road.

Tradition maintains that the cottage and shop on the west side of the road, immediately north of the bridge, was built of stone from the original Greenan Bridge. This is borne out by a stone plaque set into the north gable of the shop which appears to be the mason's stone from the original bridge. The wording on the plaque is now almost illegible and all that can be read is - 'Masons Adam Smith and James Armour'. The full wording on the plaque was originally 'This Bridge of Greenan was built by the Earl of Cassillis, Anno. Dom. 1772 - Masons Adam Smith and James Armour.'

Tradition also maintains that the mason 'James Armour', who built the bridge of 1772, was James Armour of Mauchline, father of Jean Armour and father-in-law of Burns. Jean's father was a master mason and contractor who is thought to have been involved in building work at considerable distances from Mauchline, including Dumfries House, Cumnock; Skeldon House, Dalrymple; and several bridges throughout Ayrshire. The fact that the other mason at Greenan bridge was called Adam Smith supports the tradition;

James Armour's father-in-law (Jean's grandfather) was another Mauchline master mason called Adam Smith. Armour's eldest son was called Adam after his grandfather Smith.

By coincidence, the Burnes family were living at Mount Oliphant Farm, within 2 miles of Greenan Bridge, when the poet's future father-in-law and grandfather-in-law were engaged on the building contract.

GREENFIELD AVENUE

The avenue runs parallel to the River Doon and links the A719 Ayr/Doonfoot Road with the B7024 Ayr/Maybole Road.

The poet's father, William Burnes, working under contract to Ayr Town Council, constructed the road now called Greenfield Avenue in 1755/56.

Ayr Town Council minutes for January, 1756, recorded a payment of £12.10/- to William Burnes as an instalment of the total cost of £50 for the building of the road.

Also see: Alloway.

GREENOCK WATER   Map Ref. 628 269

It joins the River Ayr from the north at the map reference shown, adjacent to the B743 Sorn/Muirkirk Road, 5 miles west of Muirkirk.

The burn was referred to in the poem THE BRIGS OF AYR - 'Or where the Greenock winds his moorland course.'

Burns was familiar with the area by passing through on his journeys between Mauchline and Edinburgh and by having visited John Lapraik at Muirsmill.

Also see: Dalfram, Muirsmill.

HAUGH   Map Ref. 497 253

A hamlet situated on the River Ayr, 1½ miles south-west of Mauchline.

It is sometimes said to have been referred to by Burns in the first stanza of the poem MAN WAS MADE TO MOURN - 'One ev'ning as I wandered forth, Along the banks of Ayr.'

The location referred to was Bridge Holm, a few hundred yards down river from Haugh.

Also see: Bridge Holm.

HIGH KIRK, KILMARNOCK   Map Ref. 430 384

Situated between Wellington Street and Soulis Street, Kilmarnock.

The kirk was built in 1731. The main building is original, only the spire and outbuildings having been added.

Minister from 1764 to 1773 was the Rev. James Oliphant, who was referred to in the poem THE ORDINATION - 'But Oliphant aft made her yell'.

From 1774 to 1800 the minister was the Rev. John Russell who was referred to as 'Black Russell' in the poem THE HOLY FAIR, 'Wordy Russell' in THE TWA HERDS and 'Rumble John' in THE KIRK'S ALARM. In the poem THE ORDINATION, he was again referred to - 'An Russell sair misca'd her'.

John Wilson, the Kilmarnock printer who printed the poet's Kilmarnock Edition, is buried in the kirkyard. Wilson had moved to Ayr in 1803 and, with his brother, Peter, started a newspaper, The Ayr Advertiser, which is still published. He died on 6 April, 1821, and was returned to Kilmarnock for burial.

Also see: Laigh Kirk; Star Inn Close; Kilmarnock.

HOGSTON FARM Map Ref. 224 087

Situated a half mile north of Maidens village.

The farm was the home of Helen McTaggart, wife of Douglas Graham of Shanter Farm. Graham was the prototype of Tam O'Shanter in the poem of that name and Helen, the prototype of Kate of the poem.

Also see: Shanter Farm.

HOGSTON FARM

HURLFORD

Situated on the A71 Kilmarnock/Galston Road at its junction with the B7073 Kilmarnock/ Mauchline Road.

Until the late 18th century, the village was called Whirlford, the name obviously arising from its location on the River Irvine.

Burns must have been familiar with the area, as the village was on his route from Mossgiel to Kilmarnock.

In his book The Ayrshire Hermit (Tammie Raeburn) and Hurlford (1875), M. Wilson quotes a contemporary of Burns as having said that the poet travelled from Mossgiel to collect coal at Norris Bank, 2 miles south of Hurlford.

The name Norris Bank has fallen into disuse; it was situated on the south bank of the River Cessnock, 200 yards east of the B7073 Hurlford/Mauchline Road, at Barleith. The contemporary said that Burns always had a book in his possession and read it during his journey.

Wilson's book also informs us that Burns was in the habit of visiting an inn which was situated on the west side of Mauchline Road, Hurlford. The innkeeper, James Aiton, was presented by Burns with a snuff box which was an item of interest for several years until eventually stolen.

65

THE MOOR

TO KILWINNING

SEAGATE CASTLE

TO STEWARTON

JEAN GARDNER'S HOUSE

DR MACKENZIE'S HOUSE

WEST BACKWAY

IRVINE
CIRCA 1786

THE GREEN

DAVID SILLAR'S HOUSE

HIGH ST

EAST BACKWAY

THE GRIP

BRIDGEGATE

AYR BANK

TEMPLETON'S BOOKSHOP

WHEATSHEAF INN

TO THE HARBOUR

TOLBOOTH

HIGH ST

TO GLASGOW

COTTON STREET

KIRKGATE

BUCHANITE'S MEETING HOUSE

GLASGOW VENNEL

PROVOST HAMILTON'S HOUSE

HECKLING SHOP

POET'S LODGING

RIVER IRVINE

KIRK VENNEL

PARISH CHURCH

TOWNHEAD

FULLARTON

GOLF FIELDS

TOLL

DREGHORN

TO

TO TROON AND AYR

HIGH STREET, IRVINE
before 1860 with the Tolbooth and Wheatsheaf Inn

IRVINE

Situated on the Ayrshire coast, at the mouth of the River Irvine, 15 miles north of Ayr.

About mid-summer 1781, when Burns was 22 years of age, he went from Lochlea to Irvine to learn flax dressing. The town was a busy seaport with a population larger than Kilmarnock or Ayr.

The popular version of the poet's sojourn in Irvine, supported by his own account, is that he went into partnership in a flax heckling workshop in Glasgow Vennel with a man related to his mother and called William Peacock. It is said that he lodged in a house in the Vennel, a few doors from the workshop. Peacock turned out to be a scoundrel. At New Year, 1782, the heckling shop was destroyed by fire and after working in other premises for a few weeks, the poet returned home to Lochlea in March, 1782. In fact, the subsequent history of the workshop in Glasgow Vennel casts doubts, not on its authenticity, but on its having been destroyed by fire.

There is additional information concerning the poet's stay in Irvine seldom taken into account although it deserves to be considered.

A man known as Robin Cummell, whose name was actually Robin Campbell (Cammell in the Ayrshire dialect), claimed to have known Burns in Irvine. Cummell was born in Kilwinning about 1745, worked at Eglinton Castle and died about 1840. He said that the poet lodged in High Street - "near the Gruip (Grip), just a wee before ye win to't comin' frae Kilwinning". Two Irvine contemporaries of Burns were recorded separately as saying that they witnessed the workshop the poet had moved into after splitting from Peacock, being destroyed by fire. Both said that the workshop destroyed had been in High Street, near the King's Arms Hotel. As the hotel is still at the High Street end of the lane called

The Grip, the premises appear to be those described by Robin Cummell.

The true story of the poet's stay in Irvine probably includes parts of various accounts and it is certain that we will never know the story exactly. The only mistake of consequence would be to neglect any account totally in favour of another, as we are in danger of doing.

To return to the reminiscences of Robin Cummell, he said that he had met regularly with - "Burns; Richie Brown, the sailor; Keelivine, the writer (lawyer); and Tammie Struggles frae the Briggate" - in The Wheatsheaf Inn, High Street. Apart from Richard Brown, little is known of the men referred to.

Cummell's account of the poet in Irvine can be read in the book The Memorables of Robin Cummell (1913) by John Service.

Richard Brown was a sailor who became friendly with the poet in Irvine and it was he who first encouraged Burns to have his poems printed. They corresponded for many years thereafter and met occasionally. Burns claimed that Brown introduced him to 'the delights of women' but Brown refuted the claim many years later when he was a married man and a respected sea captain.

The only family in Irvine with whom Burns is known to have become closely acquainted was that of Provost Charles Hamilton whose home was on the north side of the junction of Glasgow Vennel and Townhead. The house is now part of the Porthead Tavern. The Provost's son, John, later Doctor Hamilton of Irvine, was friendly with Burns and in 1786 he did not only subscribe to the Kilmarnock Edition of the poet's work, he stood surety to John Wilson, the printer, towards the costs.

In Irvine, Burns frequented James Templeton's bookshop on the east side of High Street, south of the Cross. Templeton encouraged the poet's 'thirst' for reading; he subscribed later to the Kilmarnock Edition and acted as the poet's agent by collecting all of the subscriptions due in Irvine and forwarding them to Burns.

The Rev. James Richmond, parish minister when Burns was in Irvine, said later that the poet joined the Parish Church during his stay in the town but there is no church record to confirm his statement.

The poems WINTER - A DIRGE and A PRAYER UNDER THE PRESSURE OF VIOLENT ANGUISH were composed in Irvine.

David Sillar, the poet's Tarbolton friend and fellow-rhymer, moved to Irvine and eventually opened a shop close to the Tolbooth building which stood in the middle of High Street opposite Kirkgate. He also worked briefly as a school master in the town. His fortunes fluctuated; at one time he was lodged in the Tolbooth for debt but later he inherited between £30,000 and £40,000 and as a wealthy respected citizen became a member of Irvine Town Council. He owned a block of 4 houses on the west side of High Street, north of The Cross, on the site at No. 159 now occupied by the old Post Office building. In 1814 he bought a house in Kirkgatehead, at the corner of Hill Street. He died on 2 May, 1830, and is buried in the Parish kirkyard.

Doctor John Mackenzie, the poet's friend and family physician in Mauchline, moved to Irvine. The move was at the instance of the Earl of Eglinton whose personal physician the doctor became as well as having a practice in the town. The site of Doctor Mackenzie's house is on the east side of High Street, directly opposite the north side of Seagate. The building is no longer extant. The doctor had married Helen Miller, one of *THE BELLES OF MAUCHLINE* in the poem of that name. She died in Irvine and is buried in the Parish kirkyard.

Doctor Mackenzie and David Sillar were the first President and Vice-President of Irvine Burns Club. The Club has an excellent museum at 'Wellwood', Eglinton Street, Irvine. On 15 August, 1844, the poet's surviving sons, Major James and Colonel William Burns were entertained by Irvine Burns Club in the Kings Arms Hotel, High Street.

Also see: Eglinton; Freemasonry; Glasgow Vennel; Irvine River; Monuments etc.; Sun Inn.

IRVINE RIVER   Map Ref. 303 381

The river joins the Firth of Clyde in Irvine at the map reference shown.

It is referred to in the poems *EPISTLE TO WILLIAM SIMSON* - *'While Irwin, Lugar, Ayr and Doon, Naebody sings'* - and *THE VISION* - *'There well-fed Irwine stately thuds.'*

Burns knew much of the river by his familiarity with the Irvine valley towns; by having lived for a short time with his aunt and uncle, Jean and James Allan, at Fairlie Estate, Dundonald; and by his stay in Irvine.

Also see: Fairlie House; Galston; Irvine; Newmilns; Old Rome.

JOHNIE GED'S HOLE

Referred to in the poem *DEATH AND DOCTOR HORNBOOK* - *'Waes me for Johnie Ged's Hole now'* - its meaning is probably indicated in the next stanza as being the kirkyard.

Johnie Ged is generally said to have been the name of, or nickname for, the gravedigger. The Scottish National Dictionary shows it as a name for the personification of 'Death' but as 'Death' is being addressed in the stanza concerned, that meaning is not applicable. In Scots, a 'Ged' is also a pike and a 'Ged's Hole' a pool frequented by a pike.

In Tarbolton, the scene of the poem, tradition maintains that at the time of Burns the gravedigger was one John Rodger who resided at Old House of Smithfield, known locally as Gedshall or Gedshole. According to the tradition, from the name of his home, Rodger was known as John(ie) Ged.

Old House of Smithfield is no longer extant. It was situated north of Smithfield Farm, Tarbolton and east of Tarbolton Mill, at map reference 436 276.

In the stanza in which reference is made to 'Johnie Ged's Hole', reference is also made to - 'His braw calf-ward whare gowans grew'. The latter is also a reference to the kirkyard and relates to the custom of the time whereby the minister was entitled to the grazing of the kirkyard; if he did not take up his privilege, the grazing right passed to the gravedigger.

Also see: Doctor Hornbook's House and School; Tarbolton; Willie's Mill.

KATE KEMP'S HOUSE   Map Ref. 491 254

Situated on the north bank of the River Ayr, at the east end of Barskimming Bridge, on the Mauchline/Stair Road, two miles south-west of Mauchline, the house is no longer extant. The poet and his friend, James Andrew, were both interested in a girl, Kate Kemp, who lived in the house. One evening, Burns walked from Mossgiel to Barskimming, hoping to meet Kate. Near the bridge, he met James Andrew and when Kate's father told them she was out looking for a stray cow, they went walking on nearby Bridge Holm. After some time, the poet appeared to be pre-occupied with his thoughts and, soon, left Andrew and returned to Mossgiel. His friend thought he must have offended Burns unwittingly. When they met again a few days later, the poet apologised and explained that he had been composing a poem in his mind. He then recited Man Was made To Mourn.

Also see: Barskimming Mill; Bridge Holm.

KELLY BURN Map Ref. 194 684

The burn joins the Firth of Clyde at the map reference shown, between Skelmorlie and Wemyss Bay. It forms part of the boundary between Ayrshire and Renfrewshire.

It may be the subject of the poem *KELLY BURN BRAES.*

KILBIRNIE

Situated on the A760 Largs/ Lochwinnoch Road, 10 miles east of Largs.

It is referred to in the poem *THE INVENTORY - 'The fourth's a Highland Donald hastie, A d-n'd red-wud Kilbirnie blastie.'*

The reference was to 'an insane, unmanageable beast' bought by the poet at Kilbirnie Fair from a horse-dealer called William Kirkwood of Baillieston Farm, Kilbirnie. The farm is situated north of the A760 Kilbirnie/Largs Road on the outskirts of the town.

In a copy of Johnson's Musical Museum he presented to Captain Riddell of Dumfries, the poet wrote the following footnote to the song *A MOTHER'S LAMENT - 'This beautiful tune is, I think, the happiest composition of that bard-born genius, John Riddell, of the family of Glengarnock at Ayr'.* Although the Riddells were an ancient family in the Kilbirnie area, John Riddell, a blind musician and composer was born in Ayr.

KILKERRAN HOUSE Map Ref. 304 031

Situated on the B7045 Crosshill/Girvan Road, 2 miles south of Crosshill.

It was the home of Sir Adam Ferguson of Kilkerran, who was referred to in the poem *THE AUTHOR'S EARNEST CRY AND PRAYER - 'Thee, aith-detesting, chaste Kilkerran'.* In the *SECOND BALLAD ON MR HERON'S ELECTION,* Sir Adam was referred to as *'maiden Kilkerran'.*

The house is still occupied by the Ferguson family.

KILMARNOCK

Situated at the junction of the A77 Ayr/Glasgow Road and the A71 Irvine/Edinburgh Road.

The town holds an important place in Burns lore. The poet was familiar with the town and its surrounding area but the Auld Killie known by Burns was confined generally to an area within about 200 yards in radius from The Cross. It is still easy to envisage its picturesque location on the floor of the valley of the winding Kilmarnock Water with green and wooded slopes leading out of the valley on the roads to Glasgow, Mauchline and Irvine.

Unfortunately, most of the locations associated with Burns have been obliterated by modern town centre developments.

GLASGOW

TO STEWARTON AND PAISLEY

BACK OF YARDS

BACK STREET

HIGH STREET

KILMARNOCK WATER

HIGH KIRK

SOULIS STREET

BOWLING GREEN HOUSE

BOWLING GREEN

FORE STREET

GREEN STREET

OLD COMMERCIAL INN

CROFT STREET

BRAEHEAD HOUSE

THE CROSS

HIGH GREEN

STAR INN CLOSE

LAIGH KIRK

LOW GREEN

TO MAUCHLINE

TAM SAMSON'S HOUSE

BAILIE GREENSHIELDS' HOUSE

NELSON STREET

GRANGE STREET

SANDBED STREET

BEGBIE'S

TO IRVINE

KILMARNOCK
CIRCA 1785

NETHERTON

TO AYR

71

The town's most important association with Burns is unique; it was the place in which the fruits of his poetic genius first appeared in print. In the workshop of John Wilson, Printer, in Star Inn Close, the world renowned Kilmarnock Edition was produced on 31 July, 1786. The printing workshop is no longer extant.

On the death of his father and the family's move to Mossgiel Farm, Mauchline, Burns became a farmer in his own right. Kilmarnock was his market and business town and he became a regular visitor. Through his wit and outstanding personality, he soon became a well known figure and was befriended by a group of leading citizens. The men he met in Bowling Green House, an inn adjacent to Kilmarnock Bowling Green, and who invited him to their homes, encouraged him to have his work printed and assisted in raising subscriptions for the Kilmarnock Edition.

WATERLOO STREET, KILMARNOCK (now demolished)
The Kilmarnock Edition was printed in the first attic from the right

The group of men who befriended Burns included Robert Muir, a wine merchant who was one year older than the poet and made a deep impression on him; John Goldie, businessman and religious theorist; Tam Samson, nurseryman and keen sportsman; his brother John Samson and nephew Charles Samson; Doctor William Mure, a local physician; the brothers William and Hugh Parker, landowner and banker; William Paterson, Town Clerk and businessman; Bailie Thomas Greenshield, brewer and Town Councillor; William Brown, merchant; and Sandy Patrick, Tam Samson's son-in-law and licensee of Bowling Green House.

The poet made many references to Kilmarnock in his works, the best known being; the first line of the poem *TAM SAMSON'S ELEGY* - '*Has auld Kilmarnock seen the Deil?*'; the first line of the poem *THE ORDINATION* - '*Kilmanrock wabsters fidge and claw*'; and the first line of the poem *MASONIC SONG* - '*Ye sons of Auld Killie, assembled by Willie*'.

Kilmarnock ministers featured prominently in the poet's works - Rev. James Mackinlay, Rev. John Russell, Rev. James Oliphant, Rev. John Robertson and Rev. John Mutrie. Mackinlay and Robertson are buried in the kirkyard of Laigh Kirk, Kilmarnock.

On 21 June, 1784, the poet's brother, Gilbert Burns, was married to Jean Breckenridge of Kilmarnock in a first floor flat of a house at the corner of Waterloo Street and Green Street. The site is now under the town centre 'bus terminus. The poet travelled from Ellisland Farm, Dumfries to the wedding.

It is thought that Jean Breckenridge may have been a woman of property, albeit not impressive property. The Ayrshire Register of Sasines records that in April, 1789, Jean Breckenridge, daughter of James Breckenridge, merchant, Kilmarnock, inherited a tenement property in the town.

A Kilmarnock folk character who has gained a measure of immortality through Burns is Jean Glover. In a copy of Johnson's Musical Museum given by the poet to Captain Riddell of Glenriddell, Dumfries, he wrote the following footnote to the Scottish song O'er The Moor Amang The Heather which he had contributed to the collection - 'This song is the composition of a Jean Glover, a girl who was not only a wh--e but also a thief; and in one or other characters has visited most of the Correction Houses in the west. She was born I believe, in Kilmarnock. I took the song down from her singing as she was strolling through the country with a slight-of-hand blackguard.'

Jean Glover was born in Townhead, Kilmarnock on 31 October, 1758. The daughter of a weaver, she was good-looking and had a good singing voice. While singing in Kilmarnock taverns, she met and teamed-up with a man whose surname was Richard, 'the slight-of-hand blackguard' referred to by Burns. Tradition maintains that the poet heard Jean singing in the Old Commercial Inn, Croft Street, Kilmarnock, where meetings and social evenings of Lodge St. John Kilmarnock were held. An entry in the books of St. John's Lodge, dated September, 1793, shows - 'by cash - from Jean Glover's man, 7/-.' Jean died in Letterkenny, Ireland in 1811, aged 53 years.

A.B. Todd, antiquarian and poet, recorded having interviewed several old farmers who had known Burns and met him regularly at Kilmarnock market. According to Todd, the farmers were unanimous and firm in their statements that they never heard the poet utter an oath, never saw him angry, and never saw him intoxicated.

The headquarters of the Burns Federation is in the Dick Institute, Elmbank Avenue, Kilmarnock. The Federation was established at Kilmarnock in 1885, and now has a world-wide membership of Burns clubs.

The many places in the town, of interest for their association with Burns, are dealt with separately.

Also see: Bailie Greenshield's House; Begbie's; Bowling Green House; Braehead House; Crookes's; Freemasonry (Kilmarnock); High Kirk; Laigh Kirk; Monuments etc; Museums etc.; Netherton; Riccarton; Star Inn Close; Tam Samson's House.

JAMES CUNNINGHAM
14th EARL OF GLENCAIRN

KILMAURS

Situated on the A735 Kilmarnock/Stewarton Road, 2 miles north of Kilmarnock.

In a letter dated 26 October, 1788, to Mrs. Dunlop of Dunlop, Burns expressed his intention to attend Kilmaurs Cow Fair at Hallowe'en.

The Rev. Alexander Miller, 'Wee Miller' of the poem *THE HOLY FAIR*, was minister of Kilmaurs Parish Church from 1788 to 1804 - *'Wee Miller niest, the guard relieves'*. He is buried in the kirkyard.

Another Kilmaurs minister was referred to by the poet in a letter to Peggy Chalmers, dated 26 September, 1787 - *'the preaching cant of Father Smeaton, Whig-Minister at Kilmaurs'*. The Rev. David Smeaton was Minister in the village from 1740 to about 1788.

The family seat of the poet's friend and patron, James Cunningham, 14th Earl of Glencairn, was near the village. In a letter dated 22nd March, 1787, the poet wrote to Mrs. Dunlop of Dunlop - "The noble Earl of Glencairn, to whom I owe more than any man on earth" and when the Earl died Burns composed the beautiful 'Lament for James, Earl of Glencairn'. The Earl is buried at Falmouth, having died there soon after returning from a visit to Lisbon.

It is thought that Alexander Dalziel, the Earl's factor, may have been responsible for drawing the Earl's attention to the poet's Kilmarnock Edition.

Also see: Mayville House.

KILWINNING

Situated at the junction of the A78 Irvine/Largs Road and the A737 Kilwinning//Dalry Road, 3 miles north of Irvine town centre.

The Rev. James Steven, minister of Kilwinning Parish Church from 1803 to 1828, was the minister whose sermon in Mauchline Parish Church inspired the poem *THE CALF*.

When Burns heard him preach, Steven was 25 years of age and assistant minister at Ardrossan.

The story concerning the poem *THE CALF* is of interest. Burns was in the habit of calling on his Mauchline friend, Gavin Hamilton, on his way to Sunday morning service. On calling one Sunday, he learned that Hamilton was suffering from gout and unable to go to church. Hamilton challenged the poet, for a wager, to produce a poetic account of the sermon, in no fewer than 4 stanzas, by the time he returned after the service. The Rev. Steven used as his text, Malachi Ch.IV, Verse 2 - 'And ye shall go forth, and grow up, as calves of the stall.'

Burns responded to the challenge, and won the wager with what are now verses 2 to 5 of the poem *THE CALF*. Doctor Mackenzie, Mauchline visited Gavin Hamilton while Burns was there after the service and asked for a copy of the poem. The poet sent a copy to the Doctor during the evening, by which time he had completed the poem as we know it by adding verses one and six.

The Rev. Dr. William McGill, minister of Ayr Auld Kirk, a friend to both the poet and his father, was assistant minister at Kilwinning before he moved to Ayr.

Peggy Orr, nursery maid at Stair House, who was an acquaintance of Burns and for a short time fiancee of the poet's friend, David Sillar, was born in Kilwinning where her father was a roads contractor.

Also see: Gavin Hamilton's House; Stair House; The Calf's Answer.

SPECIAL FEATURE - THE CALF'S ANSWER TO MR. ROBERT BURNS

The following is the best of several 'replies' published in the Glasgow Advertiser soon after the publication of the poem, 'The Calf' (See: Kilwinning)

(Proverbs Ch. 25, V.5 - 'Answer a fool according to his folly')

1 Not half your proofs,
   To show my hoofs,
   Dear brother Brute we're wanting;
   Come let's shake cloots,
   And leave disputes,
   Lest folk should think you're taunting.

2 Why do you blush?
   I see you wish
   The name, dear Brute, to smother;
   And Robert Burns,
   In calf skin spurns,
   The friendly name of brother.

3 But since I find
   You scorn your kind,
   I here foretell your fate, Sir;
   On stalls you'll sleep
   In skin of sheep,
   "Perhaps no distant date", Sir.

4 Or with disgrace,
   Expelled our race,
   Bound up in turkey-leather;
   Make bull and calf,
   Low out a laugh,
   To hear your goose-like blether.

5 But why deny
   Your fellow-kye,
   Your loud melodious rowte, Sir?
   For still you show,
   You're made to low,
   And ramp among the nowte, Sir.
Anon.

6 "When love, warm, young,
   Keen, shiv'ring, strong,"
   Your sturdy heart oppress'd, Sir;
   Without disguise,
   To half-shut eyes,
   You stood a bull confess'd, Sir.

KINGENCLEUGH
Map Ref. 503 255

The property is still extant. It is situated on the west side of the A76 (T) Mauchline/ Cumnock Road, almost one mile south of Mauchline Cross.

In his book The Wanderer in Ayrshire, published in 1817, Hugh Campbell wrote of the ruined Kingencleugh Castle - 'A wood near these ruins, through which runs a rivulet, is said to be the place where Burns parted from Mary Campbell.'

The wood lies between Kingencleugh and the River Ayr at the map reference shown. It is known locally as the Lily Glen and is said to have been a favourite walk of Burns.

The claim of Kingencleugh area as the location of the parting is contradicted by the first stanza of the poem *HIGHLAND MARY* - *'Ye banks and braes and streams around, The castle o' Montgomery!. . . . For there I took my last Farewell, O' my sweet Highland Mary.'*

Also see: Failford; Mauchline Burn; Stairaird.

KIRK-ALLOWAY with the poet's father's grave on the left

KIRK-ALLOWAY   Map Ref. 332 180
Situated on the B7024 Ayr/Maybole Road, 300 yards north of the River Doon. It is thought
that it was built about 1516. In 1691 it went out of regular use as a place of worship and
became dilapidated. Between 1740 and 1752 it was reroofed and taken into use again as
a place of worship and for some time as a school. By 1766 or earlier, it had become less
than wind- and waterproof and fell into disuse once more. When the antiquarian, Captain
Grose, sketched the building in 1789, it was only partially roofed.

The ruined church was the setting of the witches' dance in the poem TAM O'SHANTER
- *'Kirk-Alloway was drawing nigh, Where ghaists and houlets nightly cry'* and *'When
glimmering thro' the groaning trees, Kirk-Alloway seem'd in a bleeze.'*

William Burnes, the poet's father, is buried in the kirkyard. He died in 1784 at Lochlea
Farm, Tarbolton Parish, about 10 miles north-east of Alloway and his coffin was conveyed
to Kirk-Alloway for burial, slung from two poles between two horses in tandem. The
headstone on the grave is the third to have been erected, the first two having been mutilated
by souvenir hunters. The poet's youngest sister, Isabella Burns Begg, and her daughters,
Isabella and Agnes Begg, are also buried in the kirkyard.

David Watt, miller at Alloway Mill, and a school-fellow of Burns is accepted as having
been the last person baptised in Kirk-Alloway. He died at Alloway Mill on 22 October,
1823, aged 68 years.

Also see: Alloway; Alloway Mill; Auld Nick Horn; Bridge House; Burns Cottage; Laigh
Corton Farm; Lochlea Farm.

SPECIAL FEATURE - TAM O'SHANTER - The Story Behind the Poem

During the summer of 1789, Burns met Captain Francis Grose (1731-91), an English
antiquarian who had recently published the first of two volumes on 'The Antiquities of
Scotland' and was touring Scotland for material for his second volume. The poet met
him in Friar's Carse House, near Dumfries, home of their mutual friend, Robert Riddell,
and suggested to the antiquarian that he should include a drawing of Kirk-Alloway in his
second volume. Grose agreed, on condition that Burns would provide a 'witch-story' to
accompany the drawing.

In June, 1790, after a delay of almost a year, the poet wrote to Grose and gave him three
prose 'witch-stories...relating to Alloway kirk'. They were probably tales that Burns had
heard told by old Betty Davidson, a relation of his mother who stayed with the family
occasionally when he was a boy and had a fund of such stories.

The second story was a prose version of what we know as the tale of Tam O' Shanter,
except that the main character was not named and of the others in the poem only the
witch with the short smock was referred to. In the prose version, Tam's famous call -
"Weel done, Cutty-sark!", was the more prosaic - "Weel luppen, Maggy wi' the short
sark!"

Five months later, Burns wrote again to Grose, enclosing his masterpiece, the poem Tam
O'Shanter, which he described as 'one of the Alloway-kirk stories, done in Scots verse.'
Tam, Souter Johnnie, Cutty Sark, Kate, Kirkton Jean, the landlord and the landlady had
been added to the story and their places in literature were established for all time. The
poem was published first in The Edinburgh Magazine of March, 1791, and, later, Captain
Grose included it in his second volume beside a drawing of Kirk-Alloway.

Although the true identities of the characters in the poem have no bearing on its worth, they were the cause of great speculation amongst contemporaries. Most likely to have been true is the now traditional belief that Douglas Graham of Shanter Farm was 'Tam' and John Davidson of Kirkoswald was 'Souter Johnnie'. Both of the men were known by Burns when he was at school in Kirkoswald but conjecture that he caroused with them is fatuous; he was a penniless youth of 16 while Graham and Davidson were 37 and 47 respectively.

It has been claimed that the first draft of the poem was composed while Burns was at school in Kirkoswald but this must be regarded as fanciful. Likewise, the claim that the poem was written in one day must be considered with much scepticism. The expertise in composition, the nuances of pace and mood, the vivid sketches of character and location, and the accurate recall of people, places and stories from his boyhood, all suggest that the poet took a great deal of skilful, though subtle, care in the construction of his masterpiece. This belief is supported by his having written to a friend that the poem had - 'a final polish that I despair of excelling.'

KIRKOSWALD, circa 1900 - A Peggy Thomson's House. B Rodger's School. C Headstone for Burns's Grandparents. D Headstone for Douglas Graham and his wife. E Site of Hugh Rodger's House. F Headstone for Hugh Rodger.

KIRKOSWALD

Situated on the A77 Maybole/Girvan Road, 4½ miles south of Maybole.

The village has many associations with Burns. His family background on his maternal side was all in Kirkoswald Parish.

In 1775, at 16 years of age, the poet spent one term at school in Kirkoswald, under Hugh Rodger, schoolmaster. While attending the school, he lodged at Ballochneil Farm, 2 miles south of the village.

Although the poem TAM O'SHANTER was set in Alloway, all of the main characters were modelled on people the poet had met in Kirkoswald Parish while staying at

Ballochneil.

The present church was built in 1777, so Burns must have attended the old church which is now a ruin. The following people associated with Burns are buried in the old kirkyard:- The poet's maternal great grandparents, John Broun and his wife Agnes McGraen; the poet's maternal grandparents, Gilbert Broun and his wife Agnes Rennie; Douglas Graham and his wife Helen McTaggart, (*'Tam'* and *'Kate'* of the poem *TAM O'SHANTER*); John Davidson (*'Souter Johnie'* of *TAM O'SHANTER*) and his wife Ann Gillespie who, as a girl, was employed by the poet's maternal grandfather, Gilbert Broun; Jean Kennedy, 'Kirkton Jean' of TAM O'SHANTER; and Hugh Rodger, Kirkoswald schoolmaster.

The following anecdotes relate to the poet's time in Kirkoswald. One day, while walking up the steep Kirk Brae in the village, the youthful Burns met the minister, The Rev. Matthew Biggar, coming down.The minister enquired as to where he was going and the poet replied - "As you see, Sir, I am going heavenwards". The minister was left to contemplate on his own direction of travel.

The minister's daughters met Burns and another boy in the village. As was his habit, the poet was walking with his head bowed and did not see the ladies approaching. One of the Misses Biggar jokingly chided him on his lack of attention to the fair sex, thereby missing the opportunity to look upon and talk with ladies. The poet's quick reply was to the effect that it was right for man to contemplate the earth from whence he was taken and for woman to look upon man from whence she was taken.

Elizabeth Biggar (1757-1838) married John Graham of Dalquhat Farm, Kirkoswald, nephew of Douglas Graham (Tam O'Shanter). Louisa Biggar (1761-1846) married her father's successor, the Rev. James Inglis, and it was he who recounted the anecdotes about Burns.

The many places of interest associated with the poet are dealt with separately.

Also see: Achmachalla; Ballochneil Farm; Laigh Dalquhat Farm; Laigh Park Farm; Minnybae Farm; Rodger's School; The Ladies' House; Souter Johnie's Cottage; Peggy Thomson's House.

KNOCKHASPIE'S LAND   Map Ref. 486 288

It is referred to in the song *HIGHLAND HARRY BACK AGAIN - 'I wad gie a' Knockhaspie's Land, For Highland Harry back again'.*

The origin of the name is in doubt; Alan Cunningham, Burns biographer, wrote early in the 19th century that it was part of Mossgiel Farm and this is borne out by the fact that it is still the name of a large field on Mossgiel, two fields from the back of the steading.

In a copy of Johnson's Musical Museum given by the poet to Captain Riddell of Glenriddell, Dumfries, he wrote the following footnote to the song *HIGHLAND HARRY BACK AGAIN* - "the oldest title I ever heard to this air, was the Highland Watch's Farewell to Ireland. The chorus I pickt up from an old woman in Dunblane; the rest of the song is mine'. As Knockhaspie's Land is referred to in the chorus, it could be implied that the name was in the original song collected by Burns, probably in 1787.

It is possible that the name was given to the field on Mossgiel some time after Burns wrote the song.

Also see: Mossgiel Farm.

KNOCKSHINNOCH Map Ref. 610 129

Situated south of the B741 New Cumnock/Dalmellington Road, one mile west of New Cumnock.

The exact location of Knockshinnoch House is not known. From its position on Armstrong's 1775 map of Ayrshire, it was probably on the site occupied later by Knockshinnoch Colliery.

The poet's friend, John Logan, was designated as Laird of Knockshinnoch and the neighbouring property of Laight.

Also see: Laight.

KYLE

An ancient division of Ayrshire, being that part of the county between the Rivers Irvine and Doon. The other divisions are Carrick and Cunninghame.

The name is derived from Coil or Coilus, King of the Picts, whom legend maintains lived in Ayrshire in ancient times.

There are many references to Kyle in the works of Burns, the best known being in the song *THERE WAS A LAD* - *'there was a lad was born in Kyle'* - in which the poet wrote of his own birth.

Burns referred to Kyle as Coila in the poem *EPISTLE TO WILLIAM SIMSON* - *'We'll sing auld Coila's plains an' fells'* and *'O' sweet are Coila's haughs and woods'*. In the poem *THE VISION*, Burns gave the name Coila to his poetic muse.

An entry by the poet in his First Commonplace Book, dated August, 1784, referred to Kyle, Carrick and Cunninghame - *'My dear native country, the ancient bailieries of Carrick, Kyle and Cunningham. . . . .We have never had one Scotch Poet of any eminence, to make the fertile banks of Irvine, the romantic woodlands and sequestered scenes on Ayr, and the healthy, mountainous source and winding sweep of Doon, emulate Tay, Forth, Ettrick and Tweed'*.

Also see: Carrick; Cunninghame.

LAIGH CORTON FARM Map Ref. 352 178

Situated on Corton Road, Ayr a half mile east of the A77 Ayr/Maybole Road.

A neighbouring property to Mount Oliphant, it was farmed by John Tennant, a friend of both Burns and his father.

John Tennant later moved to Glenconner Farm, Ochiltree. He is known in Burns lore as *'auld Glen'*, derived from a reference to him by the poet in the poem *EPISTLE TO JAMES TENNANT*, which was addressed to John Tennant's son - *'guid auld Glen, The ace and wale of honest men.'*

It is generally said that John Tennant was a witness to the baptism of Burns. In fact, the man shown as a witness was probably his cousin, also John Tennant, blacksmith at Alloway, whose smiddy (smithy) neighboured the Burnes family cottage. The smiddy operated as such until after the Second World War and the dwelling at No. 6 Main Street, Alloway, is still called Smiddy Cottage. The blacksmith's wife is reputed to have been a midwife at the poet's birth and the *'gossip'* referred to in the song *THERE WAS A LAD* - *'The gossip keekit in his loof.'*

John Tennant of Laigh Corton was one of the Alloway parents who joined William Burnes, the poet's father, to bring John Murdoch, schoolteacher, to Alloway to open a school.

Also see: Auchenbay Farm; Auld Nick Horn; Barquharrie Farm; Glenconner Farm; Kirk Alloway.

The 'AULD NICK' Horn in 1985

SPECIAL FEATURE - THE AULD NICK HORN

About 1768, while the Burns family were living at Mount Oliphant Farm, Alloway, their friends, the Tennant family, in the neighbouring Laigh Corton Farm, had a large highland bullock.

One day the bullock went missing and although the Tennant boys, assisted by Robert and Gilbert Burns, searched the countryside, the animal could not be found.

A few days later, an old woman making her way on foot towards the market in Ayr with a basket of produce, was passing the partially ruined Kirk-Alloway when she was startled by a loud bellowing sound. At that time, the road past the kirk was at the end of the building farthest from the modern road and, by standing on tiptoe, the woman was able to look over a window-sill into the kirk. When she saw a pair of large horns and steamy breath, together with hearing more loud bellowing, she dropped her basket, lifted her skirts and ran off into Alloway village, proclaiming to the world - 'the deil's in Alloway kirk! the deil's in Alloway kirk!' Of course, the 'deil' was the missing bullock.

The story of the old woman having thought she had seen the devil in the kirk spread around the countryside and caused great amusement. Ever since then, tradition in the Tennant family has maintained that the incident sowed a seed in the fertile mind of the then nine years old Robert Burns, a seed that germinated many years later when he sat down to create the plot of his masterpiece, Tam O Shanter.

The story has an interesting sequel. When the boys were sent to retrieve the bullock, they found it wedged amongst the ruined pews of the kirk and while they were extricating it the animal lost one of its beautiful horns. With trepidation, the boys took the lop-side-looking bullock back to Laigh Corton. Their father, John Tennant, being pleased to have recovered the valuable animal, was understanding about the accident. He had the horn bored out and used, thereafter, as a drenching-tube for giving medicine to animals.

During the next year, the Tennant family moved from Laigh Corton to Glenconner Farm, Ochiltree, and the horn was taken with them. Several years later, Ochiltree village council needed a horn or trumpet for the use of their crier when he was making announcements around the district but they could not afford to buy one. John Tennant had the highland bullock's horn adorned with a silver mouthpiece at one end and a silver mounting at the other and presented it to the village for its crier.

Over a century later - about 1890 - John Tennant's Great Grandson, the multi-millionaire Sir Charles Tennant, head of a vast business conglomerate, decided to trace the 'Auld Nick Horn', as it had become known in the family. After a great deal of research, it was traced to London, in the possession of a descendant of an Ochiltree family. When it had been authenticated by its silver hallmarks, Sir Charles bought it back and since then it has been kept by the family. It is owned now by Lord Glenconner (Colin Tennant) and kept in Glen House, Innerleithen, Peebleshire.

In 1896, Sir Charles Tennant lent the 'Auld Nick Horn' to an exhibition of Burns memorabilia brought together to celebrate the centenary of the poet's death. Unfortunately, since then the horn has not been on view to Burns enthusiasts.

LAIGH DALQUHAT FARM   Map Ref. 222 065
Situated on the A77 Maybole/Girvan Road, 2 miles south of Kirkoswald.

It was a neighbouring farm to Ballochneil where Burns lived with his uncle while attending Kirkoswald school in 1775.

A man McTaggart, brother-in-law of Douglas Graham the model for Tam O'Shanter, farmed Laigh Dalquhat when Burns was at Ballochneil.

When Burns was in Kirkoswald, the minister was the Rev. Matthew Biggar. The minister's third eldest daughter, Elizabeth, married John Graham of Dalquhat Farm, nephew of Douglas Graham. She died in 1838, aged 82 years.

Also see: Ballochneil; Kirkoswald.

LAIGH KIRK   Map Ref. 428 379
Situated in Kilmarnock town centre, west of the Cross.

The church was extensively re-built on the same site in 1802 after a fall of plaster from the ceiling caused panic and 29 people were killed. The tower is all that remains of the original building.

The church is referred to in the poem THE ORDINATION - 'Swith! to the Laigh Kirk, ane an' a'.' THE ORDINATION was composed on the occasion of the Rev. James Mckinlay being ordained to the kirk in 1786.

The Rev. Mackinlay, Rev. John Robertson and Rev. John Mutrie, all referred to in THE

ORDINATION were ministers of Laigh Kirk.

The Rev. Mackinlay, Rev. John Robertson and Tam Samson of the poems *TAM SAMSON'S ELEGY* and *TAM SAMSON'S EPITAPH*, are buried close to each other in the kirkyard.

LAIGH KIRK

LAIGH PARK FARM   Map Ref. 223 062
Situated east of the A77 Maybole/Girvan Road, 2 miles south of Kirkoswald. The property is now called Park Farm.

It was a neighbouring farm to Ballochneil Farm and Mill where Burns lodged with his uncle in 1775 while attending Rodger's school in Kirkoswald.

Douglas Graham of Shanter Farm, Maidens, model for *'Tam'* in the poem *'TAM O'SHANTER'*, also farmed Laigh Park and the poet must have met him while living at Ballochneil. Tradition maintains that Douglas Graham died in the existing Laigh Park farmhouse.

Kate Steven or Stein, reputed to be a witch, lived in a cottage on Laigh Park. She is said to have been the model for Nannie (Cutty Sark) of the poem TAM O'SHANTER.

Also see: Ballochneil Farm; Park Farm; Shanter Farm.

LAIGHT   Map Ref. 612 117
Situated in Glen Afton, New Cumnock, 1½ miles south of the town. The house is still extant and inhabited.

It was the home of the poet's friend, John Logan, described as Laird of Laight, Afton and Knockshinnoch. Burns visited Laight and local tradition maintains that it was after a visit that he returned to his lodging in an inn at New Cumnock and composed the song *SWEET AFTON*.

In a letter dated 14 October, 1788, from Ellisland to Jean Armour at Mauchline, Burns wrote - 'You need not come on Sunday to meet me on the road as I am engaged that day to dine with Mr. Logan at Laight.' On 23 October, 1788, he wrote to Mrs. Dunlop of Dunlop - 'I breakfasted this morning at Laight, near New Cumnock.'

The first reference to the poem *THE KIRK'S ALARM* was in a letter from Burns to Logan, dated 7 August, 1789.

Also see: Afton River; Knockshinnoch; New Cumnock.

LAIGH PARK FARM

LANGLANDS FARM
Map Ref. 424 265

Situated west of the B744 Tarbolton/Annbank Road, one mile south of Tarbolton.

It was the home of John Reid whose wife was Jean Ronald of the poem THE *RONALDS OF THE BENNALS* - *'There's ain they ca' Jean, I'll warrant ye've seen, As bonnie a lass or as braw, man.'* Jean Ronald's grandson, Sir George Reid, became Prime Minister of Australia in 1904 and Australia's first High Commissioner to London in 1910.

The poet's brother, Gilbert Burns, courted Jean Ronald briefly while he lived at Lochlea Farm.

Also see: Aikenbrae Farm; Bennals Farm.

LARGIESIDE
Map Ref. 467 294

The dwelling is no longer extant and its exact location is uncertain. An early 18th century map shows it on the east side of the B733 Tarbolton/Galston Road, about 150 yards north of Largie Toll but strong local tradition maintains that it was on the north side of the same road, about 100 yards east of Largie Toll, the site now occupied by a modern bungalow. Either way it was within a mile south of Lochlea Farm.

It was the home of Elizabeth Paton who was employed at Lochlea by the Burnes family and in 1785 had an illegitimate daughter by the poet. The child was called Elizabeth Burns; she was the subject of the poem *A POET'S WELCOME TO HIS LOVE-BEGOTTEN*

DAUGHTER and was referred to as *'Dear-bought Bess' in the poem THE INVENTORY.* Elizabeth Burns was reared by the poet's mother. She married one John Bishop of Polkemmet and had seven children. She is buried in Whitburn Cemetery.

In July, 1786, when Burns was preparing to emigrate to Jamaica, he signed a Deed of Assignment in favour of his brother Gilbert. All of his property, including the anticipated profits from the Kilmarnock Edition of his poems which was about to be published, was assigned to Gilbert who was pledged to care for and support Elizabeth Burns until she was 15 years old.

The Deed was drawn up by William Chalmers, an Ayr lawyer. Chalmers was courting a young lady and he asked the poet to write a poem to help him in his wooing. The result was the poem called *WILLIE CHALMERS* or *TO WILLIE CHALMERS' SWEETHEART.*

LARGS
Situated on the north Ayrshire coast, 35 miles north of Ayr.

The town is referred to in the poem *CALEDONIA - A BALLAD - 'But brave Caledonia in vain they assail'd, as Largs well can witness and Loncartie tell'.*

The reference relates to the Battle of Largs in 1263 when King Alexander III of Scotland defeated King Haakon to end Norse domination of Scotland.

A Burns garden, incorporating the flowers referred to by the poet in his poems, is located in Douglas Park, Irvine Road, Largs.

LEEZIE'S POOL
The pool is referred to in the 26th stanza of the poem *HALLOWE'EN.* The location described, if not imagined by the poet, is unknown.

Although the poem is generally accepted as having been set in the vicinity of Culzean and Kirkoswald, Ayrshire Archaeological and Natural History Society have suggested that much of the poem, including Leezie's pool, can be closely associated with Mount Oliphant.

The Society identify the pool described in the 24th stanza of the poem as being *'Whare three lairds' lands met at a burn'*, as a pool at the meeting place of the lands of Mount Oliphant, Broomberry and Pleasantfield.

It is also suggested by the Society that the characters Rob and Nell (or Rab and Nelly) in the poem refer to the poet and his first love, Nellie Kilpatrick, whom he met at Mount Oliphant; the burn of the 25th stanza is compared with several features of Riddicks Moss Burn; and the kiln to which Merran went in the 11th stanza is seen as disused lime kilns near Leezie's pool.

The verdict on the Society's detective work must be 'Not Proven' but the evidence is very plausible and worthy of consideration. When creating the atmosphere and setting the scene for his poem, the poet would certainly draw from the full width of his experience.

Volume 5 (Ayrshire At The Time Of Burns) of the Ayrshire Archaeological and Natural History Society's Collections describes the Society's research.

LEGLEN WOOD   Map Ref. 388 230
Situated one mile south of the A758 Ayr/Mauchline Road, 2½ miles east of Ayr town centre.

The woods are on the banks of the River Ayr and are said to have been a favourite haunt and hiding place of the Scottish patriot, William Wallace.

A cairn on the south bank of the river, and on the west side of the Auchencruive/Belston Road, commemorates the two patriots, Burns and Wallace.

In a letter dated 15 November, 1786, to Mrs. Dunlop of Dunlop, Burns described how as a boy, and already a fervent admirer of Wallace, he made a pilgrimage on a Sunday from Mount Oliphant to Leglen Woods and explored every den and dell.

Mrs. Dunlop's maiden name was Wallace and she claimed descent from the patriot.

Leglen Woods Memorial Cairn to Burns and Wallace

LITTLEHILL FARM   Map Ref. 467 305

Situated one mile north of the B744 Tarbolton/Galston Road, one mile east of Crosshands on the A76 Kilmarnock/Mauchline Road.

It is a neighbouring farm to Lochlea and, according to the poet's younger sister, Isabella Burns Begg, was the home of Isabella Steven, known locally as Tibbie Stein. She also said that Tibbie was the heroine of the song *O'TIBBIE, I HAE SEEN THE DAY.*

Tibbie also lived in Tarbolton while Burns was in the area. She inherited some money and thereafter rejected the poet's advances, giving rise to the song.

Also see: Bridge House; Tibbie Stein's House.

LITTLETON FARM   Map Ref. 217 073

Situated on the unclassified road from Kirkoswald to Girvan, one mile south-east of Turnberry.

The farm is thought to have been the home of Rab McGraen, who was referred to in the poem *HALLOWE'EN* - *'Our 'stibble-rig' was Rab McGraen.'*

McGraen was related to the poet's mother, whose grandmother was called Agnes McGraen. Her grandparents, John Broun and Agnes McGraen lived at Littleton before they moved to Craigenton Farm where they were joined later by the poet's grandparents, Gilbert Broun and Agnes Rennie.

Also see: Craigenton Farm.

LOANFOOT HOUSE   Map Ref. 415 380

The house is no longer extant. It was situated about 200 yards south of Irvine Road, Kilmarnock, at Loanfoot Avenue.

It was the home of Robert Muir, Wine Merchant, Kilmarnock, subject of the poem *EPITAPH ON ROBERT MUIR*. He subscribed for 72 copies of the Kilmarnock Edition of the poet's work and 40 of the first Edinburgh Edition.

Burns and Muir corresponded and in a letter dated 7 March, 1788, the poet expressed his religious beliefs. The poet's high opinion of Muir is expressed in a letter dated 13 December, 1789, to Mrs. Dunlop of Dunlop - "Muir, thy weaknesses were the aberration of human nature, but thy heart glowed with everything generous, manly and noble; and if ever emanation from the all-good being animated a human form, it was thine."

Overlooking Lochlea from the Poet's route to Tarbolton (1985)

LOCHLEA FARM   Map Ref. 455 301

Situated on the Largie Toll/Craigie Road, 1½ miles south of the A719 Ayr/Galston Road. It was commonly spelled Lochlie at the time of Burns. Locally, it is still pronounced 'Lochli'.

It was the home of the Burnes family from 1777 to 1784, after they left Mount Oliphant Farm, Alloway and before they moved to Mossgiel Farm, Mauchline. The buildings have changed and the fields have been enclosed, but the poet would easily recognise the farm that caused the family so much worry.

The terms of the lease of Lochlea led to bitter litigation between William Burnes and his landlord, David McLure, and led to financial loss for the Burnes family.

On 13 February, 1784 the poet's father died at Lochlea aged 63 years, and his coffin was conveyed to Alloway for burial on poles slung between two horses in tandem. One of the horses belonged to the family friend, John Tennant of Glenconner Farm, Ochiltree. It is not recorded to whom the other horse belonged but we can presume it may have been the Burnes family.

The route by which the funeral left Lochlea is not known but it is generally accepted as having left by the west end of the steading and travelled by Millburn (map ref. 444 297), then south on to the 'C' class road which joins the Ayr/Galston and Tarbolton/Largie Roads; it would then turn south-west towards Mosside farm (map ref. 431 290) on a road which ran parallel to the existing road but on the south side of the plantation called The Long Wood; from Mosside the route would be by Redrae (Map Ref. 424 287) to the hamlet of Fail (Map Ref. 421 287); it would skirt the ruined Fail Monastery, ford the Water of Fail a short distance south of the existing bridge and join the Ayr/Galston Road. The route from Fail to Alloway is not known.

The poet's youngest sister, Isabella Burns Begg, revealed a scene from the father's death bed. As he was approaching death, William Burnes said that there was one of the family for whose future conduct he was afraid. Robert approached his father's bed and asked, 'O, Father, is it me you mean?' His father said that it was and Robert turned away and looked out of the window with tears in his eyes. Burns expressed the opinion some years later that his father did not like him but his brother Gilbert thought that the father's dislike was only in the poet's imagination.

It was from Lochlea that Burns frequented Tarbolton, attending a dancing class, setting up and attending the debating society called the Bachelors' Club and joining the Freemasons.

It was also from Lochlea that he went to Irvine to learn flax dressing. With his brother, Gilbert, he had grown flax on a piece of land given to them by their father. After the flax was processed for them it was spun and woven into cloth to make clothes for the family and servants. The good quality of their flax is shown by a notice that appeared in the Glasgow Mercury newspaper under the title - Gainers of the Premium for Flax Raising Crop, 1781 and showed 'Mr. Robert Burns, Lochlie farm, Tarbolton Parish - £3!' The poet went to Irvine to learn flax dressing so that the family would be able to do all of their own processing and possibly to give them another means of earning money.

An incident on the farm was recorded by the poet in the poem *THE DEATH AND DYING WORDS OF POOR MAILIE*. Gilbert told the story which inspired the composition. 'Robert', he said, 'had, partly by the way of frolic, bought a ewe and two lambs from a neighbour, and she was tethered in a field adjoining the house at Lochlea. He and I were going out with our teams, and our two younger brothers to drive for us, at midday, when Hugh Wilson (Hughoc of the poem), a curious-looking boy, clad in plaidings, came to us with much anxiety in his face, with the information that the ewe had entangled herself in the tether and was lying in the ditch. Robert was much tickled with the ewe's appearance and postures on the occasion. Poor Mailie was set to rights, and, when we were returned from the plough in the evening, he repeated to me the 'Death and Dying Words' pretty much in the way they now stand.'

Burns had started to write poetry at Mount Oliphant but it was at Lochlea that he developed from occasional rhymer to inspired poet. It is also where he started to write the first of his two common-place books.

Lochlea is worthy of a visit. Walk up to the top of the hill to the south-west of the steading and see the farm laid out below you. To your right you will see the depression which in the poet's time held the loch from which the farm took its name (when the loch was drained in the 19th century an ancient crannog/lake dwelling was revealed). From the depression, a burn still flows through the fields; imagine the brothers soaking and beating their flax in its waters. In your mind see the poet walking up over the hill and passing you on his way to Tarbolton; or see Hughoc finding Poor Mailie and running to tell his masters. Try to visualise the death-bed scene in the steading or the funeral procession leaving the farm and passing down the valley toward Millburn on your left. 'From scenes like these' a greater understanding springs.

Also see: Bachelors' Club; Glasgow Vennel; Irvine; Shawwood; Tarbolton.

SPECIAL FEATURE - THE BURNS COMMON-PLACE BOOKS

A common-place book is similar to a diary but, whereas a diary is generally a record of the occurrences of each day, a common-place book is a collection of personal opinions, observations, experiences, extracts from books, critiques, etc. Robert Burns compiled two such books, both of which give insight into his thoughts and attitudes and are of interest to all Burns enthusiasts.

The common-place books are too extensive to be reproduced here but the extracts that follow reflect the types of entries the poet made and, hopefully, might encourage the reader to seek out and read the books in full.

The poet started his First Common-Place Book in April, 1783, when he was 24 years of age and living at Lochlea Farm, Tarbolton. In a style which seems very akin to that of the Rules & Regulations of the Bachelors' Club which were written during the same period, he penned the following introduction:-

'Observations, Hints, Songs, Scraps of Poetry, etc., by Robert Burness; a man who had little art in making money, and still less in keeping it; but was, however, a man of sound sense, a great deal of honesty, and an unbounded good-will to every creature rational or irrational. - As he was but little indebted to scholastic education, and bred at a plough-tail, his performances must be strongly tinctured with his unpolished, rustic way of life; but as I believe they are really his own, it may be some entertainment to a curious observer of human-nature to see how a Ploughman thinks, and feels, under pressure of Love, Ambition, Grief, with the like cares and passions, which, however diversified by the Modes and Manners of life, operate pretty much alike, I believe, in all Species.'

In an entry dated August, 1783, the poet alludes in writing for the first time to his own literary endeavours. He refers to the circumstances which led to his first song, 'Handsome Nell' (written when he was 14), includes the poem in full, and follows it with an almost line-by-line criticism of the verses. Several more of his early works are recorded and assessed, and his literary ambition is obvious, though still tempered with doubt.

Throughout the book, quotations from numerous poets, writers and philosophers give insight into the great width of the bard's reading although he was still a young man.

The First Common-Place Book ends abruptly with an entry dated October, 1785. It is brief and unconnected with any other. - 'If ever any young man . . . . . chance to throw his eyes over these pages, let him pay a warm attention to these observations; as I assure him they are the fruit of a poor devil's dear bought experience. I have literaly (sic) like . . . . Solomon - 'turned my eyes to behold Madness and Folly' . . . . . let my pupil as he tenders his own peace, keep up a warm intercourse with the Diety.'

The Second Common-Place Book was started in Edinburgh in April, 1787. Although the wording of the first book suggests that the poet thought it might be read by others in future, the second seems to have been compiled with eventual publication in mind, a fact to be considered when the book is being read.

The second book starts with a lengthy and formally worded introduction in which Burns states his intentions regarding the contents. It begins:-

'As I have seen a great deal of human life in Edinburgh, a great many characters which are new to one bred up in the shades of life as I have been, I am determined to take down my remarks on the spot. . . . . I will sketch every character that anyway strikes me . . . with unshrinking justice. I will insert anecdotes and take down remarks. . . . . My own private story likewise, my amours, my rambles . . . . . my Poems and fragments. . . . . . I shall . . . . make one exception - the connection between two people of different sex . . . united . . . by the sacred tie of Love.'

In subsequent entries, the poet reflects on his life and measures himself intellectually and socially against the men he has met in Edinburgh society. He appraises his friends the Earl of Glencairn, Professor Dugald Stewart, Rev. Dr. Hugh Blair, Professor William Greenfield, and his publisher, William Creech.

Several of his best-known works are in manuscript in the book and it is clear that by then Burns was aware that his productions were of high literary standard and that he was assured of a permanent place in literature.

Entries in the book continued after the poet's return to Mauchline and throughout his life in Dumfries.

These summaries of the poet's common-place books are necessarily brief but they may be enough to stimulate the interest of any reader who is intent on gaining a better understanding of the complex genius, Robert Burns.

LOCHRIDGE ESTATE   Map Ref. 415 447
Situated on the A735 Kilmaurs/Stewarton Road, one mile south of Stewarton.

When the poet's uncle, Robert Burnes, moved to Ayrshire from the east of Scotland about 1748, he lived at Titwood Farm, near Stewarton.

Initially he worked at lime quarries at Lochridge but, later, he became crippled with rheumatism and moved to Stewarton.

Also see: Stewarton; Titwood Farm.

LOGAN HOUSE   Map Ref. 588 207
The house is no longer extant. It was situated on the south bank of the River Lugar, overlooking the west end of Lugar village. The site is indicated by Logan Avenue,

Cumnock, which follows the line of the main driveway to the house. It can be seen that the mature trees lining Logan Avenue are considerably older than the modern houses.

Logan was the home of Hugh Logan, designated Laird of Logan, who was probably the subject of the mock epitaph starting - 'Here lies Squire Hugh'. The poem is normally published in The Merry Muses.

In a letter to James Dalrymple of Orangefield, dated February, 1787, Burns referred to Hugh Logan, 'Let the Worshipful Hugh Logan, or Mass James McKindlay, go into their primitive nothing'.

LOUDOUN ARMS & NEWMILNS CASTLE

LOUDOUN ARMS   Map Ref. 536 373

Situated on the north side of Main Street, Newmilns, at its junction with Castle Street. The premises are still extant.

On 27 March, 1786, Burns was made an Honorary Member of Lodge Loudoun Kilwinning Newmilns No. 51 at a meeting held in a room in the Loudoun Arms. The minutes of the meeting record that 'much to the satisfaction of the Lodge', the poet was introduced by his friend and patron, Gavin Hamilton, Mauchline, then Right Worshipful Master.

Also see: Freemasonry; Newmilns.

LOUDOUN CASTLE   Map Ref. 506 377

Situated east of the A719 Galston/Glasgow Road, one mile north of Galston.

It was the home of James Mure Campbell, 5th Earl of Loudoun. When the Earl and his wife, Flora McLeod of Raasay, died within a few weeks of each other in 1786, the Earl having committed suicide because of financial difficulties, Burns composed the poem *RAGING WINDS AROUND HER BLOWING*. The poem was dedicated to Flora's sister, Isabella McLeod of Raasay.

The castle was also the home of James Henri and his wife, Susan, second daughter of the poet's friend and patron, Mrs. Dunlop of Dunlop. Mrs. Henri gave birth to a son 4 months after the death of her husband and Burns made the birth the subject of the poem *ON THE BIRTH OF A POSTHUMOUS CHILD.*

Mrs. Dunlop lived at Loudoun Castle with Mrs. Henri for a few months and Burns corresponded with her there.

Janet Little, a minor poetess known as 'The Scottish Milkmaid Poet', who corresponded with Burns and visited him at Ellisland, Dumfries. worked at Loudoun Castle dairy. She is buried in the ancient Loudoun kirkyard near Loudoun Castle.

Also see: Dunlop House; Patie's Mill.

LOUDOUN KIRK Map Ref. 537 373

Situated on the south side of Main Street, Newmilns.

The present church is not the original. It was re-erected on the site of the original in 1844.

The Rev. Dr. George Lawrie, friend and patron of Burns, was minister of Loudoun Kirk from 1763 to 1799. In 1786 he was impressed by the Kilmarnock Edition of the poet's work and brought it to the attention of Doctor Thomas Blacklock, a blind poet and influential literary figure in Edinburgh. As a result Burns delayed and later abandoned his plans to take up a post in the West Indies.

The poet became a friend of the Lawrie family and stayed with them at Loudoun manse on more than one occasion. It is probable that he attended the original church with the family.

REV. DR. GEORGE LAWRIE

Rev. George Lawrie was succeeded in the kirk by his son, the Rev. Dr. Archibald Lawrie, also a friend of the poet. Father and son are both buried in the kirkyard.

The church should not be confused with the ancient ruin called Loudoun Kirk on the north bank of the River Irvine, a short distance west of Loudoun Castle, Galston. Janet Little, a minor poetess known as 'The Scottish Milkmaid Poet', who corresponded with Burns and visited him at Ellisland, Dumfries, is buried in the ancient kirkyard.

Also see: Loudoun Manse; Newmilns; St. Margaret's Hill.

LOUDOUN MANSE, 1985

LOUDOUN MANSE   Map Ref. 527 372

The manse of the poet's time is still occupied. It is now a private house called St. Margaret's Hill, at No. 116 Loudoun Road, Newmilns.

It was the manse occupied by the Rev. George Lawrie, minister of Loudoun Parish Kirk, Newmilns. Rev. Lawrie, an accomplished man, was impressed by the Kilmarnock Edition of the poet's work and sent a copy to Doctor Thomas Blacklock, Edinburgh, blind poet and influential literary figure in the capital. As a result of Lawrie's intervention and Blacklock's acclaim, Burns delayed and later abandoned his plans to take up a post in the West Indies.

Burns was invited to the manse and became friendly with the Lawrie family. The poem *ON SENSIBILITY* or *RUSTICITY'S UNGAINLY FORM* was written to Mrs. Mary Lawrie after the poet felt that the lady had given him a mild rebuke during a visit. It was enclosed in a book sent to one of the family.

On a visit by the poet during September, 1786, one of the daughters, Christina, played the spinet; it was the first time Burns had heard the instrument and he was enthralled. Rev. Lawrie and his wife led the company in dancing and the poet danced with the other daughter, Louisa. The refined but friendly atmosphere of the manse made a deep impression on Burns. Next morning he was late for breakfast and the son of the family was sent to enquire. He met Burns on the stair and asked if he had slept well. "Not well", said the poet, "the fact is, I have been praying half the night. If you go into my room, you will find my prayer on the table". The prayer was the poem *LINES WRITTEN AT A FRIEND'S HOUSE* or *PRAYER - O THOU DREAD POWER*.

The son of the manse was later the Rev. Dr. Archibald Lawrie. He succeeded his father at Newmilns and was also friendly with Burns.

The poem *THE NIGHT WAS STILL* relates to the night of the dancing in the manse and was given by the poet to Miss Louisa Lawrie who presented it later for publication. The name St. Margaret's Hill was given to the house by the Rev. George Lawrie and it is referred to as such in some of the poet's correspondence. The house has been altered greatly since it was visited by Burns; wings were added, ceilings were heightened, attics were removed, and a bedroom used by Burns is now a passageway. The Rev. George Lawrie had the initials 'G.L.' and 'M.C.' carved in stone on the front wall of the house, and at a later date had the inscription 'Jehovah Jireh' added to it; 'G.L.' and 'M.C.' were George Lawrie and his wife, Mary Campbell. The initials and inscription are still extant.

Tradition maintains that on a window pane in the bedroom he occupied in the manse, Burns inscribed with a diamond - 'Lovely Mrs. Lawrie, she is all charms'. The window sash and pane were removed when the house was altered and are now preserved in the modern Loudoun Manse, Newmilns. Expert opinion considers the inscription to be genuine.

The Lawrie family are buried in Loudoun kirkyard, Newmilns.

Also see: Loudoun Arms; Loudoun Kirk; Monkton; Newmilns; Patie's Mill; St. Margaret's Hill.

LUGAR RIVER   Map Ref. 493 252
The river joins the River Ayr from the south, between Haugh and Barskimming, one mile south of Mauchline at the map reference shown.

It is referred to in the poem *THE BRIGS OF AYR* - '*Or stately Lugar's mossy fountains boil*' - and in the poem *EPISTLE TO WILLIAM SIMPSON* - '*While Irwin, Lugar, Ayr and Doon, Naebody sings*'.

In the song *MY NANIE, O*', Burns originally composed the first line as '*Beyond yon hills where Stinchar flows*' - and so it appeared in print until 1794. In a letter to George Thomson, song collector, in 1792, Burns wrote - 'the name of the river is horribly prosaic - I will alter it.' He then gave a choice of Girvan and Lugar. Thomson chose Lugar and so it has remained in many editions.

The date of the song and the identity of the heroine are in doubt and have caused much debate. The poet gave no clear indication.

Also see: Coldcothill Farm; Doura Farm; Girvan River; Kirkoswald; Minnybae Farm; Pinvalley; Ship Inn; Stinchar Rover.

McLELLAND'S INN   Map Ref. 497 272
Now called Loudoun Arms Hotel, it is situated on the north side of Loudoun Street, Mauchline, at its junction with Barskimming Road.

While he was living at Mossgiel Farm, the poet often attended a reading society in the inn. Gavin Hamilton, Doctor MacKenzie and other leading men in the community are thought to have been members. The society should not be confused with Mauchline Young Men's Society. The premises are now the meeting place of Mauchline Burns Club.

Also see: Ann Orr's Ale House; Mauchline.

MAIDENS VILLAGE
Situated on the Ayrshire coast, 15 miles south of Ayr.

Burns was familiar with that part of the coast now called Maidens. The village called Maidens did not appear on a map until about 1828. Previously, rocks in Maidenhead Bay had been called The Maidens of Turnberry.

The area at the centre of the present village was called Douglaston, still a familiar name, and the other parts of the area took their names from the dwellings - Ardlochan, Hogston, Jameston, Morriston, Shanter, etc.

The poet visited the area while staying at Ballochneil Farm between Maidens and Kirkoswald.

The places of interest in the area are dealt with separately.

Also see: Ardlochan; Damhouse of Ardlochan; Glenfoot; Hogston; Shanter Farm; The Cellars.

MANSON'S INN, circa 1900

MANSON'S INN   Map Ref. 432 273

A Tarbolton inn at the time of Burns; it is no longer extant. It was situated on the east side of Burns Street, at its junction with Garden Street. The site is indicated by a plaque on a small pillar in the front garden of a house at the junction.

James Manson, the innkeeper, is referred to in the poem *TO DOCTOR MACKENZIE -* '*An' taste a swatch o' Manson's barrels.*'

At a meeting of Lodge St. James Tarbolton in Manson's on 27 July, 1784, Burns was elected Depute Master. James Manson was treasurer of the Lodge.

The first man made a mason by Burns was Matthew Hall, an Ayr musician, well known throughout Ayrshire.

Manson is buried in Tarbolton kirkyard.

Also see: Freemasonry; Tarbolton.

MARY MORISON'S HOUSE   Map Ref. 497 274 and 498 273

Two locations in Mauchline are said to have been the site of Mary Morison's home. The first was in a house called 'Brownlea' which stood on the east side of Castle Street, at its junction with The Knowe. The other house was in a tenement building called 'The Place' which occupied all of the east side of the Cross.

Mary Morison lived with her father, a retired army officer known locally as Adjutant Morison. They are both buried in Mauchline kirkyard.

Mary died in 1791, aged 20 years. Her headstone, erected in 1825, records that she was the heroine of the song *MARY MORISON*. As she was only 15 or 16 years of age when the song was composed, it is now generally accepted that she was not the girl to whom the song was written. The heroine of the song is popularly thought to have been Alison (Ellison) Begbie, a servant at Carnell House between Mauchline and Kilmarnock who was courted by the poet while he was at Lochlea. This arises mainly from the poet's brother, Gilbert Burns having said that the song *MARY MORISON* was written to the same girl as the poem *BONIE PEGGY ALISON*. As the name Peggy Alison is accepted as being euphonious for Alison Begbie, on Gilbert's judgement the song *MARY MORISON* is also attributed to Alison Begbie.

Although it can not be proved, tradition in Mauchline maintains that the poet showed friendly admiration for the young Mary Morison, daughter of Adjutant Morison, whom he met at tea in a friend's home. This tradition, and the wording on Mary's headstone, were supported by the Rev. Dr. Edgar, 19th century minister of Mauchline Parish Church in his book Old Church Life In Scotland when he recorded - "I am informed, on authority, that a member of the Adjutant's family, who lived to be a grandmother, used to speak of Burns as one whom she knew personally, when he lived at Mauchline, and that she believed her sister Mary was the 'lovely Mary Morison' whom the poet admired."

In a letter dated 20 March, 1793, to George Thomson, song collector, Edinburgh, Burns wrote that the song MARY MORISON was 'one of my juvenile works'. If that is true, it is unlikely that either Mary Morison or Alison Begbie was the heroine of the song.

Mary Morison died as a result of the amputation of a foot seriously injured in an accident.

Also see: Back Causeway; Carnell House; Mauchline Kirkyard; Old Place.

MAUCHLINE

Situated at the junction of the A76 Kilmarnock/Dumfries Road and the A758 Ayr/Muirkirk Road.

The town is an important centre in the Burns Country. Although the poet lived at Mossgiel one mile north of the town, for only 4 years from March, 1784 to June, 1788, it was the period in which his poetic genius burst into full flower. In Mauchline he wrote in his finest medium, his native dialect, and on his best subjects, the people around him. The Kilmarnock Edition of his poetry, his first time in print, was published on 31 July, 1786.

After he left Mauchline, Burns returned regularly to visit his mother, brother Gilbert, and other members of the family at Mossgiel.

The town and district have changed considerably but much of both would be easily recognised by the poet.

The street now called Castle Street was Back Causeway; Loudoun Street from the Cross

MAUCHLINE
CIRCA 1784

KEY -
1 - GAVIN HAMILTON'S HOUSE
2 - MORTON'S BALLROOM
3 - NANCE TANNOCK'S INN
4 - BURNS' HOUSE
5 - DR. McKENZIE'S HOUSE
6 - SMITH'S HOUSE
7 - RICHMOND'S SQUARE
8 - BELLMAN'S SQUARE
9 - WHITEFOORD ARMS
10 - ARMOUR'S HOUSE
11 - McLELLAND'S INN
12 - ANN ORR'S ALE HOUSE

TO KILMARNOCK

TOLL

DRIVEWAY — ORIGINAL KILMARNOCK ROAD

MAUCHLINE BURN

THE KNOWE

BURNSIDE

LOAN GREEN

ELBOW TAVERN

BACK CAUSEWAY

BROWNLEA

NETHERPLACE

TO SORN

HIGH STREET

BLEACHING GREEN

BACKHOLM

CASTLE

THE PLACE

BELLMAN'S VENNEL

THE CROSS

SCENE OF THE HOLY FAIR

CHURCH

SUN INN

DADDY AULD'S MANSE

MAIN ST.

POOSIE NANCIE'S INN

WELTON ROAD

LOUDOUN STREET

OXYGATE

MANSE ST.

TO AYR

BEECHGROVE COTTAGE AND HOUSE

TANYARD

TO CUMNOCK

TO STAIR

––––– LINE OF ROADS
––––– OPENED IN 1821

97

MAUCHLINE CROSS, circa 1900, with 'The Place' on the right

Back Causeway, circa 1900, with Brownlea House on the right

to Cowgate was called Main Street; the main road through the town centre from north to south was by Back Causeway, the Cross, Main Street and Cowgate; the road through from east to west has not changed.

Earl Grey Street and Kilmarnock Road from the Cross to The Knowe were not created until about 1820. Examination of each side of Kilmarnock Road, just north of the Cross, will show the gradient of the slope from the back gardens of High Street down to Castle Street. The amount of infilling required to level the ground shows why the main road ran by Castle Street and not straight through to the Cross as at present.

The young men in Mauchline with whom Burns became most intimate were James Smith, shopkeeper; John Richmond, clerk; William Hunter, shoemaker; and John 'Clockie'

Brown, watchmaker. During June and July, 1786 he wrote to David Brice, a Mauchline shoemaker who had moved to Glasgow but nothing else is known of Brice or the friendship.

Local men older than the poet who showed him friendship and patronage were Gavin Hamilton, writer (lawyer); Doctor John Mackenzie, the family physician; Peter Morrison, cabinetmaker; and John Dow or Dove, Innkeeper.

The many places of interest in the town and district are dealt with separately..

Also See: Ann Orr's Ale House; Armour's House; Back Causeway; Ballochmyle; Barskimming; Barskimming Mill; Beechgrove Cottage; Bridge Holm; Cowgate; Haugh; Mary Morison's House; Mauchline Bleaching Green; Mauchline Burn; Mauchline Castle; Mauchline Races and Fair; Mauchline Kirkyard; Mossgiel Farm; McLelland's Inn; Nance Tannock's Inn; Netherplace; Poosie Nancie's Inn; Richmond's House; Smith's House; Whitefoord Arms.

MAUCHLINE BLEACHING GREEN   Map Ref. 498 272

The green is no longer extant as such; most of it is occupied by the garden of a private house. It was situated to the west of Back Causeway (Castle Street) and north of the 'Castle'.

The poet's wife, Jean Armour, was the daughter of James Armour, a master stone mason and contractor in Mauchline, and a man of some standing in the district.

Local tradition maintains that Burns and Jean Armour first spoke to each other on the bleaching green. The poet had attended a dance in the village on the evening of Mauchline Races in 1784. His collie dog had followed him to the village and into the dance and the poet remarked that he wished he could find a lass who would love him as faithfully as his dog. Jean was at the dance and overheard the remark.

A few days later, Jean was laying out clothes on the bleaching green when the poet went past on his way into the village. His dog ran amongst the clothes but returned to Burns when called to. Jean asked if he had yet found his faithful lass and he stopped and spoke to her.

From the meeting on the bleaching green sprang the romance of Robert Burns and Jean Armour, one of the classic romances of literature.

The accuracy of the story concerning the meeting on the bleaching green was refuted by Jean many years later, but she may have done so because the story suggests that she made the first advance.

Also see: Armour's Home.

MAUCHLINE BURN   Map Ref. 473 257

The burn flows west through Mauchline to join the River Ayr at Stairaird, at the map reference shown, 2 miles west of Mauchline. Locally, it is known as the River Chalk.

Whereas it is generally accepted that Burns and Highland Mary Campbell parted at Failford where the River Fail joins the River Ayr, as indicated by the monument on the north bank of the Fail, it has also been suggested that the parting was at Stairaird where the Mauchline Burn joins the River Ayr. A wood near Kingencleugh, Mauchline, has also been suggested as the location of the parting.

The description of the parting given by Burns - 'We met by appointment, on the second Sunday of May, in a sequestered spot by the banks of Ayr' - can be applied to the Failford, Stairaird and Kingencleugh locations. However, in the opening stanza of the poem *HIGHLAND MARY*, the poet gave another indication of the spot - '*Ye banks and braes and streams around, The castle o' Montgomery!. . . . For there I took the last fareweel, O' my sweet Highland Mary.*' This supports the claim of Failford as of the three it was the location nearest to Montgomerie House (Coilsfield).

Also see: Failford; Fail Water; Kingencleugh; Stairaird.

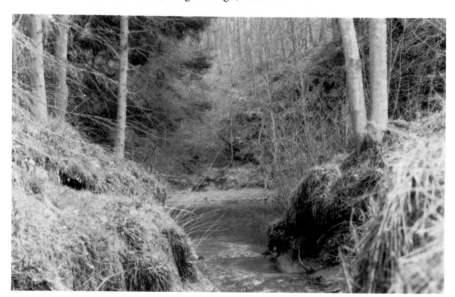

'A SEQUESTERED SPOT'
Mauchline Burn, where it joins the River Ayr at Stairaird

MAUCHLINE CASTLE

Map Ref. 497 274

Situated in Mauchline town centre, north of the kirkyard and west of Castle Street.

The 'castle' dates from the 12th century and is thought to have been associated with Melrose Abbey, the monks of which had title to the land around Mauchline.

The ruined 'castle' was a prominent feature in Mauchline when the poet lived at Mossgiel Farm and frequented the village. His youngest sister, Isabella Burns Begg, when discussing Highland Mary Campbell, said she knew little about her but had overheard the poet telling their Mossgiel employee, John Blane, that 'Mary had refused to meet him in the old castle' and presumed later that he had been referring to Mary Campbell.

The poet's friend and patron, Gavin Hamilton, lived in the house adjacent to the 'castle' on its west side and his address was normally shown as Mauchline Castle. The house is still occupied.

Also see: Gavin Hamilton's House; Mossgiel Farm.

MAUCHLINE KIRK AND CASTLE before 1827

MAUCHLINE KIRKYARD   Map Ref. 497 273

Situated in Loudoun Street, Mauchline, 50 yards west of The Cross.

The present church was built in 1827 on the site of the original. The kirkyard was the setting of the poem *THE HOLY FAIR*.

A chart on the outside wall of the church indicates the burial places of the poet's family and associates:-

1. James Hamilton - See Mossgiel Farm.

2. Gavin Hamilton - See Gavin Hamilton's House.

3. Mary Morison - See Mary Morison's House.

4. Robert Wilson - Subject of the song *THE GALLANT WEAVER*. A native of Mauchline, he moved to Paisley for several years. When Jean Armour's parents found that she was pregnant by Burns, for the first time, they sent her off to relations in Paisley. An ill-founded rumour reached the poet that Jean and Robert Wilson were to be married and it caused him to be resentful of Jean.

5. William Fisher - See Montgarswood Farm and South Auchenbrain Farm.

6. Nance Tannock - See Nance Tannock's Inn.

7. James Bryan - Referred to by Burns as *'The Godly Bryan'* in the poem 'THE COURT OF EQUITY' and again in a letter to John Richmond dated 9 July, 1786. He was a farmer at Welton Farm, one mile south-east of Mauchline. The Kirk session records show that he appeared in front of the session for 'irregularities' with girls.

8. George Gibson, his wife, 'Poosie Nancie' and daughter, 'Racer Jess'   See Poosie Nancie's Inn.

9. James Whitefoord - Infant son of Sir John Whitefoord of Ballochmyle. See Ballochmyle.

10. John Brown - Friend of Burns, referred to in the poem *THE COURT OF EQUITY* as

'*Clockie Brown*' because he was a watchmaker in Mauchline. The Brown family were well known makers of watches and clocks, especially of grandfather clocks.

11. John Richmond - See Richmond's House.

12. Rev. William Auld - See Symington.

13. Andrew Noble - School master at Mauchline and session clerk of the Parish kirk while Burns was at Mossgiel and appearing before the session for misdemeanours with Jean Armour.

14. James Humphrey - See Carngillan.

15. The Poet's children - Jean (twin of Robert, the eldest son), died September, 1786; un-named twins, died March, 1788; Elizabeth Riddell, died November, 1795.

16. 'Laird' McGavin - Referred to as '*Master Tootie, alias Laird McGaun*' in the poem *TO GAVIN HAMILTON, ESQ.* He is thought to have been a rogue cattle dealer in Mauchline.

17. Burial place of the Alexanders of Ballochmyle. Wilhemina Alexander, the '*Bonie Lass Of Ballochmyle*' is NOT buried in Mauchline but probably in a disused cemetery within the bounds of Glasgow Airport. See: Ballochmyle.

MAUCHLINE RACES AND FAIR
Mauchline Races and Fair are referred to in the poem *FIRST EPISTLE TO J. LAPRAIK* - '*But Mauchline Race or Mauchline Fair, I should be proud to meet you there.*'

At the time of Burns, Mauchline Races were held in the vicinity of the site of Burns Monument and Cottage Homes and were run from there past Mossgiel to Skeoch Hill and back.

Mauchline Fair was held at the Cross which was much the same as at present, except that Kilmarnock Road and Earl Grey Street had not been created and the houses extended from Castle Street (Back Causeway) across to High Street.

The Fair should not be confused with the religious celebration held in the kirkyard and immortalized by Burns in the poem *THE HOLY FAIR*.

MAULESIDE   Map Ref. 331 521
Situated on the A737 Dalry/Beith Road, one mile east of Beith.

William Ronald, one of the farm workers at Mossgiel referred to in the poem *THE INVENTORY*, was a farmer at Mauleside later in his life. At Mossgiel he acted as gauds boy (ploughman's assistant) when Burns was ploughing.

William Ronald's uncle, John Ronald, was the Mauchline/Glasgow carrier and probably the keeper of Ronald's Inn, Mauchline.

Also see: Mossgiel Farm; Ronald's Inn.

MAYBOLE
Situated on the A77 Ayr/Girvan Road, 10 miles south of Ayr. The poet was familiar with the town and district.

Agnes Broun, the poet's mother, lived in Maybole for about 13 years. Her mother died when she was 10 years old, in 1742, and when her father re-married 2 years later, Agnes went to live with her maternal grandmother, Mrs. Rennie, in Maybole. When her grandmother died, she moved to the home of her paternal uncle, Willie Broun, also in Maybole. The locations of the houses are not known.

The poet's parents, William Burnes and Agnes Broun, met at Maybole Fair in 1756. A bust of the poet looks down on the High Street from the apex of the gable at No. 15 and, according to local tradition, marks the site of the booth where William and Agnes met at the Fair.

The poet's friend and correspondent, William Niven (cousin of John Niven of Ballochneil), was the son of a Maybole farmer and shopkeeper and lived in the town. They met as fellow-pupils at Hugh Rodger's school, Kirkoswald in 1775. While attending the school, Burns lodged at Ballochneil Farm, south of the village but he spent weekends at William Niven's home at Maybole.

William Niven became a wealthy and avaricious businessman. He served on Maybole Town Council and was a Depute Lord Lieutenant of Ayrshire. He built himself a house in High Street, the site of which is now occupied by the Bank of Scotland at No. 67. He bought Kirkbride Farm and inherited Kirklandhill Farm from his father.

In September, 1786, the poet visited Maybole to collect subscription money for the Kilmarnock Edition of his poems. He lodged at the Kings Arms Hotel which was situated in High Street, immediately south of the District Council offices at No. 70, until it was destroyed by fire a few years ago. The poet was joined for the evening by a group of his friends, including William Niven; Hugh Rodger, his old schoolmaster; David Dunn, Maybole schoolmaster; and Thomas Piper, assistant to Doctor Hugh Logan, Maybole's only physician.

After a convivial night, some of his friends gathered next morning to say goodbye to him. Burns had hired a horse from the Kings Arms for his journey home; it was a mare called Rosinante, well known throughout the area as a broken-down nag. As was the custom, his friends went ahead of him and awaited his arrival on what is now the Maybole/Alloway High Road, a half mile out of the town. As he approached them they gave him a reception of salutes and mock heroic verses, to which the poet said, "Why all this parade of fine verses, my friends, it would have been enough to say - Here comes Burns on Rosinante, She's damned poor, but he's damned cantie".

When he returned to Mossgiel the poet wrote to William Niven in a letter dated 20 August, 1786, and sent his regards to his Maybole friends.

Also see: Ballochneil Farm; Kirkoswald.

MAYFIELD

In a letter dated 22 August, 1792, to Mrs. Dunlop of Dunlop, Burns wrote that he had been visited at Ellisland Farm, Dumfries by Mr. Baillie of Mayfield and his daughters.

Mr. Baillie's daughter, Lesley, was the heroine of the songs *SAW YE BONIE LESLEY and BLYTHE HAE I BEEN ON YON HILL.*

The Baillie family lived at Mayville, Stevenston and it must be presumed that Burns called it Mayfield by mistake. In later correspondence to Lesley Baillie, he referred to her home as Mayville.

The name Mayfield has another Burns association. Bruce Campbell, with whom Burns corresponded in a letter dated 13 November, 1788, was designated as being of Mayfield,

Milrig and Sornbeg. These properties were in Galston Parish and had no connection with the Baillie family.

Also see: Mayville House; Milrig House.

MAYVILLE HOUSE, 1985

MAYVILLE HOUSE   Map Ref. 268 422

Situated at No. 31 High Road, Stevenston, the house is still occupied.

It was the home of Lesley Baillie, heroine of the songs *SAW YE BONIE LESLEY and BLYTHE HAE I BEEN ON YON HILL*. Born at Mayville on 6 March, 1768, she married Robert Cumming of Logie and died at Edinburgh on 12 July, 1843.

Robert Baillie of Mayville erected a memorial column to his wife; Lesley's name was added to it later. It now stands on the east side of Glencairn Street, Stevenston, alongside No. 110. Originally it was erected much nearer Kerelaw Mains. It became derelict and lay in pieces for many years until restored and re-erected on its present site in 1929.

Legend in Stevenston maintains that Burns visited the Baillie family at Mayville. He did visit them but probably while they were living in a town house in Edinburgh.

The Baillie family visited Burns at Ellisland Farm, Dumfries, during August, 1792, when they were en route to England. After the visit, the poet accompanied them on horseback for the first few miles towards the border. To compliment Lesley Baillie and commemorate the visit, Burns composed the song *SAW YE BONIE LESLEY* - '*O' saw ye bonie Lesley, As she gaed o'er the border.*'

During May, 1793, Burns wrote a letter to Lesley Baillie at Mayville. According to Lesley Baillie's daughter Lesley, assisted Burns with the immortal last verse of his poem *LAMENT FOR JAMES, EARL OF GLENCAIRN*. It is claimed that originally the last two lines were - *'I'll remember gude Glencairn, And a' that he has done for me.'* On the poem being read to the Earl's sisters, the word 'gude' was objected to and the word 'great' suggested instead. Burns felt that 'great' was inappropriate but did not wish to offend the family. On a visit to the Baillie family he mentioned his dilemma to Lesley. She suggested omitting both 'gude' and 'great' and making the lines - *'I'll remember thee, Glencairn, and a' that thou hast done for me'*. Burns was delighted by the suggestion and adopted the lines for publication of the poem. The story can not be verified but it has a ring of truth.

MILNCRAIG HOUSE   Map Ref. 399 208

Situated north of the A70 Ayr/Cumnock Road, one mile west of Coylton.

It was the home of Sir William Augustus Cunninghame who was referred to as 'The Bauld Sir Willie' in the poem *THE AUTHOR'S EARNEST CRY AND PRAYER*.

MILLER'S HOLM   Map Ref. 491 254

Another name for Bridge Holm, Barskimming, Mauchline.

MILRIG HOUSE   Map Ref. 502 341

Situated east of the B744 Galston/Crosshands Road, 2 miles south of Galston.

The original house was demolished shortly after World War II. It was the home of Bruce Campbell, designated as of Mayfield, Milrig and Sornbeg. Burns corresponded with Campbell in a letter dated 13 November, 1788, and sent him subscription sheets for the Kilmarnock Edition of his poems. There is no other record of association between the men.

Also see: Mayfield.

MILTON   Map Ref. 436 236

Situated on the B730 Tarbolton/Drongan Road, at Stair Bridge. It is the correct name of the hamlet on the north bank of the River Ayr, commonly regarded as Stair.

Burns was familiar with the area and visited the nearby Stair House with David Sillar, who was courting Peggy Orr, nurserymaid to Mrs. Stewart of Stair.

In his book Burns and Stair (1927), John McVie records that Mary (Mailly) Crosbie, housekeeper to Mrs. Stewart, who had joined Peggy Orr in entertaining Burns and Sillar in the kitchen of Stair House, lived and died in a cottage at Milton. Local tradition maintains that Burns took tea in the cottage.

Mailly Crosbie's cottage is no longer extant and its exact location is unknown. It is thought to have been sited on the east side of the Tarbolton/Drongan Road, about 100 yards north of Stair Bridge.

MINNYBAE FARM   Map Ref. 234 068

Situated on the east side of the A77 Kirkoswald/Girvan Road, a half mile south of Kirkoswald.

It was the home of William Neilson who married Peggy Thomson of Kirkoswald in 1784. Peggy was the heroine of the composition *SONG - COMPOSED IN AUGUST*. The poet's sister, Mrs. Begg, said that the song *MY NANIE, O'* was written to Peggy Thomson but other girls are also suggested as the heroine of this song.

Burns visited the Neilsons, presumably at Minnybae, in 1786, shortly before he was due to leave for the West Indies. He gave Peggy a signed copy of the Kilmarnock Edition of his poems with the poem *LINES TO AN OLD SWEETHEART* inscribed on the flyleaf. The poet later recorded that William Neilson walked with him for the first 3 miles of his journey home.

Also see: Coldcothill Farm; Doura Farm; Girvan River; Kirkoswald; Peggy Thomson's House; Pinvalley; Ship Inn; Stinchar River.

REV. DR. THOMAS BURNS

MONKTON

Situated one mile north of Prestwick and a half mile west of the A77 Kilmarnock/Ayr Road.

The Rev. Andrew Mitchell, minister of Monkton Parish Church from 1775 to 1811, was referred to in the poem *THE KIRK' SALARM* as 'Andrew Gowk'. He is buried in Monkton kirkyard.

The poet's nephew, the Rev. Dr. Thomas Burns, was minister at Monkton from 1830 to 1843. He was the son of the poet's brother, Gilbert Burns, and was born at Mossgiel in 1796. His daughter, Ann Burns, great-niece of the poet, died at Monkton and is buried in the kirkyard. A plaque on the outside wall of the present Monkton Church, Monkton Road, Prestwick shows that it was - 'built 1837 by Rev. Thomas Burns, Minister from

1830 to the dissolution in 1843. In 1848 he led a party of Free Church emigrants to New Zealand and there founded the provinces of Otago and Southland.'

Another Monkton minister was the Rev. George Lawrie who was the incumbent from 1844 to 1878. He was the son and grandson of the poet's friends the Rev's. Archibald and George Lawrie of Newmilns and was born in Loudoun Manse. While at Monkton, Rev. Lawrie published a book of poems, the best known being the still popular song *HA'E YE MIND O' LANG, LANG SYNE*. He died on 14 February, 1878, and is buried in Monkton kirkyard.

Monkton kirkyard has another important association with Burns. A headstone commemorates Matthew Paterson and his wife Ann Ronald, of Aikenbrae Farm, Monkton. Matthew Paterson was an associate of Burns in Tarbolton and a member of the Bachelors' Club. Ann Ronald was one of the *Ronalds of the Bennals* and referred to in the poem of that name. The poet had been keen to court Ann but was afraid of being rebuffed because of her family's superior social standing.

Also see: Aikenbrae Farm; Bennals Farm; Loudoun Kirk; Patie's Mill.

MONTGARSWOOD FARM   Map Ref. 530 277

Situated on the south side of the B743 Mauchline/Sorn Road, 2 miles east of Mauchline.

William Fisher, farmer and kirk elder, has been described as having lived at Montgarswood Farm. There are now two Montgarswood Farms and Fisher lived at the farm now called East Montgarswood.

Fisher was immortalised by Burns as *Holy Willie* of the poems *HOLY WILLIE'S PRAYER* and *HOLY WILLIE'S EPITAPH*. He is also referred to in the poem *THE KIRK'S ALARM*.

In the 18th century the Mauchline/Sorn Road ran on the south side of the farm, not on the north as at present. The site of Fisher's dwelling was to the west of the modern steading.

William Fisher was found dead in a snow-filled ditch on South Auchenbrain Farm Road during February, 1809. He is buried in Mauchline kirkyard.

Montgarswood has another association with Burns. In the 18th century it was purchased by a Mauchline merchant, Henry Richmond, father of the poet's close friend, John Richmond. John Richmond's brother, James, took over the property in 1798.

Also see: Mauchline Kirkyard; Richmond's House; South Auchenbrain Farm.

MONTGOMERIE HOUSE   Map Ref. 446 263

The house is no longer extant; only its driveways remain. It was situated north of the A758 Ayr/Mauchline Road, one mile east of the B730 Tarbolton/Stair Road.

Between 1806 and 1809, Coilsfield House, home of the Montgomerie family, was demolished and a new mansion built on or near the site. The new residence was called Montgomerie House.

Burns was almost certainly familiar with the estate. Mary Campbell, the poet's Highland Mary, is thought to have worked at Coilsfield as a dairy maid. In the song *HIGHLAND MARY*, Burns referred to Coilsfield as 'the castle o' Montgomerie', a reference to the family, and this has led to some confusion in differentiating between the earlier Coilsfield and later Montgomerie Houses.

Also see: Coilsfield House.

MONUMENTS, MEMORIALS AND STATUES

1. Alloway - Burns Monument and Gardens.

Situated on the north bank of the River Doon, at the north end of Old Doon Bridge. The monument, designed by Thomas Hamilton, was opened on 4 July, 1823. The three-sided base represents the three divisions of Ayrshire - Carrick, Cunninghame and Kyle.

The imaginative statues of Tam O'Shanter, Souter Johnie and Nance Tannock by James Thom, the self-taught Ayrshire sculptor, are located in the beautiful gardens surrounding the monument. The monument and gardens are open to the public from April to September for a small admission charge.

Also see: James Thom, Sculptor.

2. Ayr - Burns Statue.

Situated in Burns Statue Square, Ayr, the statue by G.A. Lawson, FRSA, was unveiled on 11 July, 1891.

3. Failford - Memorial to Burns and Highland Mary.

Situated on the west bank of the Fail Water at Failford on the A758 Ayr/Mauchline Road, 2½ miles west of Mauchline.

The memorial commemorates the parting of Burns and Highland Mary Campbell. It was unveiled on 14 May, 1921.

Also see: Failford.

4. Irvine - Burns Statue.

Situated on Irvine Moor, overlooking the east bank of the River Irvine, 150 yards south of Maress Road. The statue, by Pittendrigh MacGillivray, was unveiled on 18th July, 1896.

5. Kilmarnock - Burns Monument and Statue.

Situated in Kay Park, Kilmarnock, a few hundred yards north-east of the town centre, the monument was opened on 9 August, 1879. It incorporates a museum of minor items and is open to the public by prior arrangement with the curator. The statue was sculpted by W.G. Stevenson.

6. Kilmarnock - Burns Statue

Situated at Kilmarnock Cross, the statue is by Alexander Stoddart. It is of Burns and his printer, John Wilson, together with heads of Apollo and Hermes, the Greek Gods associated with poets and traders, respectively. It was unveiled by the Princess Royal on 27th September, 1995.

7. Mauchline - National Burns Memorial and Cottage Homes.

Situated at the junction of Kilmarnock Road and Skeoch Road, Mauchline, the memorial and cottage homes neighbour the fields of Mossgiel Farm. The memorial, opened on 7 May 1898, incorporates a museum of minor relics and interesting items, and gives a panoramic view of the Burns country. The cottage homes are maintained for elderly persons by charitable Burns organisations.

SPECIAL FEATURE - JAMES THOM, SCULPTOR

Although the characters Tam O'Shanter and Souter Johnnie were created by the genius

BURNS MONUMENT, ALLOWAY

BURNS MONUMENT, KILMARNOCK

THE NATIONAL BURNS MEMORIAL,
MAUCHLINE

of Robert Burns, it was another young Ayrshireman of the next generation who produced the figures by which they are recognised throughout the world.

James Thom was born in a labourer's cottage near Tarbolton in 1799, less than three years after the poet's death. After a very basic three-R's education, he was apprenticed to a Kilmarnock stone-mason and, soon, his ability with stone was obvious. Even his leisure time was spent carving stone figures.

TAM O'SHANTER AND SOUTER JOHNIE STATUES
at National Burns Memorial Gardens, Alloway

When James was about 25, and working on a headstone in Crosbie kirkyard between Troon and Monkton, he came to the attention of a passing businessman. Mr. David Auld, Perfumier, Ayr, was a noted Burns enthusiast and on learning that the young man's hobby was sculpting, he commissioned him to produce a bust of Robert Burns. The bust, carved from a block of grey sandstone from Craiksland quarry, near Loans, and based on Nasmyth's portrait of the poet, was so well received that many more commissions followed.

Thom became a self-employed, full-time sculptor, creating more busts of Burns, statues of characters from the poet's works, and other figures as requested. A statue of Sir Walter Scott's famous character, Old Mortality - complete with his pony - spread the sculptor's fame wider. His statue of Sir William Wallace still stands in a niche in the Wallace Tower, overlooking High Street, Ayr.

Of all of the figures created by James Thom, the most popular by far were those of the characters from the poem Tam O Shanter - Tam, Souter Johnnie, the landlord and the landlord's wife - examples of which can be found throughout Britain and in the U.S.A. The best-known groups of figures are in the alehouse at the rear of Souter Johnnie's cottage, Kirkoswald, and in the grotto in the garden of the National Burns Monument, Alloway.

Thom's work was exhibited in many parts of Britain. An exhibition in London about 1830 was visited by King George IV and sculptures by Thom can still be found throughout England.

About 1832, the sculptor moved to London but his stay was brief. Examples of his work had been displayed in New York and the demand for them was such that in 1834 he moved to the U.S.A. and settled on a farm near Ramapo, New Jersey. In New York, he worked on sculptures for Trinity Church and on 17th April, 1850, he died in that city.

Several persons were suggested by contemporaries as having been Thom's models for the figures of Tam and the Souter but the sculptor left no record and the figures may have been simply products of his imagination.

James Thom's son, James Crawford Thom (1835-98), became a prominent portrait and landscape artist, exhibiting his work throughout the U.S.A. and Europe.

MORTON'S BALLROOM
The ballroom was described by a contemporary of Burns as the house nearest to Mauchline Castle on the east side. It was probably on the south-west corner of a square of houses on the site now occupied by the Parish Church Hall.

Hugh Morton, the proprietor, has been described as an innkeeper and the ballroom was probably a hall or large room in the inn. His daughter, Christina, was Miss Morton of THE BELLES OF MAUCHLINE.

Tradition maintains that Burns and Jean Armour met at a dancing class in the ballroom. The poet's dog had followed him to the dance and he remarked that he wished he could meet a lass who would love him as faithfully as his dog did. A few days later Jean was on Mauchline bleaching green when the poet passed and she asked him if he had met his faithful lass yet. So started their romance.

One traditional version of the marriage of Burns and Jean Armour maintains that it was performed in Hugh Morton's ballroom by John Farquhar-Gray, J.P. of Gilmilnscroft, Sorn. There is no official record of the place of marriage.

Also see: Gavin Hamilton's House; Gilmilnscroft; Mauchline Bleaching Green; Ronald's Inn.

MOSSGIEL FARM   Map Ref. 489 286
Situated on the 'C' class Mauchline/Tarbolton Road, one mile north of Mauchline Cross. Burns normally spelled the name Mossgiel but also used the old spelling, Mossgavill.

Burns lived at Mossgiel for 4 years, from 1784 to 1788, parts of which period he spent in Edinburgh and on tours of Scotland. It is doubtful if any man in literature has ever made a name more famous by such a brief association. The farm has given its name to a multitude of streets and houses, and even to a town in New Zealand.

The farm sits high on an exposed ridge and in the poet's time had cold, wet, unproductive soil which did little to reward hard labour. Robert Burns took it over with high hopes and good intentions - "I read farming books; I calculated crops; I attended markets" - but was soon despirited - "the first year the crops failed from buying bad seed, the second from a late harvest, we lost half of both our crops; this overset all my wisdom".

The original farmhouse still exists but would not be recognised by Burns. In 1858, the house was re-modelled and in 1870 a new storey and roof were added. The building may have changed and fields been enclosed but the poet would still be at home on the farm.

Special Bicentenary Ploughing Match at Mossgiel on 3rd March, 1996

It was during his stay at Mossgiel that the poet's genius burst into full flower and his work was published for the first time. The finest work of the period includes the following:- *THE VISION; ADDRESS TO THE UNCO GUID; THE EPISTLES TO DAVIE; THE EPISTLES TO J. LAPRAIK; HALLOWE'EN; THE JOLLY BEGGARS; THE COTTER'S SATURDAY NIGHT; THE ORDINATION; THE HOLY FAIR; THE AUTHOR'S EARNEST CRY AND PRAYER; ADDRESS TO THE DEIL; SCOTCH DRINK; HOLY WILLIE'S PRAYER AND EPITAPH; THE LASS O'BALLOCHMYLE; THE TWA DOGS; THE BRIGS OF AYR; TO A MOUSE; TO A MOUNTAIN DAISY; DEATH AND DOCTOR HORNBOOK;* and many more. A torrent of genius.

The *'daisy'* field where the 'tender stem' was crushed 'amang the stoure', and from which a mass of daisies have gone with visitors to colonise the corners of the earth, is immediately behind the steading. The 'mousie' field where the poet ploughed up 'that wee bit heap o' leaves an' stibble' is south-east of the steading, bordered on its east side by the Mauchline/Kilmarnock Road. A large field, two fields removed from the back of the steading, is known as Knockhaspie's Land, and is possibly the origin of the name Knockhaspie's Land in the song *HIGHLAND HARRY BACK AGAIN.*

Stand at Mossgiel at daybreak and see 'the rising sun o'er Blacksideen' *(A MAUCHLINE WEDDING)*, or *'upon a simmer morn - snuff the caller air'* and see *'the rising sun, owre Galston muirs' (THE HOLY FAIR)* and you know that you are in the Land of Burns. Imagine the cotter wending his weary way homewards from the back fields of Mossgiel as *'November chill blaws loud wi' angry sugh'* *(THE COTTER'S SATURDAY NIGHT)* and you will enjoy the poem even more when next you read it. See the sun setting behind Arran and you will wonder as many have done, how this great poet made no poetic acknowledgement of such magnificence. Only once did Burns make even an oblique reference to the sunset behind Arran; in a letter dated 18 November, 1786, to Miss Wilhelmina Alexander, enclosing the song addressed to her, *THE LASS OF BALLOCHMYLE*, he described the setting which inspired the poem - *'I had roved out ... to view nature in all the gaiety of the vernal years. The sun was flaming over the distant western hills.'* From Mauchline, the reference can only be to Arran.

We know more about the workers employed at Mossgiel than at any other of the Burns family farms.

MOSSGIEL, circa 1850

WILLIAM RONALD - nephew of John Ronald the Mauchline carrier was employed as a ploughman. Later in life he farmed on his own behalf at Mauleside, Beith. He spoke of the excellent way in which the poet conducted evening worship at Mossgiel.

DAVID HUTCHESON - 'wee Davoc' of the poem *THE INVENTORY* worked as herd boy. His father had been a ploughman at Lochlea but died of fever, leaving 2 boys and 2 girls orphaned. The poet took David and his sister Janet into his household. He took a special interest in the boy and looked after him until he was able to make his own way in the world. Janet worked for the poet's mother for many years.

JOHN BLANE - he worked as a gauds boy (ploughman's assistant). Many years later when he was coachman on the Cumnock/Kilmarnock coach, he was interviewed by James Grierson, Burns researcher, and claimed to have been in church with Burns when the incident occurred which inspired the poem *TO A LOUSE*. He also told of having been chastised by Burns for flicking a whip at a sparrow and removing some of its feathers. He said that the poet's manner made such an impression on him that he could never have done such a thing again.

JOHN LAMBIE - he was also employed as a gauds boy. He claimed to have been leading the plough for Burns when the poet turned over the nest of the field mouse. He had gone running after the mouse 'wi murdering pattle' until Burns stopped him. The poet had gone quiet for some time after the incident and later showed Lambie the draft of the poem *TO A MOUSE*, saying, 'Well, what do you think of your mouse now?'

JAMES HAMILTON - as a very young boy he worked at the farm and acted as the poet's messenger boy. He recalled having been sent to Mauchline with a note for Jean Armour, with the instruction to give it to no one but her. He died in Mauchline in 1862, aged 84 years, and is buried in the kirkyard.

WILLIAM PATRICK - he worked for the poet as a labourer. As an old man he lived in Loudoun Street, Mauchline, and was interviewed regularly by researchers. His reminiscences about Burns and his Mauchline associates can be read in the book Robert Burns at Mossgiel by William Joly (1881). He died in Mauchline in 1864, aged 88 years, and is buried in the kirkyard.

Also see: Galston; Knockhaspie's Land; Mauchline; Mauchline Castle; Mauchline Kirkyard; Mauleside; Stevenston.

MOUNT OLIPHANT FARM

MOUNT OLIPHANT FARM   Map Ref. 357 173

Situated a half mile south of Corton Road, and a half mile east of the A77 Ayr/Maybole Road.

The Burnes family moved from the cottage at Alloway to Mount Oliphant at Whitsun, 1766 when the poet's father, William Burnes, rented the farm from Doctor William Ferguson of Doonholm, Alloway, Provost of Ayr. At the time of the move, the poet was 7 years of age.

When 14 years of age and still at Mount Oliphant, Burns composed his first song, *HANDSOME NELL*, to a young girl called Nellie Kilpatrick of Purclewan Mill whom he met while they were working together in a harvest field.

The farm proved to be infertile and the Burnes family were close to poverty. As the eldest of the family, the poet had to labour in the fields in all weathers, adversely affecting his health for the rest of his life. In an autobiographical letter written many years later, the poet called the farm 'A ruinous bargain'.

It was from Mount Oliphant that Burns attended schools at Ayr, Dalrymple and Kirkoswald.

In 1777, the family moved on to Lochlea Farm, Tarbolton Parish. They had lived at Mount Oliphant for 11 years, considerably longer than the poet lived at any other place.

The farm buildings have changed, the fields have been enclosed and neighbouring properties have changed greatly, but the poet would still find the area reasonably familiar.

If you visit Mount Oliphant, stand and look around you. This land saw the formative years of Robert Burns. Here he *'padl'd in the burn'* and *'pou'd the gowans fine' (AULD LANG SYNE)*, from here he explored the wooded *'banks and braes o' bonie Doon'* and it was here that he dreamt his first dreams of young love. This land may have shown the Burnes family the misery of poverty and drudgery but it nurtured the God-given genius of an embryo poet.

Also see: Ayr; Dalrymple; Kirkoswald; Purclewan.

MUIRKIRK

Situated on the A70 Ayr/Edinburgh Road, 10 miles east of Cumnock.

The poet was familiar with the area by passing through en route between Mossgiel Farm and Edinburgh and by his visits to the Rhymer, John Lapraik.

Lapraik lived at Dalfram, Muirsmill, Netherwood and Nether Wellwood, all a few miles to the west of Muirkirk, and finally moved into the village. In Muirkirk, he ran an ale-house which was also the post office; it was situated in Kirkgreen, on a site later occupied by the old catholic school. He is buried in the kirkyard.

Burns referred to Muirkirk and Lapraik in the poem *(FIRST) EPISTLE TO J. LAPRAIK - 'they tauld me 'twas an odd kind chiel, about Muirkirk'*.

The Rev. John Shepherd, referred to as *'Muirland Jock'* in the poem *THE KIRK' SALARM*, was minister of Muirkirk Parish Church from 1775, probably to his death in 1799, but this can not be confirmed.

Also see: Dalfram; Muirsmill.

MUIRSMILL   Map Ref. 658 263

The house is no longer extant. The site is on the north bank of the River Ayr, almost opposite Nether Wellwood, on the A70 Muirkirk/Cumnock Road, 3 miles west of Muirkirk.

For a short period it was the home of John Lapraik, minor poet, who was an acquaintance of Burns. He was the subject of the three *EPISTLE (S) TO J. LAPRAIK*.

Burns visited Lapraik at least once and stayed overnight at Muirsmill.

Also see: Dalfram; Muirkirk.

John Murdoch's house in which Burns lodged.

MURDOCH'S HOUSE

Map Ref. 335 219

A stone plaque on the south gable of the premises at No. 58, Sandgate, Ayr, indicates the site of John Murdoch's house.

In 1765, when he was 18 years of age, Murdoch was interviewed by the poet's father, William Burnes, in Simpson's Inn, Ayr, and appointed to teach the children of Burnes and some of his neighbours, at Alloway. Murdoch was required to produce a specimen of his handwriting for examination.

The school at Alloway was held in a tenement building described as being near Burns Cottage, which was demolished in 1878.

Although the Burnes family moved 2 miles from Alloway to Mount Oliphant Farm in 1766, Robert and Gilbert continued to attend the Alloway school until about 1768. Murdoch became friendly with the Burnes family and visited them regularly.

John Murdoch left the area for a few years but returned in 1773 when he was appointed English Master at Ayr Grammar School. Shortly after his appointment, Robert Burnes attended the Grammar School for 3 weeks to improve his English and French. While at the school he lodged with Murdoch in his home in Sandgate.

In 1776, Murdoch left Ayr under a cloud; while intoxicated he had spoken out indiscreetly against the Rev. Dr. William Dalrymple, minister of Ayr Auld Kirk.

He went to London where he met the poet's brother, William Burnes. When William died he assisted with the funeral arrangements. From London, he spent some time in Paris where he met and was befriended by Colonel Fullarton of Fullarton, Troon. Colonel

Fullarton later befriended and corresponded with Burns. John Murdoch died in London and was buried in St. Andrew's Gardens burial ground, Greys Inn Road, on 20 april 1824.

Also see: Alloway; Ayr Grammar School; Fullarton House; Simpson's Inn.

MUSEUMS, DISPLAYS ETC.

1. Alloway - Burns Cottage and Museum

Situated on the west side of the B7024 Ayr/Maybole Road, in Alloway Village, 2 miles south of Ayr town centre.

Burns Cottage, the poet's birthplace, was restored and opened to the public in March, 1901. The museum has one of the world's finest collections of Burns relics; it is open from 9.00am to 7.00pm daily throughout the year.

Also see: Burns Cottage; New Gardens.

2. Alloway - Land o' Burns Centre/Tam o' Shanter Experience

Situated on the east side of the B7024 Ayr/Maybole Road, 200 yards north of the River Doon and 2½ miles south of Ayr town centre.

The centre was opened in 1977 and, on being refurbished in 1994, changed its name to The Tam O'Shanter Experience. It incorporates an audio-visual display on the life of Burns and on the poem Tam O'Shanter. It has a book and gift shop, a restaurant and a garden with a display of old farm implements. It is open to the public from 9.00am to 6.00pm throughout the year.

3. Alloway - Burns Monument

Situated on the east side of the B7024 Ayr/Maybole Road, at the north end of Old Doon Bridge, 2½ miles south of Ayr town centre.

The interior of the monument is a small museum containing some Burns relics.

It is open to the public from 9.00am to 7.00pm daily from April to October.

Also see: Monuments, Memorials and Statues.

4. Ayr - Tam O'Shanter Inn

Situated on the east side of High Street, at Nos. 230/232.

The building is an excellent example of an 18th century dwelling house and shows the type of house that was in High Street when Burns was in Ayr.

There is no evidence to suggest that it was frequented by Burns or Douglas Graham, the poet's model for Tam O'Shanter; neither is there evidence to support it as the scene of the market day carousel of Tam and Souter Johnie with the landlord and wife, as described in the poem TAM O'SHANTER.

The history of the house can be read in the beautifully produced booklet The Dwelling House of James Shearer by Joseph D. Shearer (1983).

5. Irvine - Glasgow Vennel

Situated on the east side of Townhead, about 300 yards south of the Cross. The workshop in which Burns learned flax heckling and house in which he is said to have lodged have been restored.

The heckling shop has an audio-visual display on the poet's association with Irvine and a collection of flax dressing equipment. It is connected to another restored house which contains a shop and an exhibition room. The heckling workshop, exhibition room and shop are open to the public from 10.00am to 4.00pm daily except Sunday, throughout the year.

The lodging house has been furnished in the style of the 18th century. It is also open to the public from 10.00am to 4.00pm daily except Sunday, throughout the year.

Also see: Glasgow Vennel.

6. Irvine - Irvine Burns Club Museum

Situated at "Wellwood", No. 28 Eglinton Street.

An excellent museum with a valuable collection of Burns manuscripts including Wilson the printer's copies of the poems *THE HOLY FAIR* and *THE COTTER'S SATURDAY NIGHT*. In the friendly, intimate atmosphere the average visitor is likely to get closer to a Kilmarnock Edition or a manuscript than in any other museum.

It is open to the public from 2.00pm to 5.00pm on Sundays throughout the year or at almost any reasonable time by prior arrangement with the club secretary who can be contacted at the club's telephone number.

7. Kilmarnock - Burns Monument

Situated in Kay Park, a few hundred yards north-east of the town centre.

The monument incorporates a museum of minor items. It is open to the public by prior arrangement with the Curator, Dick Institute, London Road, Kilmarnock.

Also see: Monuments, etc.

8. Kilmarnock - Burns Federation Headquarters

Situated in the Dick Institute, London Road, Kilmarnock, a few hundred yards east of the town centre.

An excellent collection of important Burns relics and manuscripts can be viewed by prior arrangement with the Curator.

Also see: Special Feature - Burns Federation.

9. Kirkoswald - Souter Johnie's Cottage

Situated on the east side of the A77 Maybole/Girvan Road in Main Street, Kirkoswald.

John Davidson, prototype of the character Souter Johnie in the poem *TAM O'SHANTER* lived in the cottage from 1785 to his death in 1806.

The cottage contains a collection of minor items and a display of souter's (shoemaker's) tools. Imaginative statues of Tam O'Shanter, Souter Johnie, the landlord and his wife, all from the poem *TAM O'SHANTER*, and sculpted by self-taught Ayrshire sculptor, James Thom, are displayed in a building in the back garden of the cottage.

The cottage is open daily from April to September.

Also see: Souter Johnie's Cottage; Special Feature - James Thom.

10. Largs - Burns Garden

Situated at the east end of Douglas Park Garden, Irvine Road.

The garden is planted with the flowers referred to in the poems and songs of Burns.

11. Mauchline - Burns House Museum

Situated in Castle Street, a few yards from the Cross.

The house in which Burns and Jean Armour started married life and the adjoining house which was owned by the poet's friend, Doctor John Mackenzie, are maintained as a museum and contain several Burns relics and items of interest. It is open daily throughout the year.

Also see: Back Causeway.

12. Mauchline - The National Burns Memorial

Situated at the junction of Kilmarnock Road and Skeoch Road.

The memorial incorporates a museum of minor relics and interesting items. It is open to the public by arrangement with the curator of the Burns House Museum, Mauchline.

Also see: Monuments, etc.

13. Mauchline - Poosie Nancie's Inn

Situated in Loudoun Street, at its junction with Cowgate.

The inn was the setting of the cantata, Love and Liberty, better known as The Jolly Beggars. it contains a museum of minor relics and interesting items and is open to the public daily throughout the year.

Also see: Poosie Nancie's Inn.

14. Tarbolton - The Bachelors' Club

Situated in Sandgate, a few yards from the Cross.

The premises in which Burns, his brother Gilbert, and 5 other young men founded the debating society called the Bachelors' Club. It was also the building in which the poet was initiated into Freemasonry.

It is furnished in the style of the 19th Century and contains several items of interest.

It is open to the public daily throughout the year.

Also see: Bachelors' Club; History, etc. of Bachelors' Club.

15. Tarbolton - Lodge St. James

The temple of Lodge St. James is situated at No. 65 Montgomerie Street. It was inaugurated in 1925.

Burns was a member of the Lodge from 1782 and Depute Master from 1784 to 1788. The Lodge possesses several valuable relics and interesting items connected with the poet's membership, including minute books entered and signed by the poet and his brother, Gilbert, a letter sent by Burns to the Lodge on 23 August, 1787, and the mallet, apron and chair used by the poet.

On 9 August, 1844, the poet's 3 surviving sons visited the Lodge and were made honorary members. Their signatures are amongst the items held by the Lodge.

The relics can be viewed by prior arrangement with the Lodge.

Also see: Freemasonry.

SPECIAL FEATURE - THE BURNS FEDERATION

Within five years of the death of Robert Burns in 1796, clubs were being formed to celebrate the anniversary of the poet's birth and to promote interest in his works. During the following eighty years, interest in the poet increased steadily until by 1884 at least 50 Burns Clubs had been formed throughout the U.K., in North America, and in many countries which were part of the British Empire.

In 1884, three Scots were walking together in Thames Embankment Gardens, London. They had been attending the unveiling of a statue of the poet in the city and as they talked, one of them suggested that a Federation of all of the world's Burns Clubs should be formed. The idea was taken up and the group met again in London in February, 1885, to draft a constitution. It was decided that the headquarters of the organisation would be in Kilmarnock and that the inaugural meeting would be held in that town, probably because two of the original group of three were from Auld Killie.

On 17th July, 1885, the Burns Federation met for the first time in the George Hotel, Kilmarnock, under the auspices of Kilmarnock Burns Club. Of the 17 men present, 14 were from the local club. Peter Sturrock, Provost of Kilmarnock, was elected as the first President, with another local man, David Sneddon, as the first Secretary.

The clubs and societies affiliated to the Federation were to be numbered consecutively and there was a lively debate as to which organisation should have the honour of being No.1. The President of the Burns Club of London, one of the original group of three, proposed that as the idea had been mooted first in London and the preliminary meeting held there, his club should have the honour, but some members felt that as Kilmarnock was to be the home of the Federation, Kilmarnock Burns Club should be No. 1. A vote went in favour of the London club.

At a later meeting, when the list of affiliated organisations was published for the first time, it was seen that while the Secretary had adhered to the result of the vote and allocated No. 1 to the Burns Club of London, he had given precedence to his own Kilmarnock club by making it No. 0. This was a piece of hypocritical sleight-of-hand, not in keeping with the character of Burns or the aims of the infant Federation. Nevertheless, it must be added that only the hard work and persistence of two Kilmarnock men, David Sneddon and David McKay, and a Kilmaurs man, Duncan McNaught, prevented the Burns Federation from foundering in the first few years and enabled it to become established as an active world-wide organisation.

The Federation's motto is 'A Man's A Man For A' That' and its objectives are:-

1. To strengthen and consolidate by universal affiliation the bond of fellowship existing amongst the members of Burns Clubs and kindred societies.

2. To purchase and preserve manuscripts and other relics connected with the poet.

3. To repair, renew, or mark with suitable inscription, any building, tombstones, etc., interesting from their association with Burns.

4. To encourage and arrange school competitions in order to stimulate the teaching of Scottish history and literature.

The Federation Headquarters is in the Dick Institute, Elmbank Street, Kilmarnock.

NANCE TANNOCK'S INN   Map Ref. 497 274

Situated in Castle Street (Back Causeway), Mauchline, a few yards out of the Cross. It was built about 1712 and is still extant but not as an inn.

The correct name of the establishment was The Sma' Inn. Nance Tannock - also spelled Tinnock or Tunnock - was the maiden name of Mrs. Agnes Weir who ran the inn.

The inn had the distinction of giving direct access to Mauchline kirkyard from its rear door. It was the place referred to as the 'change-house' in the poem *THE HOLY FAIR* - *'Now but and ben the change-house fills.'*

Burns also referred to the inn in the poem *THE AUTHOR'S EARNEST CRY AND PRAYER* - *'An drink his health in auld Nance Tinnock's.'*

In the Glenriddell Manuscript, Burns noted that the poem *TO MR. McADAM OF CRAIGENGILLAN* was composed extempore in Nance Tannock's Inn, Mauchline, on receipt of a note from that gentleman.

Nance Tannock said that Burns had been in her inn only once or twice.

Also see: Sma' Inn.

NETHERPLACE   Map Ref. 428 371

Netherplace House was demolished shortly after the Second World War. It was situated west of the A76 Mauchline/Kilmarnock Road, and north of the A758 Mauchline/Ayr Road, on the western edge of Mauchline.

It was the home of William Campbell, who was the subject of the poems *EPITAPH ON A HENPECKED SQUIRE, EPIGRAM ON SAID OCCASION* and *'ANOTHER'* - *'But Queen Netherplace of a different complexion.'*

The ancient name of the property was Cowfieldshaw or Cowfauldshaw.

At one time the road out of Mauchline to Kilmarnock ran past the front door of the house but later this road was restricted to use as the private driveway.

NETHERTON

A district of Kilmarnock, still known by that name, situated on the B7038 Kilmarnock/Ayr Road, a half mile south of the town centre.

In the 18th century it was an area, then on the outskirts of Kilmarnock, frequented by weavers. It was referred to in the poem *THE ORDINATION* - *'Or to the Netherton repair, An' turn a carpet weaver'.*

Kilmarnock weavers produced many rhymers, foremost amongst them being Gavin Turnbull who lived in poverty in Soulis Street in the town centre. Turnbull was acquainted with Burns and addressed a poem to him called *THE BARD*. He took up acting and Burns met him again when he appeared at the Theatre Royal, Dumfries. In 1793, Burns sent three of Turnbull's songs to George Thomson, song collector, for consideration for inclusion in his collection of Scottish songs. Gavin Turnbull died in America.

Also see: Kilmarnock.

NEWARK   Map Ref. 324 174

The castle and estate are situated on the west side of the B7024 Alloway/Maybole Road, a few hundred yards south of the River Doon.

Nellie Kilpatrick, the heroine of the song *HANDSOME NELL*, the first recorded composition by Burns, married William Bone, coachman to the Laird of Newark, and resided on the estate.

Also see: Purclewan.

NEW CUMNOCK
Situated on the A76 Cumnock/Dumfries Road, 6 miles south of Cumnock. Burns was very familiar with the village and surrounding district from his journeys between Mauchline and Ellisland. He had many friends in the district and stayed regularly in a local inn. Legend maintains that he wrote the song *SWEET AFTON* in the inn.

The inn cannot be traced. Local tradition maintains that the existing Castle Hotel was the inn concerned but this can not be substantiated. About 1900, the inn in which Burns had lodged was described as then being a farmhouse on the banks of the River Afton and that does not support the tradition concerning the Castle Hotel which has no history of being a farmhouse.

The Rev. James Young, *'Jamie Goose'* of the poem *THE KIRK'S ALARM* was minister of New Cumnock Parish Church from 1758 to 1795. The original church is now a ruin and Rev. Young is buried in the old kirkyard.

Also see: Afton River; Ashmark; Corsincon; Knockshinnoch; Laight; Pencloe.

NEW GARDENS   Map Ref. 335 186
Situated on the B7024 Alloway/Maybole Road, in Alloway Village, 2½ miles south of Ayr town centre.

The property now known as Burns Cottage was called New Gardens by the poet's father, William Burnes, when he built it in 1757.

William Burnes fued 7½ acres of land in Alloway from Dr. Alexander Campbell of Ayr and built the cottage with his own hands. He called it New Gardens as he intended to start a nursery. On 15 December, 1757, he married Agnes Broun and started married life in the cottage.

The poet was born there on 25 January, 1759.

Also see: Burns Cottage.

NEWMILNS
Situated on the A71 Kilmarnock/Edinburgh Road, 7 miles east of Kilmarnock, and astride the River Irvine.

Burns was familiar with the area, mainly through his friendship with the Rev. Dr. George Lawrie, minister of Loudoun Kirk, Newmilns, and by his visits to the manse.

The poet was also acquainted with John Arnot, Dalwhatswood, Newmilns, and was an honorary member of Newmilns Masonic Lodge.

Also see: Dalwhatswood; Freemasonry; Loudoun Arms; Loudoun Kirk; Loudoun Manse; Newmilns Castle; Patie's Mill.

NEWMILNS CASTLE   Map Ref. 536 373
Situated in Castle Street, Newmilns, a few yards north of its junction with Main Street.

The castle or keep was originally a residence of the Campbells of Loudoun.

It is referred to in the poem *THE NIGHT WAS STILL* - *'The night was still, and o'er the hill, The moon shone on the castle wa'.'* The poet was staying overnight with the Rev. Dr. George Lawrie and his family at Loudoun Manse and saw the moon on Newmilns Castle from his bedroom window.

Also see: Loudoun Arms; Loudoun Kirk; Loudoun Manse; Newmilns.

OCHILTREE

Situated on the A70 Ayr/Cumnock Road, 4 miles west of Cumnock.

Burns was familiar with the village and district and had several friends in the area, namely, the Tennant family at Glenconner Farm, Auchenbay Farm and Ochiltree Mill, George Reid at Barquharrie Farm, and William Simson the local schoolmaster.

The village was referred to in the poem *EPISTLE TO WILLIAM SIMSON - 'Or frosts on hills of Ochiltree, Are hoary grey'.* Simson was friend, correspondent and fellow rhymer to Burns. He was later schoolmaster at Cumnock where he died and is buried in the old cemetery.

The Rev. David Grant, *'Davie Bluster'* of the poem *THE KIRK'S ALARM*, was minister of Ochiltree Parish Church from 1786 to his death in 1791, aged 41 years; he is buried in the kirkyard. In a letter to Lady Elizabeth Cunninghame, the poet called Rev. Grant 'A designing, rotten-hearted Puritan.' John Tennant of Glenconner told Burns that his opinion of the minister was wrong. He introduced them and they became firm friends.

The poet's Kilmarnock friend, Tam Samson, who was referred to in the poems *TAM SAMSON'S ELEGY* and *EPITAPH*, was born in Ochiltree. His father was a market gardener opposite the Parish Church. His brother, John Samson, is buried in the kirkyard. In 1786, when Burns borrowed a horse from George Reid of Barquharrie Farm for his journey to Edinburgh, John Samson borrowed the horse from Burns for a journey back to Ayrshire.

John Tennant of Glenconner's eldest son, James Tennant, was miller at Ochiltree Mill. He was addressed by the poet in the poem *EPISTLE TO JAMES TENNANT OF GLENCONNER - 'Auld comrade dear and brither sinner.'*

Burns sent the poem to James Tennant by the hand of one, John Simson - *I've sent you here by Johnie Simson.'* Tradition maintains that Simson - no relation to William Simson the Schoolmaster - was an Ochiltree music and dancing teacher. In the poem, Burns exhorts Tennant to - *'Assist poor Simson a' ye can, Ye'll fin' him just an honest man.'* The Tennant family did assist Simson with the result that Ochiltree had its biggest ever dancing class.

Also see: Auchenbay Farm; Ayr Grammar School; Barquharrie Farm; Glenconner Farm; Poole; Tam Samson's House.

OLD DOON BRIDGE   Map Ref. 333 178

Situated 200 yards upstream from the modern bridge carrying the B7024 Alloway/Maybole Road; it is generally called the Brig o' Doon.

Although not open to vehicular traffic, the bridge is maintained in good repair and is open to pedestrians. The age of the bridge is uncertain but it was built not later than the 15th century and possibly as early as the 13th century.

The bridge is featured in the poem *TAM O'SHANTER* as that over which *'Tam'* was pursued by the witches and where his horse *'Meg'* gained the safety of the key-stone *'but left behind her ain grey tail.'* By its association with the poem, the bridge must be one of the most famous pieces of architecture in the world.

Also see: Kirk Alloway; Tam O'Shanter's Journey.

OLD DOON BRIDGE

OLD PLACE   Map Ref. 466 342

The property is no longer extant. It was situated south of the road leading to Cessnock Mill, Crossroads, about 200 yards west of the A76 Kilmarnock/Mauchline Road and 200 yard north of the A719 Ayr/Galston Road.

The house was an ancient home of the Campbells of Cessnock; when they built a new house near Galston, Old Place became a farmhouse. When eventually it was demolished, the land was incorporated into neighbouring farms and the site of the house is now on Shawsmill Farm.

According to John Muir, FSA (Scot.) in his booklet Burns At Galston And Ecclefechan (1896), Old Place was the home of the poet's early love, Alison (Ellison) Begbie.

In 1781, when Burns was 22 years of age and living at Lochlea Farm, he courted Alison Begbie who was then working at Carnell House which is on the River Cessnock, midway between Old Place and Lochlea. He wrote five romantic letters to her and she is thought to have been the heroine of the songs *THE LASS OF CESSNOCK BANKS and BONIE PEGGY ALISON (AND I'LL LOVE THEE YET).*

Burns proposed marriage to Alison but was rejected. In his autobiographical letter to Doctor John Moore in 1787, he wrote of the incident - "A belle fille whom I adored, and who had pledged her soul to meet me in the fields of matrimony, jilted me, with peculiar circumstances of mortification."

It is often said that the song *MARY MORISON* was written to Alison Begbie. This probably arose from the poet's brother, Gilbert Burns, having suggested that *MARY MORISON* was written to the same girl as the song *BONIE PEGGY ALISON*. It is easy to accept the euphonious name Peggy Alison for Alison Begbie but not so the name Mary Morison.

Also see: Carnell House; Mary Morison's House.

OLD ROME Map Ref. 392 361

The area is indicated by Old Rome Farm on the Earlston Road, at its junction with the A759 Kilmarnock/Troon Road, at Gatehead.

As late as the early years of this century, a map of the district showed a row of cottages called Old Rome on the east side of the Kilmarnock/Troon Road, at the south end of the bridge over the River Irvine. The area has been known as Rome, Old Rome and Rumford and in the past has had a school and a distillery.

It has been erroneously claimed that the adjacent Fairlie Estate was originally called Old Rome or Old Rome Forest. There is nothing to support this claim as the estate was called 'Dreghorn' until it was bought by the Fairlies prior to 1689 and re-named.

In 1786, Jean Armour's father, James Armour, took out a warrant against Burns, hoping to obtain money to maintain Jean and the twins she was expecting by the poet. Burns went into hiding and while doing so he wrote to his Mauchline friend, John Richmond. The letter was dated 30 July, 1786, and addressed as from 'Old Rome Foord'. The location of the ancient ford can still be traced, a short distance upstream from the modern bridge over the River Irvine at Gatehead.

The address shows that Burns was living with his mother's half-sister Jean Broun and her husband, James Allan, a carpenter on Fairlie Estate. The couple had been married in 1775 and lived in a cottage on the estate, probably near Old Rome. James died in 1789 and Jean moved into one of the houses in Old Rome cottages. She re-married an Adam Blair of Dundonald and died in 1821, aged 71 years. James and Jean's son, Sandy Allan, founded the Allan Shipping line (see the author's 'Ayrshire Heritage').

Fairlie Estate has another important connection with the Burnes family. When the poet's father, William Burnes, moved to Ayrshire from the east of Scotland in 1750, he took up employment as a gardener at Fairlie for about 2 years before he moved to Alloway.

In the Dundonald area, tradition maintains that William Burnes first met the poet's mother, Agnes Broun, while she was visiting her half-sister, Mrs. Allan. In fact, whereas William Burnes was at Fairlie between 1750 and 1752, Mrs. Allan was not born until 1750. She was 18 years younger than the poet's mother and only 7 years of age when his parents were married.

Also see: Craigenton Farm; Fairlie House.

ORANGEFIELD HOUSE Map Ref. 358 268

The house is no longer extant. Originally called Monkton House, it was situated east of the A79 Prestwick/Monkton Road, within Prestwick Airport, on the south side of the main runway. Until the new airport terminal was constructed, Orangefield was part of the terminal complex.

It was the home of James Dalrymple, patron and friend of Burns on the poet's early visits to Edinburgh. Dalrymple was cousin to two of the poet's other patrons, James Cunningham, 14th Earl of Glencairn and Robert Aiken, lawyer, Ayr. The Rev. Dr. William Dalrymple who baptised Burns, was James Dalrymple's uncle.

In a letter dated 13 December, 1786, to John Ballantine, lawyer, Ayr, the poet referred to his first visit to Edinburgh and wrote - 'I have found a worthy, warm friend in Mr. Dalrymple of Orangefield, who introduced me to Lord Glencairn...'

Although there is no record of Burns having visited Orangefield, he may have done so. In a suppressed stanza of the poem *THE VISION*, he described accurately the location of the house - *'The owner of a pleasant spot, near sandy hills'* and in a note indicated that it referred to Dalrymple and Orangefield.

Unfortunately, James Dalrymple was extravagant and dissolute and squandered his fortune. In 1791 he was declared bankrupt and amongst the trustees appointed to oversee the disposition of his property were the Rev. Dalrymple, Robert Aiken and John Ballantine. He died in Edinburgh in 1795.

Also see: Ayr Auld Kirk; Castlehill House; Whitehill.

PARK FARM   Map Ref. 223 063
Situated 200 yards east of the A77 Ayr/Girvan Road, 2 miles south of Kirkoswald.

In 1775, when Burns attended Rodger's School, Kirkoswald, and lodged at Ballochneil Farm, a fellow-pupil called Thomas Orr lived on Park Farm, neighbouring Ballochneil. The present Park Farm was then called Laigh Park. The property then called Park was probably also Laigh Park or the neighbouring property now called High Park.

Thomas Orr was the son of William Orr, farm worker, and his wife Jean Robinson. They lived in a cottage on Park and probably shared it with Jean's mother, Julia Robinson. Julia was reputed to be a witch, a reputation she probably cultivated to cover her association with smugglers.

The poet and Thomas continued their friendship after they met at school, and corresponded with each other. In 1780, Thomas visited Lochlea and helped with the harvest.

In a letter dated 3 August, 1781, the poet's father, William Burnes, wrote to Thomas Orr from Lochlea - "Thomas - I want you to be here to your harvest by Monday first, for we begin on Teusday (sic) to our wheat. My wife desires enquire, and bring her word how her brother John's wife is, - I am, yours, etc." Thomas answered the call and when he returned home he took messages from the poet to several Kirkoswald friends, including Peggy Thomson.

When Thomas was at Rodger's school he was studying navigation. He eventually went to sea in 1785 and was drowned on his first voyage.

Also see: Kirkoswald; Laigh Park.

PARK HOUSE   Map Ref. 339 209
The house is not extant. It was situated east of Carrick Road, Ayr, near what is now the junction of Bowman Road and Ballantine Drive. In the 18th century it was outwith the town.

It was the home of the unmarried Major William Logan and his sister, Miss Susan Logan, with both of whom Burns corresponded. Major Logan was addressed in the poem *EPISTLE TO MAJOR LOGAN* - *'Hail thairm-inspirin, rattlin Willie.'* Susan was addressed in the poem *TO MISS LOGAN*, which the poet sent to her with the gift of a book of poems at New Year, 1787.

The poem to Major Logan ends with a reference to the house - *'sir Bard will do himself the pleasure, To call at Park.'*

Major Logan was a fiddler of some repute and regarded as a wit and a 'character'. The following anecdote is told about him - he had been unwell and was visited by his minister who said that he would have to suffer his ailment with fortitude, to which Logan replied, "Fortitude! Aye, Minister, it would take fiftytude."

PATIE'S MILL
Map Ref. 532 370

The mill is no longer extant. It was situated on the south bank of the River Irvine. The site is at the west end of Brown Street, Newmilns, on the north side, and is now occupied by a factory car park.

In the 18th century rival locations in Ayrshire and Aberdeenshire were claimed as the subject of Allan Ramsay's Scottish song The Lass O'Patie's mill.

In a letter to George Thomson, song collector, dated 7 April, 1793, Burns referred to the song and wrote - 'The following anecdote which I had from Sir William Cunningham of Robertland, who had it from the late John, Earl of Lowdon - Allan Ramsay was residing at Lowdon Castle with the then Earl, father of Earl John, and one afternoon, riding or walking out together, His Lordship and Allan passed a sweet romantic spot on Irvine water, still called 'Patie's Mill', where a bonnie lass was "tedding hay, bareheaded on the green". My Lord observed to Allan that it would be a fine theme for a song - Ramsay took the hint; he composed the first sketch of it, which he produced at dinner.'

Burns must have been familiar with the location of Patie's Mill as it would be prominently seen from Loudoun Manse where he visited.

The mill had another very tenuous connection with the poet. It is referred to in the song HA' E YE MIND O' LANG, LANG SYNE by the Rev. George Lawrie of Monkton, son and grandson of the poet's friends Rev's Archibald and George Lawrie of Newmilns.

Also see: Loudoun Manse; Monkton; Newmilns.

PEGGY THOMSON'S HOUSE
Map Ref. 239 075

Situated in Main Street, Kirkoswald, and now part of the Shanter Hotel. Hugh Rodger's School, attended by Burns for one term in 1775, occupied what is now the south end of the hotel and Thomson's house occupied what is now the centre part of the premises.

One day in August, 1775, Burns went into the back garden of the school to take the altitude of the sun for his studies and saw Peggy in the back garden of her home.

In an autobiographical letter to Doctor Moore, dated 2 August, 1787, Burns described his encounter with Peggy - 'A charming fillette, who lived next door to the school, overset my trigonometry, and set me off at a tangent from the sphere of my studies...stepping out to the garden one charming noon to take the sun's altitude, I met with my angel.'

Thus, Peggy became the second girl to set the poet's pulse racing and as with the first, Nellie Kilpatrick, he was inspired to poetry. He composed the song HAR'STE - A FRAGMENT which he later expanded and renamed SONG - COMPOSED IN AUGUST.

In 1784, Peggy married William Neilson, Minnybae Farm, Kirkoswald. In 1786, shortly before his intended departure for the West Indies, Burns visited Peggy and William. He gave Peggy a signed copy of his newly published Kilmarnock Edition, in the flyleaf of which he inscribed the poem LINES TO AN OLD SWEETHEART. When he left, William accompanied him on the first 3 miles of his journey before they took their sad farewells of each other.

The poet's youngest sister, Isabella Burns Begg, said that the song MY NANIE, O' was written to Peggy Thomson but there are other girls suggested as the heroine of the song. Also see: Coldcothill Farm; Doura Farm; Girvan River; Kirkoswald; Pinvalley; Rodger's School; Ship Inn; Stinchar River.

PENCLOE   Map Ref. 618 095
Situated in Glen Afton, New Cumnock, one mile south of the town.

It was the home of Thomas Campbell to whom Burns wrote a letter dated 19 August, 1786, and addressed from 'Mr. J. Merry's, New Cumnock'. The letter was a farewell message from Burns to Campbell on the poet's imminent departure for Jamaica. There is no other reference to Campbell and no record of any other association with the poet.

Burns had several friends in Glen Afton and it is generally thought that the friendships were established when the poet was journeying between Mauchline and Ellisland, Dumfries. As the poet paid his first visit to Ellisland in February, 1788, and took it over in May 1788, the date and address on the letter to Campbell show that he had visited New Cumnock before he was concerned with Ellisland.

Also see: Afton River; Ashmark; Laight; New Cumnock.

PINVALLEY   Map Ref. 331 951
Situated about 3 miles east of Barr, and north of the Nick of the Balloch, on the Crosshill/ Newton Stewart Hill Road.

The poet's aunt, Mrs. Brown of Kirkoswald, wife of his maternal uncle, Samuel Brown of Ballochneil Farm, said that Burns wrote the song *MY NANIE, O'* to a girl called Agnes McIlwraith of Pinvalley.

According to his aunt, Burns met Agnes McIlwraith at Kirkdamdie Fair. The Fair, also called Kirkdominie Fair, was the largest feeing fair in south Ayrshire and was very ancient in origin. It was held annually on the last Saturday in May in the grounds of the ruined Kirkdominie which stands on the north bank of the River Stinchar, 1½ miles south-west of Barr.

In all editions of his work up to and including 1794, Burns made the first line of the song *MY NANIE, O'* - *'Behind yon hill where Stinchar flows.'* In a letter dated 26 October, 1792, to George Thomson, song collector, the poet wrote of the song - "The name of the river is horribly prosaic, I will alter it." He then gave a choice of Girvan and Lugar and observed - "Girvan is the river that suits the idea of the stanza best".

As Stinchar was the original choice and, of the others, Girvan suited the idea best, it is easy to conclude that the song was set in south Ayrshire. If the poet composed the song at Mount Oliphant or Kirkoswald, the setting sun would first darken the east, roughly where the upper reaches of the Stinchar and Girvan Rivers flow *'Mang moores an' mosses many, O'*, as in the first verse of the song. If south Ayrshire was the location, the otherwise unknown Agnes McIlwraith could have been the heroine.

It is generally accepted that the heroine was Agnes Fleming of Coldcothill or Doura Farms, neighbouring Lochlea. If she was, it is incredible that the poet chose Stinchar or Girvan as suitable rivers for his introduction, as neither of them bears any relationship to the sun setting in the west or first darkening the east as seen from Lochlea.

The poet's brother, Gilbert Burns, said that the heroine was Agnes Fleming; his youngest sister, Isabella Burns Begg, said that it was Peggy Thomson of Kirkoswald; in Girvan, local tradition maintains that it was Agnes Brown, daughter of the proprietor of the Ship Inn, Girvan; and Rev. Hamilton Paul, a 19th century Burns scholar said that it was an Agnes Sheriff of Kilmarnock.

The poet gave no indication of the identity of the heroine. In his first Commonplace Book he commented - 'Whether the following song will stand the test, I will not pretend to say, because it is my own; only I can say it was, at the time, real.'

Also see: Coldcothill Farm; Doura Farm; Girvan River; Kirkoswald; Lugar River; Minnybae Farm; Ship Inn; Stinchar River.

POOLE   Map Ref. 497 212

Situated 200 yards north of Watston Farm, Ochiltree, which is a quarter mile west of the village and to the north of the A70 Ayr/Cumnock Road.

The home of Thomas Walker, tailor, was in the vicinity but its exact location is unknown. Walker was addressed in the poem *REPLY TO A TRIMMING EPISTLE RECEIVED FROM A TAILOR*. Walker was a friend of William Simson, schoolmaster, Ochiltree, subject of the *EPISTLE TO WILLIAM SIMSON*. He composed verses and sent them to Burns who did not reply. He then wrote to the poet and attacked his morals, prompting the poet to compose his 'Reply'.

Walker later gained some fame for a widely distributed religious pamphlet, A Picture Of The World. He died at Sorn Bridgend in 1833, aged 82 years, and is buried in Sorn kirkyard.

Also see: Ochiltree.

POOSIE NANCIE'S INN, circa 1890

POOSIE NANCIE'S INN   Map Ref. 498 274

Situated in Loudoun Street, Mauchline, at its junction with Cowgate. It is open to the public as a public house and museum. It was the setting of the cantata *LOVE AND LIBERTY*, better known as *THE JOLLY BEGGARS* - '*Ae night at e'en a merry core, O' randie, gangrel bodies, In Poosie-Nancie's held the splore, To drink their orra duddies.*'

When Burns was in Mauchline, the landlord was George Gibson referred to as *'Black-bearded Geordie'* in the poem *ADAM ARMOUR'S PRAYER*. The name by which the inn was known is now unknown. Poosie-Nancie was the name given by the poet to Gibson's wife, Agnes Ronald. Their daughter Janet Gibson was referred to as *'Racer Jess'* in the poem *THE HOLY FAIR* - *'there Racer Jess and twa-three whores, Are blinkin at the entry'*; the name *'Racer'* was derived from her fleetness of foot and her habit of running errands for payment and races for wagers. Their son Jock was referred to as *'Haveril'* (half-witted) Jock in the same poem.

An entry in Mauchline kirk session minutes for 1773 records that Agnes Ronald was habitually drunk and troublesome to her neighbours. She was summoned to appear before the Session and did so, only to tell them that she was determined to continue in her disorderly ways.

A later entry in the same year records that George Gibson kept a disorderly house and that his wife and daughter were guilty of resetting stolen goods.

Agnes Wilson, servant to George Gibson, was referred to as *'Geordie's Jurr'* in the poem ADAM ARMOUR'S PRAYER and was probably the *'Tozie Drab'* of the poem *LOVE AND LIBERTY*. An entry in the kirk session minutes refers to her as being 'of lewd and immoral practices and the occasion of the late disturbance.' The disturbance was probably the incident which Burns made the subject of the poem *ADAM ARMOUR'S PRAYER*. Jean Armour's brother, Adam, and a number of other young men subjected Agnes Wilson to the custom of 'riding the stang'; - for her prostitution and probably for spreading disease, they tied her astride a rough pole and carried her through the village.

Poosie Nancie should not be confused with Nance Tannock, keeper of the Sma' Inn, Mauchline.

Burns did not frequent Poosie Nancie's.

Also see: Mauchline Kirkyard; Museums, etc; Nance Tannock's Inn.

PURCLEWAN MILL, 1985

PURCLEWAN Map Ref. 379 158

Situated between the A713 Ayr/Dalmellington Road and the B742 Dalrymple/Coylton Road, a half mile south of their junction.

When the Burnes family lived at Mount Oliphant Farm, Purclewan was a hamlet with a mill and a smiddy, less than 2 miles away. It was the home of Nellie Kilpatrick, heroine of the poet's first published song, *HANDSOME NELL*. Her father was the miller at Purclewan. Burns and Nellie met while working together in a harvest field in 1773, at which time Burns was 14 and Nellie 12 or 13 years of age. Nellie sang a song composed by a local laird's son and Burns tried to impress her by composing words to her favourite tune. Several years later, he wrote of the incident - 'thus with me began Love and Poesy.'

Nellie Kilpatrick married William Bone, coachman to the Laird of Newark, and lived at Newark Estate. She died about 1820.

The blacksmith at Purclewan was Henry McCandlish. He lent the youthful Burns a copy of the book The Life of Wallace which fired him with a patriotic fervour that lasted all of his life.

The blacksmith's son, James McCandlish - he later dropped the 'Mc' - was the poet's lifelong friend. He studied medicine at Glasgow University and settled firstly in Edinburgh and later in Mauchline. He married Jean Smith of Mauchline, sister of the poet's friend James Smith; Jean was referred to in the poem *THE BELLES OF MAUCHLINE* - '*Miss Smith she has wit.*' Burns corresponded with Candlish. In a letter dated March, 1791, to Peter Hill, he described Candlish as 'the earliest friend except my brother that I have on earth and one of the worthiest fellows that ever any man called by the name of friend.'

Also see: Coylton; Leglen Woods; Newark Castle.

RATTON-KEY Map Ref. 335 223

A quay of Ayr Harbour, situated in South Harbour Street, opposite Fort Street. It is no longer extant.

It is referred to in the poem *THE BRIGS OF AYR* - '*And from Glenbuck, doon to the Ratton-Key.*' In a note to the poem, Burns indicated that it referred to - 'a small landing place above the large quay.'

RICCARTON

Situated on the B7038 Kilmarnock/Ayr Road, 2 miles south of Kilmarnock town centre.

In the poem *THE VISION*, Sir Adam Wallace of Riccarton is referred to as '*Bold Richardton.*' Sir Adam was a cousin of William Wallace, the Scottish patriot.

The Rev. Alexander Moodie, '*Singet Sawnie*' of the poem *THE TWA HERDS*, was minister of Riccarton Parish Church from 1761 to 1799. He was also referred to in the poem *THE HOLY FAIR* - '*For Moodie speels the holy door.*'

The present church was built in 1823. Rev. Moodie is buried in the kirkyard.

RICHMOND'S HOUSE Map Ref. 498 274

Situated at No. 3 High Street, Mauchline. The house is still extant. Local tradition maintains that it was the home of John Richmond, close friend and confidant of Burns.

Richmond's father was a merchant in Mauchline and also owned Montgarswood Farm, Mauchline, which was for several years farmed by 'Holy Willie' Fisher.

Born in 1765, probably at Montgarswood Farm, Richmond was educated at Newmilns school. He started work as a clerk to the poet's friend and patron, Gavin Hamilton, Mauchline. In 1785 he moved to Edinburgh and when Burns paid his first visit to the capital in 1786 he shared Richmond's lodging. About 1789, he returned to Mauchline, married a local girl, Jenny Surgeoner, and set up business as a lawyer.

Jenny Surgeoner had had an illegitimate child by Richmond in 1784, for which they had to appear before the church session and congregation. Richmond would not marry her at that time but did so 6 years later. In a letter dated 1 September, 1786, Burns chastised Richmond for his treatment of Jenny.

Burns, Richmond and their friends James Smith and William Hunter formed the bachelor association called the Court of Equity, subject of a bawdy poem of the same name. Burns, Richmond and Smith were together in Poosie Nancie's Inn, Mauchline, when they saw the riotous scene which inspired Burns to write the poem *LOVE AND LIBERTY*, better known as *THE JOLLY BEGGARS*.

Richmond died in 1846, aged 82 years, and is buried in Mauchline kirkyard.

Also see: Elbow Tavern; Mauchline; Mauchline Kirkyard; Montgarswood Farm.

High Street, Mauchline, with Richmond's house second from the left, circa 1900

ROBERTLAND HOUSE   Map Ref. 441 471
Situated on the B769 Stewarton/Glasgow Road, a half mile east of Stewarton. The present house was built shortly before 1820.

It was the Ayrshire home of Sir James Hunter Blair, who was referred to in the poem *ELEGY ON THE DEATH OF SIR JAMES HUNTER BLAIR*. Sir James was born James Hunter, son of an Ayr merchant, and added Blair to his name on marriage. He was Lord Provost of Edinburgh from 1784-86 and when Burns paid his first visit to Edinburgh in 1786, Sir James received him and gave his assistance.

The house was owned later by Sir William Cunningham of Robertland and Auchinskeith. Lady Cunningham is thought to have been the 'Mrs C.' referred to by Burns in a letter dated 3 April, 1786, to Robert Aiken, Ayr.

In a letter dated 16 October, 1789, to Captain Riddell, Glenriddell, Dumfries, from Ellisland, the poet asked for an enclosed letter to be forwarded to Sir William Cunningham.

Burns visited Robertland and tradition maintains that during a visit the poet confirmed that Douglas Graham was the model for Tam O'Shanter in the poem of that name. When asked about the identity, he is said to have replied - "Tam! It was none else but the guid man of Shanter."

The poet's uncle, Robert Burnes, who lived in Stewarton, may have been Land Steward for Robertland Estate but this cannot be confirmed.

Also see: Auchinskeith; Patie's Mill; Stewarton.

RODGER'S SCHOOL   Map Ref. 239 075

Situated in Main Street, Kirkoswald, and now part of the Shanter Hotel. A plaque on the outside wall of the building commemorates the school. In 1775, Burns went from his home at Mount Oliphant Farm, Alloway, to attend the school run by Hugh Rodger for one term - 'to learn Mensuration, Surveying, Dialling, etc.' - to quote the poet.

While attending the school, the poet lodged at Ballochneil Farm and Mill, 2 miles south of the village. The farmer/miller was Robert Niven and the poet's maternal uncle, Samuel Broun, was married to Niven's daughter, Margaret. Burns probably lodged with his uncle but he referred to Robert Niven's son, John, as his bedfellow, suggesting that he may have at least slept with the Nivens.

Later in life, Burns claimed that during his time at Kirkoswald, he - 'learned to look unconcernedly on a large tavern bill and to mix without fear in a drunken squabble.' His claim was certainly an exaggeration; a penniless 16 year old lodging 2 miles south of the village would be unlikely to be involved in the circumstances described.

Hugh Rodger's home was on the south side of Kirkbrae, Kirkoswald, which is directly opposite the gate of the old kirkyard. The house is no longer extant.

In Kirkoswald, Burns met his second known sweetheart, Peggy Thomson, a girl of about his own age who lived in the neighbouring house to the school. He went into the back garden of the school house to take measurements and saw Peggy in the garden of her home. He described the meeting - 'stepping out to the garden one charming noon to take the sun's altitude, I met with my angel.'

Amongst his fellow pupils at the school were three members of the Niven family, cousins to each other. John Niven of Ballochneil Farm and Mill was the boy referred to by the poet as his bedfellow; he succeeded his father in the farm and married Jean Rodger, daughter of his old schoolmaster; he was made a Freeman of Maybole for his generosity and benevolence to the people of the town at a time of difficulty. William Niven was the son of a Maybole shopkeeper who also owned Kirklandhill Farm west of the town; he became a very wealthy and avaricious businessman; he was appointed to Maybole Town Council and appointed a Depute Lord Lieutenant of Ayrshire. While they were attending Rodger's School as boys, Burns occasionally spent his weekend break at William Niven's home in Maybole. Alexander Niven belonged to Girvan; he became a minister; as a student, he was tutor to the children of John Hamilton of Sundrum; in a letter to William Niven from Lochlea, dated 12 June, 1781, Burns wrote - 'Our communion was on Sunday se'en night, I mention this to tell you that I saw your cousin there, with some of Mr. Hamilton's sons. You cannot imagine how pleased I was to steal a look at him, and trace the resemblance of my old friend. I was predisposed in favour...by that ingenuous modesty...which is so apparent in his manner.' Alexander Niven visited Burns at Mossgiel.

Tradition maintains that Burns and William Niven joined the school on the same day and, as was the custom, they took the schoolmaster to the local inn and treated him to a refreshment. The inn was 'The Ladies' House immortalised by the poet later as *'The Lord's House'* in the poem *TAM O'SHANTER*.

Another tradition concerning the poet's time at Rodger's school maintains that outwith the classroom, Burns and William Niven, both bright pupils and well read for country youths, tested each other's mettle in friendly debating jousts on a wide variety of subjects. Mr. Rodger became aware of the contest and looked on their supposed debating skills with contempt. One day, in class, he sneeringly asked what the subject of debate had been for that day and on being told it was whether a great General or a respectable merchant made the greater contribution to society. Rodger laughed derisively. Burns suggested that the master should choose the side of the argument he favoured and he, Burns, would adopt the opposite stance. Rodger chose to support the General and led off the debate in front of the class. It soon became obvious to Rodger and his pupils that Burns was his superior in debating. Pupils recalled later that Rodger had abruptly closed the debate and dismissed the class in a state of agitation at having been defeated.

Also see: Ballochneil Farm and Mill; Kirkoswald; Maybole; Minnybae Farm; Peggy Thomson's House; The Ladies' House.

RONALD'S INN
Map Ref. 498 272

This Mauchline inn is accepted, generally, as having been in the square west of Castle Street, on the site now occupied by the Parish Church hall, although it has been described as having been in Loudoun Street, on the site of the shop at No. 57.

A Mrs. Alexander of Mauchline, daughter of John Richmond and Jenny Surgeoner, close friends of Burns and Jean Armour, claimed that the poet and Jean were married in Ronald's Inn. Although her information came from her parents it cannot be deemed to be totally accurate as her father was in Edinburgh at the time of the marriage. Although there is no evidence to support Mrs. Alexander neither is there evidence to refute the claim.

The innkeeper was John Ronald, which was also the name of the Mauchline/Glasgow carrier, and the same man may have fulfilled both roles. In a letter from Edinburgh dated 17th September, 1787, the poet wrote to his brother Gilbert at Mossgiel - "I am thinking to cause my old mare to meet me, by means of John Ronald, at Glasgow."

Another man, William Ronald, a Mauchline tobacconist, was the man referred to by Burns in a letter dated 10th November, 1789, to his brother William as having gone bankrupt. In November, 1786, the poet sent two copies of his Edinburgh Edition to his friend George Reid of Ochiltree, care of the tobacconist.

John Ronald, the carrier, was the uncle of William Ronald who worked for the poet at Mossgiel and later farmed at Maulside, Beith.

Also see: Gavin Hamilton's House; Gilmilnscroft House; Mauleside; Morton's Ballroom; Richmond's House.

RYE WATER   Map Ref. 299 499
The river joins the River Garnock from the north, at the map reference shown, at the east end of Dalry, Ayrshire.

There has been much specualtion as to whether the word 'Rye' of the song *Comin thro' The Rye*, refers to the Rye Water or to the cereal crop, rye.

There is nothing recorded by the poet to prove the matter either way. The most significant evidence is that when he submitted the song to Johnson for his Scots Musical Museum, the poet spelled Rye with a small 'r', which indicates that it did not refer to the river.

The song was very old, with several bawdy versions, before Burns improved it.

ST. MARGARET'S HILL   Map Ref. 527 372
The name given by the poet's friend the Rev. Dr. George Lawrie to his home, Loudoun Manse, Newmilns. The house is still occupied though no longer the manse. It is situated at No. 116 Loudoun Road, Newmilns.

In a letter dated 13 November, 1786, to the Rev. Dr. Lawrie, the poet wrote - 'I think the peaceful unity of St. Margaret's Hill can only be excelled by the harmonious concord of Apocalyptic Zion.'

Writing from Edinburgh to Rev. Lawrie on 5 February, 1787, Burns wrote - 'My compliments to all the happy inmates of St. Margaret's.'

On 15 November, 1788, the poet wrote from Mauchline to the son of the manse, Archibald Lawrie, later a minister and incumbent of Loudoun Kirk and Manse - 'Please return to me by Connel, the bearer, the two volumes of songs I left last time I was at St. Margaret's.'

Also see: Loudoun Manse.

ST. QUIVOX
A hamlet situated a half mile north of the A758 Ayr/Mauchline Road at Auchincruive, one mile east of the A77 Ayr By-pass.

The Rev. William McQuhae, referred to in the poem *THE TWA HERDS* as - '*That curs'd rascal ca'd McQuhae*' - was minister of St. Quivox from 1764 to 1823. He is buried in the kirkyard.

The church is still extant and used for worship.

The poet's friend, John Tennant, Auchenbay Farm, Ochiltree, later farmed at Shields Farm, St. Quivox, west of the A77 Ayr By-pass.

Also see: Auchenbay Farm.

SHANTER FARM   Map Ref. 218 074
The farm occupied by Douglas Graham, model for Tam O'Shanter in the poem of that name, was not the existing Shanter Farm, Maidens.

The 18th Century farm steading was demolished during the 19th century. It was situated east of the A719 Ayr/Turnberry Road, a half mile south-east of Maidens village. The house was close to the east side of the disused Ayr/Girvan railway line and near the ancient mote (mound) at the location.

Local tradition maintains that Burns got his inspiration for much of *TAM O'SHANTER* during a visit to Shanter Farm. As a 16 year old, he went from Mount Oliphant to attend Hugh Rodger's school at Kirkoswald and lived at Ballochneil Farm between Kirkoswald and Maidens. According to the tradition, the school's annual summer holiday was on the first Thursday of July, the day of Ayr's annual horse fair. On the holiday, Burns and his school friend John Niven of Ballochneil set out to go fishing at the coast. They went to Maidenhead Bay and embarked on a small boat belonging to Douglas Graham of Shanter Farm and called 'The Tam'. When they were out in the Firth a strong wind got up and threatened to blow them too far out to sea. Niven wanted to return to the shore but Burns refused to do so 'Tho' the wind was blowing strong enough to blaw the horns aff the kye.' At length they returned to the shore and went to Shanter Farm where they were entertained by Douglas Graham's wife, Helen McTaggart. Graham was at Ayr attending the horse fair. Helen was noted for her quick temper and harsh tongue and having expected her husband home early in the evening she became angry when he failed to return. She launched into a tirade of abuse against her husband's character and intemperate habits and prophesied that one day he would fall into the River Doon. In her temper she also spoke against her husband's friend John Davidson, the local shoemaker, who normally went to Ayr with him and shared his escapades. The tradition concludes with the suggestion that Burns returned to Ballochneil and next morning produced his first draft of the poem *TAM O'SHANTER*.

The story of the fishing trip and visit to Shanter Farm may be based on fact but the drafting of TAM O'SHANTER can only be fantasy. Without doubt the immortal poem was based on an amalgam of such experiences of people and places but it took many more years before the poet produced work even approaching such brilliance.

Also see: Ballochneil Farm and Mill; Glenfoot; Kirkoswald; Laigh Park Farm; Park Farm; Rodger's School; Souter Johnie's House.

SHAWWOOD   Map Ref. 405 260

The house is still extant as the dwelling-house of Shawwood Farm. It is situated about a half mile north of the A758 Ayr/Mauchline Road, a half mile east of Mossblown.

It was the home of David McLure, a merchant in Ayr. He bought the property in 1774 and was forced to sell it in 1788 after he had lost money in the collapse of the Ayr Bank.

McLure owned Lochlea Farm, Tarbolton and leased it to the poet's father, William Burnes, in 1777.

The rent of Lochlea was high and the land poor. The Burnes family worked hard and lived frugally but were unable to make enough to pay the rent. The terms of the lease had not been properly recorded and in 1783, after a lengthy dispute, McLure took out a warrant of sequestration against William Burnes. Burnes defended the action and eventually took his case to the Court of Session, Edinburgh; the decision was mainly in his favour but by then both his health and finances were exhausted.

At one stage of the dispute, John Hamilton of Sundrum Castle was appointed referee between the parties. James Grieve, Boghead Farm, Tarbolton, acted as arbitrator on behalf of McLure and Charles Norval, gardener, Coilsfield House in the same capacity for William Burnes. Grieve was the subject of a satirical mock epitaph.

Also see: Boghead Farm; Coilsfield House; Lochlea Farm; Sundrum Castle.

SHIP INN   Map Ref. 186 983

The inn is no longer extant. It was situated on the west side of Old Street, Girvan, a short distance south of the wall of the old cemetery.

Burns is reputed to have visited the inn but this cannot be verified. Local tradition maintains that he met the innkeeper's daughter, Nannie Brown, at Kirkdamdie Fair and escorted her home to the inn.

The tradition also maintains that Nannie Brown was the heroine of the song *MY NANIE, O'*, an honour also attributed to amongst others, Agnes Fleming of Coldcothill or Doura Farms. Tarbolton and Agnes McIlwraith of Pinvalley, Barr.

Kirkdamdie Fair was the largest feeing fair of south Ayrshire and was held annually on the last Saturday of May. It was a very ancient fair and was held in the grounds of a ruined church called Kirkdominie on the north bank of the River Stinchar, 1½ miles west of Barr.

Also see: Coldcothill Farm; Doura Farm; Lugar River; Pinvalley; Stinchar River.

Ship Inn, Girvan, circa 1890, said to have been visited by Burns

SIMPSON'S INN
Map Ref. 338 222

The Black Bull public house, River Street, Ayr, close to the north end of the Auld Brig, is, at least, on the site of Simpson's Inn; all or part of the existing premises may be the original building but the inn may have been totally replaced about the late 18th or early 19th century. It has not been possible to prove the history of the inn.

When the poet's father, William Burnes, and other parents, were looking for a school teacher for Alloway, Burnes arranged to meet the 18 year old John Murdoch of Ayr in Simpson's Inn and required Murdoch to produce a sample of his handwriting for examination.

Burns referred to the inn in the poem *THE BRIGS OF AYR* - '*And down by Simpson's wheel'd the left about.*' In a note to the poem he indicated that Simpson's was 'a noted tavern at the Auld Brig end.' The River Street area was then known as Brigend of Ayr.

A letter dated September, 1786, from Burns to John Ballantine, Ayr, accompanying a manuscript copy of the poem *THE BRIGS OF AYR*, was addressed as having been written at 'Simpson's.'

In the legal dispute between William Burnes and his landlord, David McLure, over Lochlea Farm, some of the legal documents were witnessed by John Simpson innkeeper, Brigend of Ayr, which suggests that they were drawn up in the inn.

Also see: Water-Fit.

Probably the original Simpson's Inn, circa 1890

SMA' INN   Map Ref. 497 274

The Sma' Inn was the name of the establishment commonly known as 'Nance Tannock's.' Nance Tannock was the maiden name of Mrs. Agnes Weir who ran the inn.

Also see: Nance Tannock's Inn.

SMITH'S HOUSE AND SHOP   Map Ref. 498 274

The building which included the house and shop in which the poet's friend, James Smith, lived and worked, was situated at the north side of Mauchline Cross. It was in line with the north sides of Castle Street and High Street, facing on to the Cross.

The building was demolished about 1820 when the new road to Kilmarnock was constructed northwards from the Cross. The road is still known locally as New Road.

The poems *EPISTLE TO JAMES SMITH* and *EPITAPH FOR A WAG IN MAUCHLINE* were addressed to James Smith.

Burns, Smith, John Richmond and William Hunter formed the bachelors' association called *THE COURT OF EQUITY*, referred to in the poem of that name. It should not be confused with Tarbolton Bachelors' Club.

James Smith's sister, Jean, was one of the girls referred to in the poem *THE BELLES OF MAUCHLINE* - *'Miss Smith she has wit.'* She married the poet's lifelong friend, Doctor James Candlish. The doctor, originally called McCandlish, was born and reared at Purclewan, near Mount Oliphant.

The father of James and Jean Smith died and their mother re-married James Lammie, an elder of Mauchline Kirk. The stepfather was very strict and disapproved of James Smith and his associates.

James Smith eventually emigrated to Jamaica where he died c.1823.

Also see: Richmond's House; Purclewan.

SOUTER JOHNIE'S COTTAGE

SOUTER JOHNIE'S COTTAGE Map Ref. 240 076

Situated on the east side of Main Street, Kirkoswald.

Built in 1785 for John Davidson, prototype of Souter Johnie of the poem Tam O'Shanter, he occupied it until his death in 1806. One room served as his shoemaking workshop and the roof space gave extra sleeping accommodation.

Davidson and his wife, Ann Gillespie, lived previously at Glenfoot, Maidens, and the poet probably knew them when he lodged with his uncle at Ballochneil in 1775. He would know that Mrs. Davidson had assisted his mother, Agnes Broun, with family duties at Craigenton Farm after the death of his grandmother. He may have visited the cottage when he passed through the village in 1786.

Davidson's descendants owned the cottage until 1920 when they handed it over to a local committee which had it restored. It was taken over by the National Trust for Scotland in 1932. The cottage is open to the public.

Statues by James Thom of Tam O'Shanter, Souter Johnie, the landlord and the landlady, all from the poem, are in a restored ale house in the garden behind the cottage.

Also see: Auchenblane; Glenfoot; Kirkoswald; Museums, etc; James Thom, Sculptor.

SOUTH AUCHENBRAIN FARM   Map Ref. 522 305

Situated east of Auchmillan Road, Mauchline, one mile south-west of the B7037 Galston/Sorn Road.

William Fisher, farmer and kirk elder, referred to by Burns in the poems *HOLY WILLIE'S PRAYER, HOLY WILLIE'S EPITAPH and THE KIRK'S ALARM*, lived for most of his life at Montgarswood Farm on the Mauchline/Sorn Road. Subsequently, he moved to Tongue and Briggs Farms, east of the B7037 Galston/Sorn Road.

On the evening of 13 February, 1809, aged 72 years, Fisher attended a meeting in Mauchline and set out in a snowstorm on the 4 miles walk home. At a part of the road near South Auchenbrain Farm he went off the road, fell into a ditch and died.

A.B. Todd, Ayrshire poet and antiquarian, who was born at Craighall near South Auchenbrain, gives the following account of Fisher's death in his Reminiscences Of A Long Life (1906) - "It is a curious fact that in the *EPITAPH ON HOLY WILLIE*, Burns says of him - 'His soul has ta'en some ither way, I fear the left-hand road' - and that Fisher, on his way home that night actually took the left-hand side of a fence and ditch near the farm of Meikle Auchenbrain and so was drowned, for had he taken the right-hand and proper side he would have been safe." Todd's father had been one of a party of neighbours who had searched for and found Fisher. He had also arranged for the body to be taken by horse and cart to Fisher's home at Tongue and went on ahead to tell the widow.

William Fisher is buried in Mauchline kirkyard.

Also see: Mauchline Kirkyard; Montgarswood Farm.

SPITTALSIDE FARM   Map Ref. 425 277

Situated on the west side of the B730 Tarbolton/Dundonald Road, a half mile north of Tarbolton Cross.

The poet's friend, David Sillar, was born at Spittalside in 1760 and lived there until about 1785. The poet corresponded with him and he was addressed in the two *EPISTLE(S) TO DAVIE.*

Although not a founder member of Tarbolton Bachelors' Club, he joined in 1781. Like Burns, he was a rhymer and after the success of the Kilmarnock Edition he had a book of mediocre poetry published by John Wilson, Kilmarnock, in 1789. It has probably been more popular for its curiosity value through his connection with Burns than it was when first published.

Sillar also played the fiddle and tried his hand at composing music. In a note to Johnson's Musical Museum, regarding the song A Rosebud By My Early Walk, Burns wrote -

'This air is by David Sillar, quondam merchant, and now a school master, Irvine.'

In Tarbolton, David Sillar worked as a temporary school teacher but the permanent appointment went to John Wilson, previously school master at Craigie. Wilson was immortalised by Burns as *'Doctor Hornbook'* in the poem DEATH AND DOCTOR HORNBOOK. Having been unsuccessful in Tarbolton, Sillar started an adventure school at Commonside between Tarbolton and Annbank but it soon failed. He then moved to Irvine where he tried his hand as a shopkeeper but he went bankrupt and landed in the town jail as a debtor. He became a school teacher, again, this time in Irvine.

Eventually, Sillar inherited £30,000 or £40,000 and as a prosperous citizen became a member of Irvine Town Council. In 1826 he became a founder member and first Vice-President of Irvine Burns Club. He died on 2 May, 1830, aged 70 years, and is buried in Irvine Parish kirkyard.

Also see: Commonside; Glasgow Vennel; Irvine; Robert Burns by David Sillar; Stair House.

SPECIAL FEATURE - 'ROBERT BURNS' BY DAVID SILLAR
David Sillar (1760-1830), who had a close friendship with Burns while the poet was living at Lochlea Farm and frequenting Tarbolton, recorded his impression of his friend:

'Mr. Robert Burns was some time in the parish of Tarbolton prior to my acquaintance with him. His social disposition easily procured him acquaintance; but a certain satirical seasoning, with which he and all poetical geniuses are in some degree influenced, while it set the rustic circle in a roar, was not unaccompanied by its kindred attendant - suspicious fear. I recollect hearing his neighbours observe he had a great deal to say for himself, and that they suspected his principles. He wore the only tied hair in the parish; and in the church, his plaid, which was of a particular colour, I think fillemot (yellowish brown), he wrapped in a particular manner round his shoulders. These surmises, and his exterior, had such a magical influence on my curiosity, as made me particularly solicitous of his acquaintance. Whether my acquaintance with Gilbert was casual or premeditated, I am not now certain. By him I was introduced not only to his brother, but to the whole family, where, in a short time, I became a frequent, and, I believe, not unwelcome visitant.

After the commencement of my acquaintance with the bard, we frequently met upon Sundays at church, when, between sermons, instead of going with our friends or lasses to the inn, we often took a walk in the fields. In these walks I have frequently been struck by his facility in addressing the fair sex; and many times, when I have been bashfully anxious how to express myself, he would have entered into conversation with them with the greatest ease and freedom; and it was generally a death-blow to our conversation, however agreeable, to meet a female acquaintance. Some of the few opportunities of a noontide walk that a country-life allows her laborious sons, he spent on the banks of the river (Ayr), or in the woods in the neighbourhood of Stair, a situation peculiarly adapted to the genius of a rural bard. Some books (especially one of those mentioned in his letter to Mr. Murdoch) he always carried, and read when not otherwise employed. It was likewise his custom to read at table. In one of my visits to Lochlea, in time of a sowen supper, he was so intent on reading, I think 'Tristam Shandy', that his spoon falling out of his hand, made him exclaim, in a tone scarcely imitable, "Alas, poor Yorick!" He had in his youth paid considerable attention to the arguments for and against the doctrine of original sin, then making considerable noise in the neighbourhood of Ayr; and having perused Dr. Taylor's book on that subject, and also a book called 'Letters concerning the Religion essential to Man', his opinions, when he came to Tarbolton, were consequently favourable to what you Ayr people call the "moderate side." The religion of the people of Tarbolton at that time was purely that of their fathers, founded on the 'Westminster Confession', and taught by one generation to another, uncontaminated by reading, reflection, and conversation; and although divided into different sectaries, the 'Shorter Catechism' was the line which bounded all their controversies. The slightest insinuation of Taylor's opinions made his neighbours suspect, and some even avoid him, as a heretical and dangerous companion. Such was Burns, and such were his associates, when, in May, 1781, I was admitted a member of the Bachelors' Club.'

Part of Sillar's opinion was borne out by a Tarbolton family of the time who often walked to and from Tarbolton kirk with the poet. They said that on such Sabbath walks, and also in the kirkyard before the services Burns delighted in 'getting up an argument' and that his opinions usually startled and sometimes irritated his rustic antagonists, sorely 'puzzling their Calvinism.'

STAIRAIRD
Map Ref. 473 257

Situated on the River Ayr, a half mile south of the A758 Ayr/Mauchline Road, 2 miles west of Mauchline Cross.

It is commonly accepted, though occasionally disputed, that Highland Mary Campbell worked at Coilsfield House, Tarbolton, after leaving the employment of the poet's friend and patron, Gavin Hamilton, Mauchline. It has been suggested that Mary did not work at Coilsfield but at Stairaird Farm which overlooks the River Ayr where it is joined by the Mauchline Burn. Neither of the claims can be substantiated.

Whereas it is generally accepted that the final parting of Burns and Highland Mary Campbell was near Failford, a tradition maintains that the parting was at Stairaird, where the Mauchline Burn joins the River Ayr. A description of the location given by Burns can be applied equally to Stairaird - 'We met by appointment, on the second Sunday of May, in a sequestered spot by the banks of Ayr.' However, the first stanza of the poem *HIGHLAND MARY* indicates that, as the location nearer to Montgomerie House (Coilsfield), Failford must be favoured - 'Ye banks and braes and streams around, The castle o' Montgomery, for there I took the last fareweel, O' my sweet Highland Mary.'

A wood near Kingencleugh, Mauchline, is also said to have been the location of the parting.

Doctor Thomas Armour, a descendant of the Armour family of Mauchline and relation of Jean Armour, occupied Stairaird Farm in the 1890's.

Also see: Coilsfield; Failford; Kingencleugh; Mauchline Burn; Montgomerie House.

STAIR CHURCH
Map Ref. 439 236

The present church was built in 1864 on the site of the original.

Mrs. Catherine Stewart of Stair House and Afton Lodge, the poet's early patron, and James Andrew, friend of the poet and miller at Barskimming Mill, are buried in the kirkyard.

Also see: Afton Lodge; Barskimming Mill; Bridge Holm; Stair House.

STAIR HOUSE

STAIR HOUSE
Map Ref. 440 238

Situated on the south bank of the River Ayr, 300 yards east of the B730 Tarbolton/Drongan Road at Stair. The house is still occupied.

It was the home of Mrs. Catherine Stewart of Stair and later of Afton Lodge, the first member of the 'gentry' to befriend and encourage the poet.

Burns and his friend, David Sillar, visited the kitchen of Stair House where Sillar was courting the nurserymaid, Peggy Orr. In the kitchen they were in the company of Peggy and the housekeeper, Mary (Mailly) Crosbie, and Burns was amusing them by singing and reciting some of his compositions. Mrs. Stewart heard the sound of singing and laughing and sent for her housekeeper. On being told that Robin Burns from Mossgiel was the cause of the hilarity, Mrs. Stewart invited him up to the drawing room and thus began a long friendship and patronage.

Peggy Orr was referred to in the poem *(FIRST) EPISTLE TO DAVIE* - *'You hae your Meg, your dearest part, And I my darling Jean.'* Peggy and Davie were engaged, but only briefly.

In Stair parish, tradition maintains that the poem *FAREWELL TO ELIZA* was written to a servant at Stair House called Betty Campbell. Nothing is known about the girl to support or refute the tradition. It is generally accepted that the poem was addressed to Miss Betty Miller, one of the girls referred to in the poem *THE BELLES OF MAUCHLINE*.

David Sillar eventually moved from Tarbolton Parish to Irvine. He inherited wealth of between £30,000 and £40,000 and was able to lend £4,000 to the daughters of Mrs. Stewart.

Also see: Afton Lodge; Kilwinning; Milton; Stair Church.

STAR INN CLOSE, circa 1920

STAR INN CLOSE
Map Ref. 429 380

The close is no longer extant. It was on the north side of Waterloo Street, Kilmarnock, a few yards out of the Cross. The site is now under the modern shopping complex called The Kilmarnock Centre.

John Wilson's printing workshop in which the poems of Robert Burns first appeared in print in the Kilmarnock Edition in July, 1786, was in the attic of a two-storied building entered from Star Inn Close. Six hundred and twelve copies were printed, all of which were sold in just over a month. The employee who actually printed the books and spoke with pride of having done so for the rest of his life was Walter Graham of Kilmarnock.

Tradition maintains that Burns first asked Messrs. Dunlop and Wilson of Glasgow, the West of Scotland's leading printers and booksellers, to print his poems but they declined.

In 1803, Wilson moved to Ayr and, with his brother, Peter, started Ayrshire's first newspaper, The Ayr Advertiser. He died on 6 May, 1821, and was buried in the kirkyard of Kilmarnock High Kirk.

There has been much debate as to whether or not Wilson was the subject of the poem ON WEE JOHNIE. A Mauchline bookseller, also called John Wilson, was possibly the person to whom the poem referred. The poet gave no indication of the person concerned.

Also see: High Kirk, Kilmarnock; Kilmarnock.

STEVENSTON
Situated on the A78 Irvine/Greenock Road, 5 miles north of Irvine.

Mayville House, No. 31 High Road, was the home of Lesley Baillie, the poet's 'Bonie Lesley'. Miss Baillie was the heroine of the songs *SAW YE BONIE LESLEY* and *BLYTHE HAE I BEEN ON YON HILL*. She was born at Mayville on 6 March, 1768, and died in Edinburgh on 12 July, 1843.

A memorial column erected by Lesley Baillie's father, Robert Baillie, to the memory of his wife and family, stands on the east side of Glencairn Street, alongside No. 110.

Local tradition maintains that Burns visited the Baillie family at Mayville. He did visit them but probably while they were in Edinburgh.

John Lambie, a native of Stevenston who returned there later in life, worked for Burns as a gaudsman at Mossgiel and claimed to have been leading the plough when Burns turned over the nest of the fieldmouse, which inspired the poem *TO A MOUSE*.

Also see: Mayville; Mossgiel Farm.

STEWART KYLE
The ancient division of Ayrshire called Kyle is sub-divided into King's Kyle and Stewart Kyle. Stewart Kyle is that part of Ayrshire between the Rivers Irvine and Ayr. King's Kyle is the part between the Rivers Ayr and Doon.

Stewart Kyle was referred to in the poem *THE MAUCHLINE LADY* - *'When first I came to Stewart Kyle, My mind it was na steady.'*

Also see: Carrick; Cunninghame; Kyle.

STEWARTON
Situated on the A735 Kilmarnock/Lugton Road, 4 miles north of Kilmarnock.

When the poet's uncle, Robert Burnes, moved to Ayrshire from the east of Scotland, he settled in the Stewarton area. For several years he lived at Titwood, west of the town, and worked at lime quarries at Lochridge. Eventually, he was crippled with arthritis or rheumatism and moved into Stewarton, living first in a house in the Buck's Head Close and later in another house, the location of which is unknown.

Robert Burnes died on 3 January, 1789, and is buried in Stewarton kirkyard. On 9 January, the poet wrote from Ellisland to his cousin, James Burness of Montrose, with the news of their uncle's death - 'We have lost poor uncle Robert...His son, William has been with me this winter, and goes in May to bind himself to be a mason with my father-in-law...His other son, John comes to me, I expect in summer...His only daughter, Fanny, Has been with me ever since her father's death.'

On 24 September, 1910, Stewarton Literary Society erected a memorial in Stewarton kirkyard to the poet's uncle Robert and his eldest son, John, who died on 17 February, 1846. The memorial, still in good condition, is situated against the boundary fence on the right on entering the main gate of the kirkyard.

Frances (Fanny) Burns married Jean Armour's brother, Adam Armour, builder, Mauchline who was referred to in the poem *ADAM ARMOUR'S PRAYER*. They lived in Mauchline and had 5 sons and 4 daughters.

The poet was familiar with the town and district of Stewarton by visiting his uncle, visiting Robertland House, and passing through on his way to Dunlop House.

It is claimed locally that the poet's *EPIGRAM ON ROUGH ROADS* related to the road from Kilmarnock to Stewarton. It is more likely to have been written during his Highland tour.

Also see: Dunlop House; Lochridge; Robertland; Titwood.

STINCHAR RIVER   Map Ref. 079 815
The river flows south-west through Ayrshire and enters the Firth of Clyde at Ballantrae, at the map reference shown.

In all editions of his work up to and including 1794, Burns made the first line of the song *MY NANIE, O'* - '*Behind yon hills where Stinchar flows.*'

In a letter to George Thomson, song collector, in 1792, Burns wrote - 'The name of the river is horribly prosaic. - I will alter it.' He then gave the choice of Girvan and Lugar. Thomson chose Lugar and so it has remained in many editions. Burns also commented in his letter - '*Girvan is the river that suits the idea of the stanza best.*'

As Stinchar was the first choice and, of the others, Girvan suited the idea best, it appears that the song was set in south Ayrshire. If the poet composed the song at Mount Oliphant or Kirkoswald, the setting sun would first darken the sky in the east where the Stinchar and Girvan Rivers flow 'Mang moors an' mosses many o' as described in the first verse of the song.

It is generally accepted that the heroine of the song was Agnes Fleming of Coldcothill or Doura Farms, neighbouring Lochlea. If she was, it is incredible that the poet chose Stinchar or Girvan as suitable for his introduction, as neither of them have any relationship with the sun setting in the west or darkening the eastern sky as seen from Lochlea.

The poet's brother, Gilbert Burns, said that Agnes Fleming was the heroine; his youngest sister, Isabella Burns Begg, said that it was Peggy Thomson of Kirkoswald; the poet's aunt, Mrs. Brown of Kirkoswald said that the heroine was Agnes McIlwraith of Pinvalley; local tradition in Girvan maintains that it was Agnes Brown, daughter of the proprietor of the Ship Inn, Girvan; and Rev. Hamilton Paul, 19th century Burns scholar said that it was an Agnes Sheriff of Kilmarnock. The poet gave no indication of the identity of the heroine of his song. In his First Commonplace Book he commented - 'Whether the following song will stand the test, I will not pretend to say, because it is my own; only I can say it was, at the time, real.'

Also see: Coldcothill Farm; Doura Farm; Girvan River; Kirkoswald; Lugar River; Minnybae Farm; Pinvalley; Ship Inn; Stinchar River.

SUN INN   Map Ref. 498 273
The inn is no longer extant. It was situated on the south side of Mauchline Cross, in line with the south side of Loudoun Street, and was removed when Earl Grey Street was constructed.

It was owned by John Miller whose daughters Elizabeth (Betty) and Helen were two of the girls referred to in the poem *THE BELLES OF MAUCHLINE* - '*Miss Betty is braw*' and '*Miss Miller is fine.*'

The poet was briefly infatuated with Elizabeth Miller and she was probably the heroine of the poem *FROM THEE ELIZA*, written while he was contemplating departure for the

West Indies. She married William Templeton, a Mauchline shopkeeper, and died young in childbirth.

Helen Miller married the poet's friend and physician, Doctor John Mackenzie, who lodged in the Sun Inn until he was married. They moved to Irvine where she died and is buried in the parish kirkyard.

The Miller family were referred to in the poem *A MAUCHLINE WEDDING* which was inspired by the marriage of John Miller's son, William, to a sister of a local man called Alexander Bell who had made a fortune in Jamaica.

Also see: Back Causeway; Blacksidend; Irvine; Stair House.

SUNDRUM CASTLE   Map ref. 411 212
Situated one mile north of the A70 Ayr/Cumnock Road, 1½ miles west of Coylton. The castle is still extant.

It was the home of John Hamilton, businessman and agricultural improver, who was appointed as referee in the dispute between the poet's father, William Burnes, and his landlord, David McLure, over Lochlea Farm. Hamilton found mainly in favour of Burnes.

In a note to a suppressed stanza of the poem *THE VISION*, Burns indicated that the following lines relate to Sundrum - *'Where hid behind a spreading wood, An ancient pict-built mansion stood.'* The 'female pair' referred to in the stanza were John Hamilton's daughters, Lilias and Margaret.

Also see: Lochlea Farm; Rodger's School.

SYMINGTON
The village is situated on the A77 Ayr/Kilmarnock Road, 4 miles south of Kilmarnock.

The Rev. William Auld, minister of Mauchline Parish Church when the poet was at Mossgiel Farm, was born at Ellanton (Helenton), Symington. His father was Laird of Ellanton.

The Rev. Auld was referred to as *'Daddy Auld'* in the poem *THE KIRK'S ALARM*. In his introduction to the poem *HOLY WILLIE'S PRAYER*, and in a letter dated December, 1787, to Gavin Hamilton, Mauchline, the poet referred to the minister as *'Father Auld.'*

It was before Rev. Auld, his session and his congregation that Burns and Jean Armour were required to do penance for their illegitimate children.

Also see: Mauchline Kirkyard.

TAM O'SHANTER'S JOURNEY
Armstrong's 1775 map of Ayrshire shows two roads from Ayr to the River Doon and south-west Ayrshire; one route follows the line of the B7024 Ayr/Alloway/Maybole Road and the other the line of the A719 Ayr/Doonfoot/Dunure Road. In addition, Greenfield Avenue, joining the two roads, had been constructed by the poet's father, William Burnes, in 1755/56.

Although the poem *TAM O'SHANTER* was not composed until 1790, Burns set it in a time before the new roads were constructed. Poetic licence also played a part in the account of Tam's route.

Having left the High Street, Ayr, by Cow Vennel (Alloway Street) or Carrick Vennel (Carrick Street), Tam -

'Weel mounted on his grey mare Meg'

made his way across the rough common land between the modern Dalblair Road/Alloway Street area and the Curtecan (now Slaphouse) Burn. The burn still flows west under Monument Road, through Belleisle Park and under Doonfoot Road to the sea.

It is not generally realised that some of the important landmarks highlighted by Burns in *TAM O'SHANTER* did exist and that some still do.

Let us take up the story of Tam O'Shanter's journey as he approached Alloway and -

'Kirk-Alloway was drawing nigh,

Where ghaists and houlets nightly cry.'

The route ran parallel to Monument Road, along the east side of Belleisle Park until it reached the Slaphouse Burn -

'By this time he was cross the ford,

Whare in the snaw the chapman smoor'd.'

In fact, the burn had been bridged by the mid 17th century but the poet preferred to have Tam ford it. The ford was probably about 100 yards west of Monument Road.

Tam pressed on towards Alloway -

'And past the birks and meikle stane,

Where drunken Charlie brak's neck-bane.'

The Cairn - 'Whare hunters fand the murder'd bairn'.

The meikle stane is no longer extant. It was situated on what is now the east side of Belleisle Park, about 100 yards south of the Monument Road entrance.

The route then veered slightly to the west and passed to the west of Burns Cottage, until it went-

'...thro' the whins and by the cairn,

Whare hunters fand the murder'd bairn.'

The ancient cairn was situated on what is now the site of a house in Cairn Crescent, a few hundred yards south-west of Burns Cottage. To allow building development, the cairn was removed from its original site in 1964 and on its removal was found to have covered an ancient burial kist (grave). By arrangement with the building contractor, part of the cairn and stones from the kist were used in 1965 to erect a small commemorative cairn on the north footpath of Cairn Crescent, between numbers 5 and 7 (map ref. 329 185), close to the original site.

After the cairn, Tam passed -

'Near the thorn, aboon the well,

Where Mungo's mither hang'd hersel.'

The well still exists at map reference 332 181 and is called St. Mungo's Well, supposedly after the patron saint of Alloway. It is situated on the steep north bank of the River Doon, alongside the north end of the disused railway bridge which crosses the river a short distance down-stream from the modern Doon Bridge. To see the unmarked and neglected well, walk down the embankment of the disused railway line which runs parallel to the road leading to the Tam O'Shanter Experience, go through the tunnel under the main road, and as you emerge from the south end of the tunnel look over the west parapet on to the steep north bank of the river. The thorn tree is no longer extant.

The Well - 'Where Mungo's mither hang'd hersel'.

149

There is no local legend of a hanging at the well and we must presume that the poet's licence turned St. Mungo's Well into the place where an imaginary Mungo's mother met her end.

When he had reached the well on the bank of the river, Tam saw -

'Before him Doon pour(s) all his floods'

heard -

'The doubling storm roar(s) thro' the woods'

and was astonished to see that -

'...glimmering thro' the groaning trees,

Kirk-Alloway seem'd in a bleeze.'

Once more poetic licence had taken over. In fact, on Tam's route, the ruined kirk would be reached before the well and the river. When Tam fled from the kirk, pursued by the witches, Meg did 'her speedy utmost' and won 'the key-stane of the brig' to reach safety. Like Tam O'Shanter in the poem, the account of the journey ends on the old Doon bridge.

It is strange that the cairn and the well, two of the most widely known features in the works of Burns, indeed in all of English literature, are unmarked and unpublicised within a stone-throw of the Tam O'Shanter Experience, hub of the Burns Heritage Trail.

TAM SAMSON'S HOUSE

TAM SAMSON'S HOUSE
Map Ref. 432 379

The house is no longer extant. The site is indicated by a plaque on a wall at the south side of London Road, Kilmarnock, at its junction with Braeside Street.

The house was called 'Rosebank' and was almost certainly visited by Burns.

Tam Samson was born in Ochiltree. He was a nurseryman in Kilmarnock, and was the subject of the poems *TAM SAMSON'S ELEGY* and *TAM SAMSON'S EPITAPH*.

Tam Samson was a keen sportsman, especially fond of shooting. One day Burns was in their favourite Kilmarnock tavern, Bowling Green House, which was conducted by Tam's son-in-law, Sandy Patrick. Tam was out shooting and late in returning. His nephew was present and told Burns that Tam had always said that he would be happy to die out shooting on the moors and perhaps his wish had been granted. The poet retired from the company for a short time. By the time Tam returned, Burns was able to read to the company the poem *TAM SAMSON'S ELEGY*. Tam protested that he did not like the story and would prefer the world to know that he was hale and hearty. After a few minutes, Burns restored Tam's confidence and remedied the situation by reading out *TAM SAMSON'S EPITAPH* and its 'per contra.'

Tam Samson died 7 months before Burns and is buried in the Laigh Kirkyard, Kilmarnock. The Epitaph is inscribed on his headstone.

When Burns borrowed a horse from George Reid, Barquharrie Farm, Ochiltree, for his journey from Mauchline to Edinburgh in 1786, Tam Samson's brother, John, borrowed the horse for a journey back to Ayrshire.

Also see: Bowling Green House; Dalsangan Mill; Kilmarnock; Laigh Kirk; Ochiltree.

TARBOLTON
Situated on the B730 Dundonald/Coylton Road, one mile north of the A758 Ayr/Mauchline Road.

The town is an important centre in the Burns Country and has many important associations with the poet.

Burns moved into Lochlea Farm in Tarbolton Parish in 1777, aged 18 years, and moved out to Mossgiel Farm, Mauchline, in 1784. While he was at Lochlea, the village became the centre of his social life; he joined a dancing class, helped to found the Bachelors' Club, and became a freemason. After he left the parish, he retained some of his connections with Tarbolton, especially as Depute Master of Lodge St. James Tarbolton.

His time in the parish was an important period in the development of Burns as a poet. When he moved in he had already composed some poetry and when he left he had begun to show poetic ability of some worth.

The Rev. Dr. Patrick Wodrow was minister of Tarbolton from 1738 to his death in 1793. He was referred to in the poem *THE TWA HERDS* - '*Auld Wodrow lang has hatch'd mischief.*' He is buried in the kirkyard. The present church was built on the site of the original. Rev. Wodrow's manse stood on the east side of Burns Street, at its junction with Sandgate.

The Rev. John McMath, who was addressed in the poem *TO THE REV. JOHN McMATH*, was assistant to Rev. Dr. Wodrow in Tarbolton from 1782 to 1791. He supported the poet's friend, Gavin Hamilton of Mauchline, in his dispute with Mauchline kirk session and asked Burns to send him a copy of the poem *HOLY WILLIE'S PRAYER* which relates to the dispute. Although he had been chosen to be Rev. Wodrow's successor in Tarbolton, McMath became a heavy drinker and had to demit office prematurely in 1791, before the death of Rev. Wodrow.

John Wilson, Tarbolton school teacher, immortalised by Burns as '*Doctor Hornbook*' in

the poem *DEATH AND DOCTOR HORNBOOK*, was also session clerk of Tarbolton church and secretary of Lodge St. James, Tarbolton.

Alexander 'Saunders' Tait, who wrote and circulated several rhymes attacking Burns and his friend David Sillar, was a bachelor tailor in Tarbolton. The location of his house is in dispute; it has been reliably described as 'originally a small two-storied cottage, later modernised and partly rebuilt, on the west side of Montgomerie Street, a short distance above the entrance to the school.' Tait published a book of poems in 1790.

James Findlay, a Tarbolton excise officer, is thought to have instructed Burns in the subjects required for excise duties. He married Jean Markland, one of the *'BELLES OF MAUCHLINE'* in the poem of that name - *'Miss Miller is fine, Miss Markland's divine.'* Tradition maintains that the couple were introduced by the poet. They moved to Greenock where Jean is buried.

John Lees, a shoemaker in the village, recounted that as a youth he had acted as 'blackfoot' for Burns in his pursuit of local girls. A 'blackfoot' was a go-between or chaperon between a young man and the girl whose acquaintance he wished to make. Lees said that once he had attracted a girl out of her home on the poet's behalf, Burns would say to him - 'Now, Jock, you can gang awa' hame now.'

William 'Souter' Hood, an elder of Tarbolton Church and also a shoemaker, was the subject of a mock epitaph by the poet. Burns recorded it in his First Common Place Books as *EPITAPH ON WM. HOOD, SENR. IN TARBOLTON* and it is sometimes called *EPITAPH ON A CELEBRATED RULING ELDER.*

The many places in the village and parish connected with Burns and his associates are dealt with separately.

Also see: Adamhill Farm; Bachelors' Club; Coilsfield House; Cross Keys Inn; Doctor Hornbook's House and School; Freemasonry (Tarbolton); Johnie Ged's Hole; Langlands Farm; Lochlea Farm; Manson's Inn; Montgomerie House; Spittalside Farm; Tibbie Stein's House; Tarbolton Mill; Willie's Mill.

TARBOLTON MILL   Map Ref. 435 274
Situated south of the B744 Tarbolton/Galston Road, on the eastern edge of Tarbolton village.

In the poem *DEATH AND DOCTOR HORNBOOK*, Burns referred to it as *'Willie's Mill'*, after his friend, William Muir, the miller - *'I was come round about the hill, An' toddlin down on Willie's Mill.'*

Gilbert Burns the poet's brother, referred to it as 'Tarboth' Mill, a local corruption of Tarbolton. He said that Burns was in the habit of meeting 'Montgomerie's Peggy,' the otherwise unknown heroine of the song of that name, at the mill.

Also see: Coilsfield; Tarbolton; Willie's Mill.

THE CELLARS   Map Ref. 216 082
A cottage situated at No. 53 Ardolochan Road, Maidens. It is still occupied and is thought to be the oldest house in the village.

Local tradition maintains that it is called The Cellars because it was originally an ale-house and that Burns visited the house in 1775 while he was living at Ballochneil Farm, Kirkoswald Parish, and attending Hugh Rodger's school in Kirkoswald village.

Part of the cottage may have been used as a smiddy (smithy), either at the time of Burns or later. It is sometimes said to have been occupied by John Niven, model for the smith in the poem *TAM O'SHANTER*. It is generally accepted that Niven's smiddy was at or near Damhouse of Ardlochan, a half mile north of The Cellars.

Also see: Ardlochan; Ballochneil Farm; Damhouse of Ardlochan; Douglaston; Maidens.

Kirkton Jean's House as Kirkoswald Smiddy, circa 1900

THE LADIES' (LEDDIES') HOUSE Map Ref. 239 075

The house is no longer extant. It was situated on the west side of Main Street, Kirkoswald, a few yards north of the kirkyard. For the last few years of its existence it was a smiddy (smithy).

When Burns was at school in Kirkoswald in 1775, it was an ale house conducted by two sisters, Jean and Anne Kennedy. The sisters were rather refined and conducted their premises likewise, with the result that it was known as The Ladies' House.

In the poem *TAM O'SHANTER*, Burns changed the name to 'The Lord's House', probably to make the line scan properly, and referred to Jean Kennedy as 'Kirkton Jean' - *'That at the Lord's house, even on Sunday, Thou drank wi' Kirkton Jean till Monday.'*

The name 'Kirkton' was applied throughout Scotland to a 'town' (hamlet or village) with a kirk.

When the poet started at Hugh Rodger's school in the village, he did so with William Niven, the son of a Maybole merchant and nephew of Robert Niven of Ballochneil Farm,

Kirkoswald, where Burns was lodging. As was the custom when boys of their age entered a school, Burns and William Niven took Rodger to The Ladies' House and treated him to a draught of ale.

William Niven became a very wealthy businessman and landowner. He was a Bailie, Town Councillor and Depute Lord Lieutenant of Ayrshire, but with a reputation for meanness. Burns and Niven were lifelong friends.

Also see: Kirkoswald; Maybole; Rodger's School.

TIBBIE STEIN'S HOUSE Map Ref. 431 273

The house is no longer extant. It was situated on the west side of Burns Street, Tarbolton, at its junction with Garden Street and directly opposite the site of Manson's Inn. It was the home of Isabella Steven, known locally as Tibbie Stein.

Burns courted Tibbie but she inherited a legacy of £75 and turned her attention to another, probably a more prosperous suitor. Local legend maintains that one night Burns called at her home and the door was answered by a member of the household who said that Tibbie was entertaining another gentleman. The poet left the house and never returned. It was soon afterwards that he wrote the song *O' TIBBIE, I HAE SEEN THE DAY*.

Later in her life Tibbie was pleased to acknowledge that she was the heroine of the song. She married and became a Mrs. Allan.

The poet's youngest sister, Isabella Burns Begg, said that Tibbie Stein lived at Littlehill Farm, neighbouring Lochlea. Tibbie has been described as the daughter of a small farmer so it is possible that she lived at Littlehill before she moved to Tarbolton.

Burns was about 18 years old when he wrote the poem. As Mrs. Begg was 12 years younger than the poet, her information can not be regarded as reliable.

Also see: Littlehill Farm; Tarbolton.

TITWOOD FARM Map Ref. 403 433

Situated a half mile west of the A735 Kilmaurs/Stewarton Road, one mile north of Kilmaurs.

When the poet's uncle, Robert Burnes, moved to Ayrshire from the east of Scotland he lived at Titwood Farm and worked at lime quarries at Lochridge, Stewarton.

The exact site of his home is not known.

TUNNOCH Map Ref. 308 097

Situated on the eastern outskirts of Maybole, north of the B7023 Maybole/Crosshill Road.

It was the parental home of Captain Matthew Henderson with whom Burns was acquainted while both were in Edinburgh. Henderson was the subject of the poem *ELEGY ON CAPTAIN MATTHEW HENDERSON*. The poem was subtitled 'A Gentleman who Held the Patent for His honours immediately from Almighty God.'

Burns wrote complimentary remarks about Henderson in letters to Professor Dugald Stewart, Robert Cleghorn and Robert Graham of Fintry.

The estate, as it was classed in the time of Burns, was then spelled Tannoch.

Captain Henderson was also Laird of Tannochside in Lanarkshire.

WALLACE TOWER

Map Ref. 338 218

Situated in High Street, Ayr at its junction with Mill Vennel.

The present tower was built on the site of the original in 1834. The original tower was very ancient, the date of building being unknown; in 1673, Ayr Town Council bought it from the Cathcarts of Corbieston.

The tower and its clock are referred to in the poem *THE BRIGS OF AYR* - *'And Wallace Tower had sworn the fact was true.'*

WATER-FIT

It is referred to in the poem *THE HOLY FAIR* - *'Peebles, frae the Water-Fit.'*

The name Water-Fit referred to Newton-on-Ayr and is descriptive of its location at the mouth of the River Ayr; it is that part of Ayr north of the river and was originally a separate parish.

The Rev. Dr. William Peebles was minister of Newton-on-Ayr and clerk to Ayr Presbytery. He moved to Newton in 1778 and remained there until his death on 11 October, 1826. Peebles Street, Newton-on-Ayr, commemorates the minister's long association with the parish.

In 1786, in the midst of the controversy in the Church Of Scotland between the 'Auld Licht' (established) and 'New Light' (modern/liberal) approaches to religious beliefs, the Rev. Dr. William McGill of Ayr published a 'New Licht' essay on The Death Of Jesus Christ. He was attacked as a heretic by Peebles, an 'Auld Licht' fanatic. Burns and his father had both held McGill in high regard during their time near Ayr and the poet stepped into the midst of the controversy with his scathing attack on the *'Auld Licht'* clergy in his poem *THE KIRK'S ALARM.*

Peebles thought he had some poetic ability and had published mediocre poems on religious subjects. In the poem *THE KIRK'S ALARM,* Burns referred to him as 'Poet Willie' and the stanza relating to him is a sarcastic attack on his attempts at poetry.

Peebles disliked Burns, even after the poet's death, and in 1811 published a bombastic, unchristian attack on the growing cult of Burns appreciation in an essay called "Burnsomania - The celebrity of Robert Burns considered in a Discourse addressed to all real Christians of every Denomination." He denounced the poet's work as 'vile scraps of indecent ribaldry.'

WHITEFOORD ARMS

Map Ref. 498 273

The inn is no longer extant. The site is indicated by a plaque on the east gable of the building in Loudoun Street, Mauchline, at the west side of its junction with Cowgate.

It was frequented by the poet and his friends and was the meeting place of the bachelor group called *THE COURT OF EQUITY* referred to in the poem of that name.

The innkeeper was John Dove or Dow, nicknamed Johnie Doo or Johnie Pigeon by Burns. He is referred to in the poem *TO GAVIN HAMILTON, ESQ.* as *'Paisley John'* and is the subject of the poem *EPITAPH ON JOHN DOVE, INNKEEPER.* In the poem to *JOHN KENNEDY, DUMFRIES HOUSE,* the inn is referred to in the lines - 'please step to Dow's, And taste sic gear as Johnie brews.'

Jean Armour's house was situated in Cowgate, behind the Whitefoord Arms, and separated from it by a lane.

Loudoun Street, Mauchline, with Poosie Nancie's and the site of the Whitefoord Arms, circa 1920

WHITEHILL
Map Ref. 364 183

Situated west of the A713 Ayr/Dalmellington Road, at the Asylum Brae. The original house is no longer extant. The name of the property and its modern house have been changed to 'Glenparks'.

In 1778, when he was 39 years of age, Robert Aiken, an Ayr lawyer, purchased what was later described as 'the considerable estate of Whitehill.'

Robert Aiken was one of the poet's best friends. Burns dedicated the poem *THE COTTER'S SATURDAY NIGHT* to him and in the poem *THE KIRK'S ALARM* he was referred to as *'Orator Bob.'* In letters to their mutual friend, John Ballantine, the poet called Aiken 'my first poetic patron' and 'my first kind patron.'

The support and encouragement given by Aiken to the poet is illustrated best by the fact that of the 612 subscriptions for the Kilmarnock Edition, 145 were arranged by Aiken.

Tradition maintains that John Hunter, another Ayr lawyer who later bought Doonholm House, was responsible for drawing Aiken's attention to the poetic genius of Burns. It must be probable that Aiken knew of the poet through his maternal uncle, the Rev. Dr. William Dalrymple, minister of Ayr Auld Kirk, who baptised Burns and was friendly with the poet and his father. Aiken was cousin of James Dalrymple of Orangefield, another of the poet's patrons.

The poem *EPISTLE TO A YOUNG FRIEND* was addressed to Robert Aiken's son, Andrew Hunter Aiken. Andrew Aiken's eldest son, Peter Freedland Aiken, became a noted Burns scholar and in 1876 produced a book called Memorials of Robert Burns and his Contemporaries.

Robert Aiken had one daughter called Grace who was born on 12 January, 1777, and died on 13 October, 1857. As a girl she delighted in the poet's visits to her home and to listening to him reciting his compositions. In March, 1796, four months before the poet's death, she met him in Dumfries and was distressed by his emaciated appearance and obvious ill-health. Her nephew, Peter Freedland Aiken, recounted that the poet had said to her - "The fire in me is almost extinguished; I am the shadow of my former self".

Although it cannot be proved, tradition maintains that there was one shadow over the relationship between Burns and Aiken. In 1786, Burns gave Jean Armour a letter in which he either declared them to be married or, at least, promised to marry her. The ultimate fate of this letter is unknown and the exact wording has not been recorded. It appears to have been regarded by Burns as a marriage contract. Jean told her parents that she was pregnant by Burns and showed them the letter. Her father, James Armour, was furious and did not want Jean associated with the poet. According to tradition he took it to Robert Aiken who cut the names of Robert and Jean out of the letter, rendering it valueless as a contract. Burns was both angry and hurt and blamed Jean. As a result of Robert Aiken's involvement there was a temporary coolness between Burns and his friend.

Robert Aiken, who had been born on 23 August, 1739, died in 1807 and is buried in Ayr Auld Kirkyard. The poet's friend, James Dalrymple, was his cousin, and the Rev. Dr. William Dalrymple, who baptised Burns, was his uncle.

Also see: Ayr Auld Kirk; Orangefield House.

WHITESTONE COTTAGE
Map Ref. 258 107

Situated on the west side of the A719 Ayr/Turnberry Road, about a half mile south of its junction with the B7023 Maybole/Culzean Road. The exact location is indicated by the ruined gable of the cottage in the wood on the west side on the road, 250 yards south of the large lay-by created by road re-alignment south of the B7023 junction.

Tradition maintains that the poet's mother, Agnes Broun, was born in the cottage on 17 May, 1732.

Agnes Broun's parents, Gilbert Broun of Craigenton Farm, Kirkoswald Parish, and Agnes Rennie of Maybole, were married on 7 May, 1731. Gilbert is said to have been employed as a forester on Culzean Estate and on his marriage to have set up home in Whitestone Cottage on the estate.

The family moved to Craigenton Farm when Agnes was an infant.

Also see: Craigenton Farm.

WILLIE'S MILL
Map Ref. 435 274

Situated south of the B744 Tarbolton/Galston Road, on the eastern edge of Tarbolton.

It was the home of William Muir, miller, close friend of the poet and his father. In 1788, when Jean Armour's parents put her out of their home for being pregnant by Burns for a second time, she was befriended and given a home by Willie Muir and his wife.

William Muir is the subject of the very complimentary poem *EPITAPH ON WM. MUIR OF TARBOLTON MILL*.

The mill is referred to in the poem *DEATH AND DOCTOR HORNBOOK* - '*I was come round about the hill, An toddlin down on Willie's Mill.*' The location of the supposed encounter with Death is still easily recognisable from the description; it is indicated by a plaque on the south verge of the Tarbolton/Galston Road, a few yards west of the road leading to Willie's Mill.

As indicated in the title of the *EPITAPH ON WILLIE MUIR*, the proper name of the mill was, and still is, Tarbolton Mill.

Gilbert Burns, the poet's brother, said that the poet was in the habit of meeting 'Montgomerie's Peggy', the otherwise unknown heroine of the song of that name at Tarboth Mill. Tarboth was a local corruption of Tarbolton.

Also see: Tarbolton.

WILLIE'S MILL, circa 1900

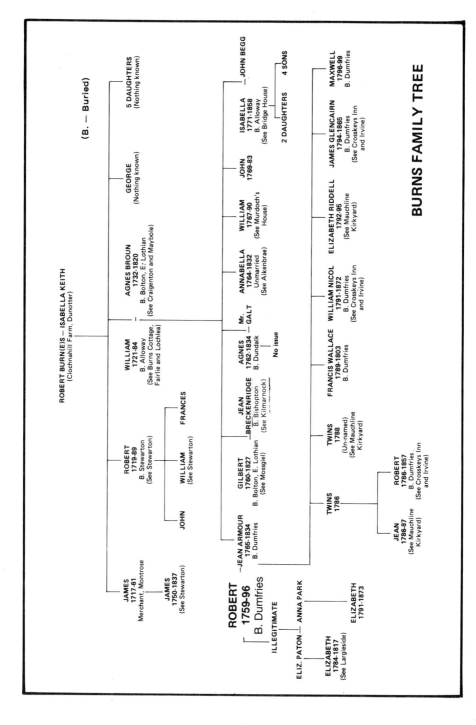

BURNS FAMILY TREE

ROBERT BURN(E)S — ISABELLA KEITH
(Clochnahill Farm, Dunotter)

(B. — Buried)

INDEX

INDEX

INDEX

INDEX

Jean Armour with a granddaughter

Tho I were doom'd to wander on,
Beyond the sea, beyond the sun,
Till my last weary sand was run,
Till then—and then—I'd love thee!